On
Purposeful
Systems

On
Purposeful
Systems

An Interdisciplinary Analysis of Individual and Social Behavior as a System of Purposeful Events

Russell L. Ackoff
Fred E. Emery

With a new introduction by Brent D. Ruben

ALDINETRANSACTION
A Division of Transaction Publishers
New Brunswick (U.S.A.) and London (U.K.)

Library of Congress Catalog Number: 2005054854
ISBN: 0-202-30798-0
Printed in the United States of America

Library of Congress Cataloging-in-Publication Data

Ackoff, Russell Lincoln, 1919-
    On purposeful systems : an interdisciplinary analysis of individual and social behavior as a system of purposeful events / Russell L. Ackoff & Fred E. Emery ; with a new introduction by Brent D. Ruben.
      p. cm.
    Originally published: London : Tavistock Publications, 1972.
    Includes bibliographical references and indexes.
    ISBN 0-202-30798-0 (pbk. : alk. paper)
      1. Social sciences—Methodology. 2. Social systems. I. Emery, F. E. (Frederick Edmund) II. Title.

H61.A38   2006
302.3—dc22   2005054854

To E. A. Singer, Jr., Thomas A. Cowan, and C. West Churchman, who gave us the material to work with.

Contents

AldineTransaction Introduction

To have written a book that colleagues would want to read, let alone reissue, some thirty-five years after its original publication is an enviable accomplishment to say the very least. And so it is with *On Purposeful Systems*. First published in 1972 by Tavistock Publications, this landmark work by Russell L. Ackoff and Fred E. Emery helped to provide the foundation for the area that is traditionally referred to as general systems theory. Along with notable scholars like Ludwig von Bertalanffy, Norbert Wiener, C. West Churchman, Magorah Maruyama, James G. Miller, and Anatol Rapaport, Ackoff and Emery contributed to the articulation of a more integrative way of thinking about and studying the universe. The systems paradigm advanced a framework that focused on commonalities in structure and process. In so doing, it offered concepts that transcended and unified diverse disciplines and the phenomena upon which they focus. With a generic focus on concepts such as organization, communication, relationship, wholeness, and purpose, systems theory at once spanned and linked the study of atoms and galaxies, cells and higher order organisms, individuals and societies.

Systems theorists offered a formidable challenge to the accepted views of causality, which emphasized the search for causal linkages, where independent and dependent variables were linked in linear—"the former causes the latter"—sequences. Alternative explanations emphasized the possibility of the dynamic interplay of variables in mutually-causal, deviation-reducing, and/or deviation-amplifying relationships, where no linear sequences are discernible, and indeed, questioning the very premise on which the search for linear sequences is based.

In its more orthodox form, classical systems theory was a search for isomorphies—identities—in process and structure across multiple levels and domains. Often, it was the goal of these approaches to represent these universals with mathematical or formulaic models. In its more liberal applications, systems theory was characterized by the pursuit of analogies and similarities in structure and process that

ix

would cross and link varying levels of analysis and disciplinary domains. Thus, in the case of communication processes, for example, there were theorists who sought to develop and apply universal conceptualizations of the phenomenon. Information theory represented one of the more familiar examples. Other communication scholars who applied a system-theoretic perspective focused their attention on functional similarities and parallels in communication processes at a cellular, organismic, individual, group, organizational, and societal level, and on communication relationships among these levels. At the risk of oversimplification, the orthodox approach to systems theory can be seen as a quest for identities and universals across systems levels and types; the more liberal view a search for functional parallels and useful analogies.

Both epistemological approaches to systems theory—indeed nearly all facets of systems theory—challenge the logic and value of the traditional preoccupation with a disciplinary approach to knowledge acquisition, dissemination, and application. As Ackoff and Emery note:

> Nature does not come to us in disciplinary form. Phenomena are not physical, chemical, biological, and so on. The disciplines are the ways we study phenomena; they emerge from points of view, not from what is viewed. Hence the disciplinary nature of science is a filing system of knowledge. Its organization is not to be confused with the organization of nature itself. (p. 4)

While acknowledging that disciplinary segmentation evolved as a way of coping with the complexity of the universe and the study of it, systems theorists challenge the presumption that the world is best understood by segmenting our investigation of it into discrete disciplinary areas, each of which specializes in a particular perspective, level of analysis, or phenomena. Systems theorists argue that such an approach may not be the most appropriate one for meaningfully addressing the complexity of life, and also point to the limitations this structure imposes on the advancement of general and integrative knowledge. Perhaps, one of the most tangible manifestations of this problem can be seen in the curriculum of the average undergraduate student, which offers up a biological view of life first hour, a psychological view second hour, a communication view third, sociological fourth, political science fifth, and so on, as if human behavior could be best comprehended when compartmentalized in such a manner.

From the perspective of traditional systems theory, *On Purposeful Systems* represents an ambitious effort to offer a systems view of human behavior. In a craftsman-like manner, Ackoff and Emery painstakingly create and assemble the building blocks of a formalized and formulaic model of human life. In fewer than 300 pages, the authors manage to address many of the fundamental concepts and issues of concern in the disciplines the work transcends.

Viewed more broadly, *On Purposeful Systems* is a work of historic and contemporary relevance. It provides a useful summary of many of the foundational concepts of systems theory. At the same time, the book provides a helpful background for more recent applications of systems theory. Particularly concepts like wholeness, order, feedback, complexity, and interaction, so central to systems theory, have found their way into the literature of various disciplines, and into popular articles, textbooks, and trade publications in fields as seemingly diverse as philosophy, biology, communication, anthropology, engineering, neuroscience, physics, education, and management science.

While the influence of classical systems theory is apparent in many contemporary writings across various fields, it is also the case that the intellectual roots and full richness of the systems framework is often understated in many of these same publications. Because of its historical significance and no less than because of its continuing relevance, the reissue of *On Purposeful Systems* represents a most significant contribution to the literature of the social sciences. Few works provide as eloquent a statement of the rationale, concepts, insights, promise, and continuing challenges of the general systems approach. With its republication, a great book becomes accessible once again.

Brent D. Ruben
Rutgers University

Preface

Work on this book began in 1941. Then Associate Professor Thomas A. Cowan of the Department of Philosophy of the University of Pennsylvania suggested to Instructor C. West Churchman and Assistant Instructor Russell L. Ackoff that they try to extend the work of Professor E. A. Singer, Jr., the grand old man of the department, who had befriended and taught all three. Singer had developed a conceptual system designed to show the compatibility of teleology and mechanism and had carried his work to the edges of psychology. (His work was later published posthumously as *Experience and Reflection,* ed. C. West Churchman [University of Pennsylvania Press, Philadelphia, 1959].) Cowan urged Churchman and Ackoff to carry this work deeply into the behavioral sciences. Shortly after initiating their effort, Churchman and Ackoff were separated by World War II, during which they carried on as best they could by correspondence, much to the dismay of military censors. In 1946 Ackoff returned to Pennsylvania, where he rejoined Churchman who had returned a few months earlier. They completed the first version of this manuscript that year. Ackoff used a portion of it as his doctoral dissertation in philosophy. The full work, *Psychologistics,* was issued as a monograph in 1947.

Churchman and Ackoff continued to work on the manuscript at Wayne University (1947–1951) and at Case Institute of Technology into the mid-1950s. They extended the work into areas not previously covered and re-worked much of what had been done. Portions of this work were published in article form.

Churchman moved to the University of California (Berkeley) in the late 1950s. He incorporated part of the work he had done with Ackoff in *Prediction and Optimal Decision* (Englewood Cliffs, N.J.: Prentice-Hall, 1961). Ackoff worked on extending the system to include some aspects of psychology that they had not previously included, and to cover communication, conflict, and organization. Portions of this work also appeared in article form in the late fifties and early sixties.

In 1964 Ackoff returned to the University of Pennsylvania, and shortly thereafter received from the National Science Foundation a grant that made possible his preparation of a new version of the work, *Choice, Communication, and Conflict*, which appeared as a report of the Management Science Center in November 1967.

About the time this second version appeared, Ackoff began collaborating with Fred E. Emery (then at the Human Resources Centre, The Tavistock Institute, London) in applying some of the conceptual system that had been developed to explain patterns of drinking behavior, which Emery had uncovered in his studies in Europe. Emery also brought to the collaboration his long concern with open systems in general and sociotechnical systems in particular, and a deep appreciation of the work of G. Sommerhoff. This collaboration spread into one directed at revising, extending, and updating *Choice, Communication, and Conflict*. This third version is an outcome of that collaboration.

Although only three people have put their hands to this book at its various stages, many have put their heads to it. Three in particular have played critical roles in its development. Leon Pritzker, who in 1946 suffered through the first seminar given on its content, made numerous subsequent contributions to its development. Thomas A. Cowan, who started the whole thing, played a large role in the thinking that went into both the first and second versions. Eric Trist was a most constructive critic of the second version, and many of his ideas significantly influenced this third effort.

Several students have helped greatly along the way — in particular, Anthony C. Scoville, James R. Emshoff, and Robert W. Cort. It was the enthusiasm, interest, and hard work of such students that kept the work warm during its long gestation.

It should be apparent that this book is not a final report on work that has been completed. Rather, it is a progress report of a program we hope will continue for many years and will involve an ever-increasing circle of collaborators.

Over the thirty years this book has been in the making, the relevant literature has been combed many times. In earlier versions proper displays of familiarity with that literature were provided. They were also included in the early draft of this version. But the manuscript became prohibitively long, and we elected to eliminate all references not essential to the development of our argument. We hope this will not be interpreted as a lack of respect for, or appreciation of, the ideas of many persons, which we have used liberally.

The references in the early chapters tend to be older than those in later chapters, because we begin with behavioral concepts that have been of concern for some time, so basic contributions to their understanding are likely to be older than similar contributions to the development of concepts more recent to scientific inquiry. Where possible, our citations refer to the seminal work rather than to more recent restatements of it.

Even without frequent references to the literature, the manuscript remained too long, so we often resorted to a telegraphic style in order to reduce it further. There are many other shortcomings in our presentation. The complexity of the content does not excuse all of them. The result is a book that cannot be read easily. It requires study. We hope that some will have the patience and inclination to do so.

On Purposeful Systems

I

Foundations

In this part we lay the foundations on which our conceptual system is built. Chapter 1 sets the background of our effort. In Chapter 2 we begin to construct our system, starting with mechanics and working our way up to the concept of purpose. The essential properties, components, and parameters of purposeful systems are considered in Chapter 3.

1

On Human Behavior as a System

This book presents neither a theory of behavior nor a set of generalizations that explain why people behave as they do. Nor does it describe their behavior. Nor is it another of the increasing number of efforts to mathematize or formalize the study of human behavior. What this book does attempt to do is provide *a way of looking at human behavior as systems of purposeful (teleological) events.*

Our way of looking at behavior is derived from the conviction that the principal function of the philosophy of science ought to be to make possible scientific investigation of types of phenomenon not previously susceptible to such inquiry.[1] Historically each branch of science emerged out of philosophical analysis of its subject matter and methods of inquiring into it. This historical role of philosophy, which is the basis for calling it "the mother of the sciences," can now be carried out with considerably more sophistication, because we now have a much better understanding of what science is. It is therefore possible to open new areas of inquiry, such as will be attempted here, in a rigorous scientific way. Whether such an effort is best called philosophical, scientific, or methodological is a matter of personal preference.

Philosophy has traditionally had another role in science. In the nineteenth century it was commonly believed that philosophy's principal function was to synthesize the findings of the various scientific disciplines into one cohesive body of knowledge about natural phenomena.[2] This view was epitomized in the encyclopedic work of Herbert Spencer, who attempted to unify science around the concept of evolution. More recent efforts along these lines have been made by Richard L. Schanck (1954), using the concept of dynamic equilibrium, and Ludwig von Bertalanffy (1951 and 1968) and his followers,

1. This point of view is developed and illustrated in Churchman (1948) and Churchman and Ackoff (1950).
2. The biggest barrier to such synthesis is the difference between living and nonliving systems, not just the diversity of disciplines.

3

who use the concept of structural isomorphism in the development of general systems theory.

The need to synthesize findings in the many disciplines of science arises because these disciplines have been developed with relatively unrelated conceptual systems. Scientific development has resulted in the grouping of phenomena into smaller and smaller classes, and in the creation of disciplines specializing in each. As disciplines multiply, each increases in depth and decreases in breadth. Collectively, however, they extend the breadth of scientific knowledge.

Nature does not come to us in disciplinary form. Phenomena are not physical, chemical, biological, and so on. The disciplines are the ways we study phenomena; they emerge from points of view, not from what is viewed. Hence the disciplinary nature of science is a filing system of knowledge. Its organization is not to be confused with the organization of nature itself.

Over time our concept of nature has broken, like Humpty Dumpty, into bits and pieces, and, like all the king's men, we are having trouble putting it back together again. The rapid growth and segmentation of science prompted Colin Cherry (1957) to observe:

> Leibnitz, it has sometimes been said, was the last man to know everything. Though this is most certainly a gross exaggeration, it is an epigram with considerable point. For it is true that up to the last years of the eighteenth century our greatest mentors were able not only to compass the whole science of their day, perhaps together with mastery of several languages, but to absorb a broad culture as well. But as the fruits of scientific labor have increasingly been applied to our material betterment, fields of specialized interest have come to be cultivated, and the activities of an ever-increasing body of scientific workers have diverged. Today we are most of us content to carry out an intense cultivation of our own little scientific gardens (to continue the metaphor), deriving occasional pleasure from a chat with our neighbors over the fence, while with them we discuss, criticize, and exhibit our produce (p. 1).

In brief, the need to assemble knowledge of our world into one cohesive view derives from the necessity to take it apart in order to penetrate it in depth.

The modern philosopher of science, E. A. Singer Jr. (1924 and 1959), tried to see the "whole picture" and show the relationship between the various disciplinary points of view. He observed that if we conceive of science as *a system of related points of view* we do not have the task of reassembling these points of view. The task of synthesis assumed by some philosophers and scientists derives from the confusion of taking the results of disciplinary analysis as the starting points of experience, rather than taking conceptual analysis of holistic experience as the starting point of scientific disciplinary analysis.

In this book we take a holistic view of human behavior and hence necessarily a functional, teleological, or purposeful view. Yet, following Singer and

Rosenblueth and Wiener (1943 and 1950) and Sommerhoff (1950), we try to make all the functional concepts employed as objective, as measurable, as capable of use in experimentation as any structural concepts produced by the mechanistic (so-called *behavioristic*) view of human behavior.

Perhaps no one has made so strong a case for a teleological approach to behavioral research—an approach that is complementary, not antithetical, to mechanism—as has Singer. Early in the century he began to develop a basis for studying purposeful behavior in an objective and experimental way. He was motivated by his recognition that the mechanistic point of view failed to deal adequately with the nature of *life, mind, society*, and *value*. The fruitfulness of his approach was not generally recognized until it was stated in another context by Rosenblueth and Wiener, who, as far as we know, were unaware of Singer's work.

Rosenblueth and Wiener, and later Wiener alone (1961), began to see the fruitfulness of looking at mechanisms as functional entities. They were concerned with how mechanisms functioned, with mechanisms that served a function, with *teleological mechanisms*. They found it more useful to proceed conceptually from functionally conceived wholes to structurally conceived parts than conversely. (Singer had shown that structure itself was a functional concept.)

Prior to the work of Rosenblueth and Wiener, designers of mechanisms tended to get their conception of the whole by assembling analyses of parts. Since then designers increasingly tend to develop their conceptions of the parts by decomposing their conception of the whole. This orientation has come to be known as the *systems point of view*. (See Churchman, 1968, and Emery, 1969.)

Put another way, before the revolution in thought that made possible the use of teleological concepts as a methodological key to open doors previously closed to science, scientists tended to derive their understanding of the functioning of the whole from the structure of the parts and the structural relationships between them. Today we increasingly tend to derive our understanding of the structure of the parts of a system from an understanding of the functioning of the whole.

Sommerhoff, like (but independently of) Singer, was preoccupied with making the teleological study of *life* compatible with the prevailing mechanistic point of view taken by most scientists. He developed a conceptual system that is expressed in terms quite different from Singer's, but one that is almost identical to Singer's where they overlap in subject matter.[3]

Sommerhoff formalized the insights of Rosenblueth and Wiener, and rigorously showed how *goal-directed behavior* could be made conceptually compatible with a deterministic mechanical conception of nature. However,

3. For a brief exposition of Sommerhoff's work and an analysis of it in the context of the social sciences, see Nagel (1956).

he stopped short of *purposeful behavior*, although he recognized the need to
go further.

> . . . since we . . . know that an action does not necessarily have to be consciously
> purposed in order to be goal-directed in the objective sense of the term, it is
> advisable to maintain a strict distinction between "purposive" in the subjective
> sense and "goal-directed" in the objective sense. The present papers deal only
> with the latter. This does not preclude the possibility of making a transition to the
> subjective aspects of behavior at a later stage . . .
>   Any exact science must start with objective data. The essence of scientific con-
> cepts is that they are definable in terms of public operations and observations.
> This is the very secret of their power. The exact sciences, therefore, cannot proceed
> from things of which we have only private awareness. They must start with
> objective and public events. But there is no reason why it should not be possible
> at a later stage to interpret subjective events in terms of such objective events.
> (p. 6 of undated manuscript)

Singer did consider purposeful behavior but he did not penetrate it in any
detail. This work attempts to do so. In a sense, using Singer's insights into the
nature of purpose, we attempt to do for the behavioral sciences what Sommerhoff did with Rosenblueth and Wiener's insights into the nature of goal-
directed behavior for biology.

The objective teleology developed here is not intended to replace the
objective ateleology (mechanism) that preceded it. Following Singer and
Somerhoff, we shall try to show that mechanistic and teleological viewpoints
are completely compatible or, as Neils Bohr believed, that there is a *complementarity* between them. We only argue that the mechanistic point of view is
not so fruitful as is the teleological in the study of human behavior.

Consider the characteristics of an objective teleology in more detail.
Centuries ago, Aristotle invoked teleological concepts to explain why
things, inanimate as well as animate, behaved as they did. Among those on
the contemporary scene who carry on in his spirit are some psychologists
who, for example, try to explain human behavior by invoking such concepts
as beliefs, attitudes, traits, instincts, and drives. Thus they employ a *subjective*
teleology. In an *objective* teleology, conversely, beliefs, attitudes, and traits
are attributed to an individual because of what he does. These properties are
derived from *perceived regularities of behavior under varied but specified
conditions*. Such concepts do not lie behind behavior; they lie *in* behavior.
Hence, in an objective teleology functional characteristics of human behavior
are not treated as intervening variables subjectively fabricated to conceal
our ignorance; they are objectively derived from what we can observe. An
objective teleology is in no way constrained to the study of subjective
purposiveness.

The objective part of objective teleology refers not only to the derivation of
functional properties from observable behavior but also to the observations
involved being reproducible by different observers. Introspection is not

required. This opens to public examination the study of the mind's inner workings. In order to accomplish this study it is necessary to provide *idealized operational* definitions and measures of functional concepts – definitions that provide *standards* in the same sense that the ateleologically oriented sciences provide standards for structural concepts (for example, length, density, and energy in physics).

An idealized operational definition of a concept provides a standard if it consists of an explicit statement of the conditions under which, and the operations by which, questions concerning the concept *ideally* ought to be answered. This type of operational definition differs from that proposed by P. W. Bridgman (1928), S. S. Stevens (1935), and E. G. Boring (1945). Their concern was with definitions in terms of simple operations that could *actually* be performed, not with ones we would *ideally* like to perform.[4]

Even though it may be impossible to meet the specifications contained in an idealized operational definition, they serve an important scientific purpose by enabling comparison of observations made under different sets of conditions but relevant to the same concept. Such observations can be *adjusted* back to the standard. That is, however research involving a concept is conducted, inferences should be drawn from what was observed to what would have been observed if the idealized specifications contained in the standard had been met. In order to make such inferences it is necessary to formulate explicitly how the conditions in which observations were made differ from those specified in the standard, and to employ appropriate theory to adjust the observations for the effects of these differences.

For example, in the idealized conditions formulated in physics for measuring the length of an object, the temperature of the environment in which observations should be made is specified. If the temperature under which observations actually are made differs from that specified, then the coefficient of linear expansion appropriate to the object measured can be applied to adjust the observations. Analogous coefficients and theories on which to base them are rare in the behavioral sciences. Thus the formulation and use of standards points up the need for theories that can be used to adjust data. Without the ability to make such adjustments, different researchers on the same subject cannot effectively compare their work, and without the ability to relate different studies of the same thing, results do not build up cumulatively or so rapidly as they should.

A standard can only be idealized in a relative sense – relative to our current state of knowledge. A standard is neither immutable nor absolute. Hence as our understanding of a concept increases, we change our formulation of how it ought to be observed and measured. This has been the case, for example, with respect to length. Therefore, at this stage in the development of the

---

4. For a discussion of the shortcomings of traditional (as contrasted to idealized) operational definitions, see Ackoff (1962, pp. 142–46).

behavioral sciences it is not necessary to develop ultimate (or even long-lasting) definitional standards, but to provide *some* standards. We cannot hope to provide generally acceptable operational definitions of behavioral concepts, but we do hope to provide definitions that will provoke constructive discussion, leading to their rapid improvement.

In developing the content of the definitions offered here, we have tried to take into account both historic and current usage; but usage is often confused, obscure, ambiguous, and inconsistent. We cannot hope to resolve all the conflicts inherent in such usage. We can only hope to reduce it.

Why bother to construct idealized operational definitions for a large number of behavioral concepts? Surely, it will be argued, we have only to draw on the existing concepts, methods, and findings of the behavioral sciences. The reason is that in a systems-oriented era — an era when we are becoming increasingly more interested in wholes than in their parts — that human behavior is still conceived, observed, analyzed, experimented on, and otherwise treated in a piecemeal way.

Human behavior is studied by psychologists, social psychologists, anthropologists, sociologists, political scientists, psychiatrists, philosophers, and others, and within each of these disciplines there are points of view as distinct and disparate as those between the disciplines. For example, some psychologists study *only* perception, or conception, or traits, or attitudes, or learning, or communication. Most psychologists make little or no effort to relate their work to that of others outside their own area of specialization, even if it is still within their discipline. As a result we have a very large number of very thin slices made through the sphere of human behavior, but nothing approaching a conception of it in the round.

What we have said of the study of human behavior in the large is also true of it in the small. For example, consider the study of human communication. In Colin Cherry's important book, *On Human Communication* (1957), he reveals a large number of ways in which such communication has been studied. But these appear to be almost completely unrelated despite Cherry's considerable effort to pull them together.

Alfred Smith's more recent effort (1966) is no more successful in this respect. Using two classification schemes, he attempted to relate many individually useful contributions to our understanding of human communication. These schemes allowed him to organize his selections but not to relate or synthesize the findings contained in them.

Communication itself has been divided into smaller and smaller subsystems — for example, coding, transmission, data processing, storage and retrieval, indexing, and so on. Not only is human communication a system too great to permit its parts to be understood in isolation from one another, but it is also a *sub*system too great to be treated fruitfully in isolation from other aspects of human behavior. Put another way, in order to develop a system of concepts that would relate the wide variety of studies of human communication, we found it necessary to imbed such a system in a more inclusive one involving all of purposeful behavior.

What is true of the study of communication is also true of the study of conflict, cooperation, and competition. In both areas, many of the results that have been obtained not only are unrelated but also are trivial or incapable of use in dealing with any real situations. For example, much small-group research has been directed toward determining whether cooperative or competitive groups are better in solving problems or in completing some other type of task. In a review of their own work and that of others on this question, Raven and Euchus (1963) came to the conclusion that in situations in which group members' actions do not affect each other's performance, competition is likely to produce better results than cooperation; but if members' actions are interdependent, then cooperation is likely to be more effective. *Sic*!

Raven and Euchus go on to observe that if group performance is the sum of independent individual performances, and these determine individual rewards, then the "competition (for reward) might add additional interest to what might otherwise be a dull task" and "motivation would be great in the competitive situation" (p. 308). More trivial results are hard to imagine.

A great deal of contemporary scientific paraphernalia has been applied to the study of choices — that is, decision making. This has produced an illusion of accomplishment greater than has actually been so. Regarding what has been accomplished, we find ourselves in agreement with Thomas A. Cowan (1963), who observed that

> . . . the teleology of decision making is more powerful than its logic in shaping the course of decision . . . intuition has a more important role to play in even simple and apparently trivial decisions than the rational constraints of present-day decision procedures allow . . . since it seems to me that every true *decision*, as distinct from an *inference*, involves an element of individual choice, the constraints imposed by general logic and generalizing mathematics upon decision procedures virtually rule out the study of truly creative decisions and tend to restrict decision science to mechanical, and, therefore, dull and repetitive instances of decision making . . . (p. 1069).

Some have criticized the behavioral sciences with less charity. For example, William Gomberg (1966) reviewed a prominent summarizing work in the field as follows.

> Recently Berelson and Steiner[5] wrote an inventory of scientific findings on human behavior that attempts to summarize those aspects of human behavior that are entitled to the honorific term "scientific" . . .
>
> As the pages of the book are reviewed, what is most striking is the banality of its "scientifically established findings" . . .

5. B. Berelson and G. A. Steiner, *Human Behavior, An Inventory of Scientific Findings* (New York: Harcourt Brace, 1964).

The fruitfulness of their investigation is hobbled because they have failed to distinguish what is needed for a description of social nature from their self-imposed rituals. They have engaged in a decision making ritualistic prescription for scientists to act in certain ways rather than in others. . . .

Professor Henry[6] is even rougher with Berelson and Steiner. He states that the book ought to be called "The Nature of Intellectual Failure in the Behavioral Sciences." He charges the entire field with:

1. An inability to distinguish truism from discovery
2. Insensitivity to platitude
3. Insensitivity to tautology
4. Confusion of causal sequences
5. The delusion of precision
6. The drawing of simple-minded parallels (pp. 9–11).

This quotation reflects how some observers of the behavioral sciences view the results of applying mechanistic and unsystematized concepts, and the methodology derived from them, to the subject of human choice. These concepts and methodology have dictated the kinds of studies that fill much of the literature. But we are not so concerned with the past as we are with the future – with the kinds of human behavior study that ought to be conducted, and with developing the concepts and methods that make them possible. We hope to show that an objective teleology expressed in the form of a conceptual system can serve as a foundation for significant research into such phenomena as choice, communication, conflict, and other types of social interaction.

The kinds of operational definitions of functional concepts developed here suggest general and rich hypotheses about human behavior. Furthermore, such definitions provide a basis for designing adequate tests for these hypotheses and for relating test results to each other, because the definitions form a network of concepts.

A principal hope behind this effort is that it will facilitate consideration of behavioral variables in the evaluation and design of social systems, including those involving machines as well as men. The models of such systems currently used in systems science, management science, operations research, systems engineering, and other systems-oriented interdisciplines frequently contain behavioral variables. But these variables are almost always treated ateleologically rather than teleologically. For example, in the study of service processes (such as check-out counters at supermarkets or toll booths at bridges or tunnels) the arrival rate of customers and the service rate of servers are important variables, but there is nothing particularly human about the way they are treated. This is not to say that in studying queues behavioral variables should be treated teleologically; it is to say that in those processes where such treatment would be desirable, it is seldom done. In models of

6. Jules Henry, "Revue of Human Behavior," *Scientific American*, July 1964, pp. 129–33.

most communication, advertising, and marketing processes, for example, people's responses are at best treated statistically, not as outputs of individual decision processes. In general we tend to treat behavior collectively, leaving the resulting statistic unexplained; hence, we do not increase our understanding and potential control over the process under study. To predict behavior is not enough; we must explain it.

For example, even very significant correlations between alcoholism and socioeconomic characteristics do not explain this disease and do not help to prevent or cure it. Accident statistics and knowledge of associated characteristics of bad drivers do not help us to prevent accidents.

Humans are typically treated by systems researchers as statistics-generating machines, or as entities that respond to stimuli in a mechanical way. Sometimes the human is completely excluded. In his model of the communication process, Claude Shannon (1949) excludes the human communicator. His contribution is not belittled in pointing up the need to bring human purposes into the study of phenomena involving human behavior. Thus, to improve communication processes we must understand *why* individuals choose to communicate in the way they do. We cannot start our analysis with the messages they have produced; we must begin with the process by which messages are produced. This is a matter of *choice*. Choice must be an integral part of any complete model of communication.

Finally it should be emphasized that what is attempted here is only secondarily intended to provide systems-oriented scientists and engineers with additional quantitative tools and techniques for their kits; it is primarily intended to provide them with a new kit for new and old tools and techniques. We try to provide a new way of thinking about and dealing with behavioral variables by constructing well-defined measures, not by attempting to add to the already numerous ill-defined indexes of such variables. Our efforts will not make it easy for others to deal rigorously and objectively with the richness, subtlety, and complexity of human behavior, but, if successful, they will make it possible.

REFERENCES

Ackoff, R. L. *Scientific Method: Optimizing Applied Research Decisions.* New York: John Wiley & Sons, 1962.
Bertalanffy, L. von. "Problems of General System Theory." *Human Biology* 23 (1951): 302–12.
———. "Conclusion." *Human Biology* 23 (1951): 336–45.
———. *General System Theory.* New York: George Braziller, 1968.
Boring, E. G. "The Use of Operational Definitions in Science." *Psychological Review* 52 (1945): 243–45.
Bridgman, P. W. *The Logic of Modern Physics.* New York: The Macmillan Co., 1927.

Cherry, Colin. *On Human Communication.* New York: John Wiley & Sons, 1957.

Churchman, C. W. *Theory of Experimental Inference.* New York: The Macmillan Co., 1948.

_____. *The Systems Approach.* New York: Delacorte Press, 1968.

Churchman, C. W., and R. L. Ackoff. *Methods of Inquiry.* St. Louis: Educational Publishers, 1950.

Cowan, T. A. "Decision Theory in Law, Science and Technology." *Science,* 7 June 1963, pp. 1065–75.

Emery, F. E. *Systems Thinking.* Harmondsworth, England: Penguin, 1969.

Gomberg, William, *The University and Business Education.* Working Paper No. 16, Department of Industry, Wharton School of Finance and Commerce, University of Pennsylvania, March 1966.

Nagel, E. *Logic without Metaphysics* , pp. 247–83. Glencoe, Ill.: Free Press. Also in F. E. Emery, *Systems Thinking,* pp. 297–329. Harmondsworth, England: Penguin, 1969.

Raven, B. H., and H. T. Euchus. "Cooperation and Competition in Means-Independent Trials." *Journal of Abnormal Psychology* 67 (1963): 307–16.

Rosenblueth, A., and N. Wiener. "Purposeful and Non-Purposeful Behavior." *Philosophy of Science* 17 (1950): 318–26.

Rosenblueth, A., N. Wiener, and J. H. Bigelow. "Behavior, Purpose, and Teleology," *Philosophy of Science* 11 (1943): 18–24.

Schanck, R. L. *The Permanent Revolution in Science.* New York: Philosophical Library, 1954.

Shannon, C. E., and W. Weaver. *The Mathematical Theory of Communication.* Urbana: The University of Illinois Press, 1949.

Singer, E. A., Jr. *Mind as Behavior.* Columbus: R. G. Adams, 1924.

_____, *Experience and Reflection.* Ed. C. W. Churchman. Philadelphia: University of Pennsylvania Press, 1959.

Smith, A. G. *Communication and Culture.* New York: Holt, Rinehart, & Winston, 1966.

Somerhoff, G. *Analytical Biology.* London: Oxford University Press, 1950.

_____. "Papers on Analytical Biology and Cybernetics." Undated and Mimeographed.

_____. "The Abstract Characteristics of Living Systems." in F. E. Emery, *Systems Thinking,* pp. 147–202. Harmondsworth, England: Penguin, 1969.

Stevens, S. S. "The Operational Basis of Psychology." *American Journal of Psychology* 47 (1935): 323–30.

Wiener, Norbert. *Cybernetics.* 2nd ed. New York: John Wiley & Sons, 1961.

2

Structure, Function, and Purpose

DECIDE, *v.i.* To succumb to the preponderance of one set of influences over another set.

AMBROSE BIERCE, *The Devil's Dictionary*

Introduction

Cybernetics, information theory, communications engineering, computer science, general systems theory, systems engineering, operations research, and related scientific and engineering efforts have brought with them a new respectability for such teleological concepts as *function* and *purpose*. They have shown the fruitfulness of conceiving of at least some phenomena in other than a mechanistic framework such as dominated the scientific thought of the nineteenth and early twentieth centuries. As noted by Miller, Galanter, and Pribram (1960), this development has even had an effect on the traditional mechanistic thinking of the behavioral sciences.

> Once a teleological mechanism could be built out of metal and glass psychologists recognized that it was scientifically respectable to admit that they had known it all along (p. 43).

Whenever a set of concepts such as purpose and communication become critical in many different fields of science and technology, there is danger that their definitions may become oriented to the special interests of their formulators, thereby restricting their applicability to other types of study. The process goes somewhat as follows. Cyberneticians define purpose and information so that they are admirably suited to the types of study in which cyberneticians are engaged. They then suggest that these definitions are equally applicable in other fields. For example, some cyberneticians believe the concept of purpose as used in their field is equally applicable in the behavioral sciences. Some psychologists and sociologists, however, realize that the phenomena they are concerned with are not captured in the cybernetician's definitions; hence, they look at his offerings simply as metaphors or analogies. Therefore, some behavioral scientists ignore work that could be at least very suggestive to them. Others have taken literally the definitions

13

offered by cyberneticians and have produced analyses of human behavior that miss much of its richness and subtlety. Both tendencies mitigate against interdisciplinary studies of human behavior such as Wiener (1961) called for.

To be more specific, consider Rosenblueth's and Wiener's formulation of "some criteria for the distinction between purposeful and nonpurposeful behavior" (1950). All these criteria were concerned with establishing some connection between the purposeful object and its environment and goals. Thus, for them, the purposeful object must be "coupled to" certain features of the environment, as well as "oriented to and guided by" the goal. Tests of purpose must be made by changing the environmental conditions, and so on. The general idea is that an object behaves purposefully if it continues to pursue the same goal by changing its behavior as conditions change.

Although this concept can be applied to some behavioral problems, it clearly cannot be applied to all. For example, the psychologist Koehler observed that simians learned how to use instruments to obtain food that was beyond their reach. Such animals were observed in unchanging environments, and yet their actions would generally be regarded as purposeful. Again, on the social level, a governmental agency may, in unchanging conditions, try many different tactics to get enacted some legislation that it wants. This, too, would generally be regarded as purposeful behavior.

In effect, Rosenblueth and Wiener found a useful concept of goal-directed activity in the study of mechanisms. But it is not advisable to assume that this concept captures all the meanings of purpose in human or even machine behavior. Sommerhoff (1969) has provided a well-worked-out example to arrive at the same conclusion.

> I approach the door of my house and enter. Here the approach towards the door might possibly be interpreted as an error-controlled movement in which visual and proprioceptive impulses provide the basis of an error computation which is then used in determining the corrective output. But it does not apply to my choice of this door as distinct from the other doors of the street . . . even if we just look at the movements involved in approaching the chosen door, all we can say strictly speaking on the observed facts of the case is that these movements are *error eliminating*—not that they are *error controlled*—in the strict sense of the term in which this implies a mechanism based on the initial computation and setting up of an error signal reflecting the magnitudes and direction of the discrepancy between the actual and desired state of the system. The final output of the central nervous system reflects this discrepancy, of course. But we have no evidence that explicit error signals are set up at any of the intermediate stages in the processing of the sensory inputs in this particular context. In fact the plasticity required of the nervous system in adaptive activities of this particular kind argues against the employment of mechanisms requiring such error computations. The familiar "comparators" of the servo-engineer imply functional rigidities that are difficult to reconcile with the degree of plasticity required in the central nervous system. And it is, of course, well known that the only evidence we have of a servo-mechanism

in the strict sense in the nervous system involves merely the purely mechanical action of the stretch reflex.

It cannot be stressed enough that the indiscriminate application of engineering concepts to biological situations is fraught with danger. Only extreme caution and careful analysis can save us from many possible pitfalls (pp. 198–199).

What is needed is a system of concepts and measures that goes beyond the findings of cybernetics and encompasses the concerns of the behavioral scientist, psychological or social. Such a system of concepts should be general enough to cover inquiries into many types of phenomena by different disciplines and, hopefully, lead to genuinely interdisciplinary research.

To develop such an appropriate system we begin with an analysis of the concept of structure as it has emerged in the physical sciences. Structural considerations enable us to define the mechanical image of strict determination that is fundamental to the physical sciences and to identify the probabilistic relation of producer–product that is basic to the biocentric sciences.

Classifications based on the common properties of production enable us to define the concepts of *function, goal-seeking,* and *purpose* with all the rigor of the concepts used in the physical sciences, and yet retain the core of meaning these terms have gained over the ages. This, unless we are mistaken, settles the question of whether such terms are admissible to scientific discourse (for example, the debate between Rosenblueth and Wiener, and Taylor [in Buckley, 1968, pp. 221–42]). The lack of more recent debate seems to us no more than scholarly collusion in agreeing not to raise embarrassing questions. To go beyond this classification to the detailed conceptual framework required for the study of concrete purposive behavior, we introduce in Chapter 3 the linking concept of purposive state. From such states at time t_0 issue the purposive behaviors and environmental settings at a later time t_1, and the outcomes or goal-states at a still later time t_2. The concept *purposive state* parallels the role of the coenetic variable in Sommerhoff's model of goal-directedness, but in order that it serve studies of concrete purposive behavior it has had to be defined in much more detail.

The program carried out in this chapter derives the concept *purpose* from the structural concept *deterministic causality* and thus shows their compatibility or complementarity. So doing unifies the conceptual foundations of the natural and behavioral sciences. The program does *not* demonstrate the primacy of structural concepts, although it may appear to. It does not, because it is possible to reverse the program carried out here and derive structural concepts from functional ones. (This is done in Chapter 15.) Hence, construction of a hierarchy of concepts is *not* our objective. We have proceeded from structure to function for two reasons. First, the progression corresponds to the historical development of structure and function, and hence the older structural concepts are more familiar and more widely understood than are functional ones. Second, the purpose of this effort is to delve into functional not structural, concepts. We maintain, however, that the concepts of science are interrelated with a symmetrical interdependence; any set of concepts can be used to illuminate any other set regardless of the order of their historical development. History and logic should not be confused.

The second aspect of this chapter's program consists of developing: (1) the · concept *system* out of that of an *individual*, and (2) a classification of types and levels of functional systems. We will show that a system is a type of individual and, hence, that all properties attributable to functional individuals are also attributable to functional systems.

The Concept of Structure

The meaning of *purpose* depends on the meaning of *function* and function is used throughout this book in contrast with *structure*. Structure is a very general concept that includes geometric, kinematic, mechanical, physical, and morphological concepts. Therefore, we treat these aspects of structure first, then derive the meaning of structure from them.

Euclid's geometry begins with a set of concepts and properties of which the most elementary are *point* and *line*. Concepts of other geometric entities and properties are built out of these basic building blocks.

2.1.   *Geometric class:* two or more sets of (geometric) points that have one or more geometric properties in common.

Whether or not such sets are said to be members of the same geometric class depends on whether the property or properties they have in common are of interest to the person doing the classification. Two sets that are alike with respect to a property of no interest to the investigator will not be said to be members of the same class if they differ with respect to another property that is of interest to him.

Mechanics, like geometry, begins with certain basic concepts. For example, in classical mechanics these were the Euclidean three-dimensional space-coordinate system, a time coordinate, and two mechanical properties — mass and acceleration.

2.2.   *Mechanical point:* a point that has geometric (spatial), kinematic (temporal), and basic mechanical properties (defined in 2.23).

In classical mechanics, such points were called point-particles. The exact nature of these particles (be they atoms, molecules, electrons, or what not) is not relevant to the concept, nor is it relevant whether or not they be considered to be divisible.

2.3.   *Mechanical class:* sets of equal numbers of mechanical points whose corresponding members have one or more mechanical properties in common.

2.4.   *Physical individual:* a set of two or more mechanical points that occupies a specified volume of space at (or over) a specified (period of) time.

The bodies or things we deal with daily are, therefore, physical individuals.

2.5. *Envelope and region* of a physical individual: the *envelope* is that part of a specified volume of space (V) at a specified moment of time that together with the part occupied by the physical individual, its *region*, exhausts V.

2.6. *Physical property* of a physical individual: a property that can be expressed as a function of the geometric, kinematic, and basic mechanical properties of the mechanical points of which the physical individual is composed.

For example, the temperature of an object is one of its physical properties because it can be expressed as the mean squared velocity of its point particles. Similarly, the mass of a body is equal to the sum of the masses of its point particles.

2.7. *Physical class:* a set of two or more physical individuals that have one or more physical properties in common.

Note that two sets of mechanical points that are alike in all respects except their locations must have the same physical properties. But two bodies with the same physical property need not consist of sets of mechanical points in the same mechanical class. Two sets (consisting of different numbers) of mechanical points in which no pair of points, one from each set, have the same mechanical properties may nevertheless form physical individuals with the same temperature or mass.

2.8. *Morphological property:* a set of physical properties — each the same function of the same geometric, kinematic, and basic mechanical properties — the values of which lie in the range $v \pm k$, where v is a value on a scale used to measure the physical property, and k is on that scale a value greater than zero.

Morphological properties are the ones the physical sciences usually deal with. When we say that two bodies have the same temperature we do not usually mean *exactly* the same temperature; their temperatures fall within some specified interval (say, $70° \pm 0.5°F$.) within which differences are of no significance to the investigator. The size of the interval used depends on our purposes. For some purposes we may want to consider as the same two bodies whose temperatures fall within the same $10°F$ interval; for others a $1°F$ interval may be required. When we classify people by age, each class is based on a morphological property. Here, too, the size of the interval will vary with our purposes. For one purpose it may be sufficient to consider only minors and adults (for example, in determining who can purchase alcoholic beverages), for another, age at the nearest birthday (as in the census).

2.9. *Morphological class:* a set of two or more physical individuals that have one or more morphological properties in common.

Note that two physical bodies with the same physical property must have the same morphological property defined on the scale used to measure that physical property. Clearly, however, two bodies with the same morphological property need not have the same corresponding physical property.

2.10. *Structural property:* any geometric, kinematic, mechanical, physical, or morphological property.

2.11. (*Structural*) *individual* or *object* (x or y): a physical individual with one or more specified physical or morphological properties.

2.12. *Structural environment* ($\bar{x}$ or $\bar{y}$) of an object (x or y): the envelope of x or y with one or more specified physical or morphological properties.

Note that the region occupied by x is the envelope of $\bar{x}$, and $\bar{x}$ can be treated as an individual and x as its environment. Hence object and environment are relative concepts.

2.13. *Structural class:* a set of two or more objects (X) or environments ($\bar{X}$) that have one or more structural properties in common.

Thus structure is a general concept applicable to geometric, kinematic, and mechanical properties, and to any properties that can be expressed as functions of them.

Systems

2.14. *System:* a set of interrelated elements, each of which is related directly or indirectly to every other element, and no subset of which is unrelated to any other subset.

Hence, a system is an entity composed of at least two elements and a relation that holds between each of its elements and at least one other element in the set. The elements form a completely connected set that is not decomposable into unrelated subsets. Therefore, although a system may itself be part of a larger system it cannot be decomposed into *independent* subsystems.

2.15. *Abstract system:* a system all of whose elements are concepts.[1]

2.16. *Concrete system:* a system at least two of whose elements are objects.

Languages, philosophic systems, and number systems are examples of abstract systems. *Numbers* are concepts, but the symbols that represent them, *numerals*, are physical things. Numerals, however, are not elements of a number system. The use of different numerals to represent the same numbers does not change the nature of the system.

2.17. *State of a system at a moment of time:* the set of relevant properties that system has at that time.

Any system has an unlimited number of properties. Only some of these are relevant to any particular research. Hence, those that are relevant may change with changes in the purpose of the research. The values of the relevant properties constitute the state of the system. In some cases we may be interested in only two possible states (such as off or on, or there or not there).

1. Concept is defined in 10.7.

In other cases we may be interested in a large or unlimited number of possible states (such as a system's velocity or weight).

2.18.   *Environment of a system:* a set of elements and their relevant properties, which elements are not part of the system, but a change in any of which can cause or produce a change in the state of the system.

The concepts *cause* and *produce* are treated in the next sections but do not presuppose this definition.

A system's environment, then, consists of all variables that can affect its state. External elements that affect irrelevant properties of a system are not part of its environment.

2.19.   *State of a system's environment at a moment of time:* the set of its relevant properties at that time.

The state of an element or subsets of elements of a system or its environment can be similarly defined.

Although concrete systems and their environments are *objective* things, they are also *subjective* to the degree that the particular configuration of elements that form both is dictated by the interests of the researcher. Different observers of the same phenomena may conceptualize them into different systems and environments. To one researcher an object may be a system, but to another the object may be an environment of one of its molecules, which he treats as a system.

A system consists of a set of individuals but, in addition, is itself an individual. (Not all individuals need be treated as systems.) Therefore, a structural individual may be treated as a system if we are concerned with the interactions of its parts (say, mechanical points), and some systems can be treated as structural individuals.

Cause–Effect and Producer–Product

Using the structural concepts developed thus far, it is possible to make explicit the meaning of a *natural mechanical system* (or mechanical image of nature) and the concept of *causality* that derives from it. The basic element of such a system is called a *time-slice*.

2.20.   *Time-slice:* a bounded part (volume) of space at a moment of time.

A time-slice is that part of the natural world that interests an investigator. Just how large or small it should be depends on the purpose of the investigation and the required precision of the results. For absolute precision the time-slice would have to contain the entire universe. In effect, what is excluded from a time-slice is what is considered to be irrelevant to the subject under investigation.

The researcher assigns certain bodies to the natural environment of interest to him. In any given investigation he does not include all possible mechanical points. The selection of points in space to which he assigns mechanical properties, like the size of the closed system, depends on the precision he wants to obtain.

Each time-slice contains a (finite or infinite) set of mechanical points, all of which have the same time property. Time-slices can be ordered along the time scale; if t_1, t_2, ... represents a sequence of moments of time, then s_1, s_2, ... represents an ordered set of time-slices if s_1 is a time-slice at t_1, s_2 at t_2, and so on.

All time-slices are individuated by time. The space-time system used may or may not be relativistic. Pictorially we can conceive of time-slices as three-dimensional discs forming a progression along a time axis. (A two-dimensional version is shown in Figure 2.1.) We will use (t_1-t_2) to represent a closed interval of time running from t_1 to t_2.

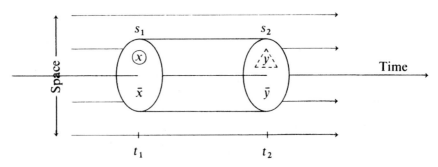

Figure 2.1.   Schematic Mechanical Image

2.21. *Laws of a natural mechanical system:* a set of assertions that, when given the spatial, temporal, and mechanical properties of any time-slice, determine the spatial and mechanical properties of any other time-slice consisting of the same volume in space.

For example, the universal law of gravitation relative to a system of centers of gravity of the planets was designed to enable the astronomer to determine the position of any one of the planets at any moment of time, given the space-time coordinates of each component of the system and its mechanical properties at any other given moment of time.

2.22. *Natural mechanical system:* a formal system composed of time-slices and a set of laws applicable to these time-slices.

Now we can define *basic mechanical properties* used in defining *mechanical points* (2.2).

2.23. *Basic mechanical properties* of a natural mechanical system: the minimal set of properties, other than spatial and temporal, that together with these properties is sufficient for application of the laws of the system to its time-slices.

2.24. *Cause–effect:* one time-slice s_1 is the *cause* of another time-slice s_2, its *effect*, if both time-slices belong to the same natural mechanical system and s_1 precedes s_2 along the time axis.[2]

Put in other words, s_1 is the cause of s_2 if it is the *necessary and sufficient* condition of s_2 — that is, if s_1 occurs, s_2 must follow, but if s_1 fails to occur, s_2 cannot follow. If one thing is both necessary and sufficient for another thing, then the two things can be conceptualized as time-slices in a closed natural mechanical system.

A time-slice can be considered to be composed of an object (x) and its structurally defined environment ($\bar{x}$) — that is, $s_i = (x + \bar{x})_i$, where i refers to the moment of time, t_i. We can now make explicit the sense in which an object at one moment of time can be said to be either necessary or sufficient for another object at a later moment of time.[3]

2.25. *Necessity:* an object x of class X in an environment $\bar{x}$ of class $\bar{X}$ at time t_1 is *necessary* for the presence of another object y of class Y in an environment $\bar{y}$ of class $\bar{Y}$ at a later time t_2 if: (1) $(x + \bar{x})_1$, s_1, is the cause of $(y + \bar{y})_2$, s_2, and (2) x were replaced by a structurally different object x' in $\bar{x}$ at t_1 without changing $\bar{x}$, y would not occur at t_2.

The second condition can be put in another way:

$$(x' + \bar{x})_1 - > (y' + \bar{y})_2,$$

where $- >$ means "is the cause of."

An acorn in a particular environment is necessary for an oak in a later environment if it can be shown that the acorn and its environment are the cause of the oak in its environment, and that had the acorn been removed from its environment and replaced by a non-acorn the oak would not have occurred in the later environment.

In order to determine whether x is necessary for y, it is *not* necessary to actually replace x in $\bar{x}$; the replacement required is virtual (that is the non-occurrence of y follows deductively from the absence of x in $\bar{x}$ *and the laws of the system*).

2.26. *Sufficiency:* an object x of class X in an environment $\bar{x}$ of class $\bar{X}$ at

---

2. It should be noted that if cause–effect applies to two time-slices of a natural mechanical system — of times t_1 and t_2, respectively — then the same relationship exists between two time-slices separated in time by an interval less than any given interval. If we follow common usage and regard the cause–effect relation as existing when the time-difference reaches the limit of zero, then the relation has the property of reflexivity, the one logical property that it does not share with the producer–product relation to be defined below. To use cause–effect in this way is analogous to saying that the shape of a balloon and the shape of the gas it contains determine each other. For further discussion of this point, see Singer, 1959, p. 289f.

3. These meanings are reflected in John Stuart Mill's (1862) first two canons of induction. In the first, the Method of Agreement, Mill attempted to specify how to determine whether one thing was sufficient for another. In the second canon, the Method of Difference, he attempted to specify how to determine whether one thing was necessary for another. For a discussion of the inadequacies of his treatment, see Ackoff, 1962, p. 312f.

time t_1 is *sufficient* for the presence of another object y of class Y in an environment $\bar{y}$ of class $\bar{Y}$ at a later time t_2 if x in any environment at t_1 is always followed by y in $\bar{y}$ at t_2. x in $\bar{x}$ at t_1 is *insufficient* for y in $\bar{y}$ at t_2 if there exists an environment of the non-$\bar{X}$ class, $\bar{x}'$, such that x in $\bar{x}'$ at t_1 would never be followed by y in $\bar{y}$ at t_2: $(x + \bar{x}')_1 - > (y' + \bar{y})_2$.

An acorn is insufficient for an oak because in a number of environments it cannot cause an oak — for example, in waterless sandy soil.

Note that if x were sufficient for y at a later time, its environment $(\bar{x})$ would be irrelevant. Thus x could then be considered to be a time-slice of a natural mechanical system.

Now we can turn to what is probably *the* most critical concept in this book.

2.27. *Producer–product*: an object x of class X in an environment $\bar{x}$ of class $\bar{X}$ at time t_1 is the *producer* of another object y — the *product* — of class Y in an environment $\bar{y}$ of class $\bar{Y}$ at a later time t_2 if x in $\bar{x}$ at t_1 is necessary but insufficient for y in $\bar{y}$ at t_2.

Producer–product is thus a special case of cause–effect. It applies when we consider the relationship between parts of time-slices (such as objects) rather than time-slices as wholes. An acorn, which was shown to be necessary but insufficient for an oak, is thus a producer of an oak, its product.

A further and important step can now be taken. We have defined producer–product relations for individual structures represented by x and y, which could denote acorns and oaks, boys and men, and like things or objects. However, if x in $\bar{x}$ at t_1 is a producer of y in $\bar{y}$ at t_2, the environment $(\bar{x})$ is also a producer of y. Given that $(x + \bar{x})_1$ is the cause of $(y + \bar{y})_2$, it follows from the necessity of x for y that $\bar{x}$ is insufficient for y, and from the insufficiency of x for y that $\bar{x}$ is necessary for y. This is not a surprising conclusion, because within the natural mechanical system represented each x and $\bar{x}$ is the environment of the other.

Note that a property (p_x) of an object (x) at one moment of time can be the producer of another object (y) or one of its properties (p_y) at a later moment of time. If the class (X) an object belongs to is defined as a set of objects with property p_x, and if x is a producer of y, then p_x is a producer of y. For example, since a female chicken produces chicken eggs the property *femaleness* is a producer of chicken eggs; it is necessary but not sufficient for such eggs. Similarly, *hot* water is a producer of *cooked* eggs. Hence *hotness* is a producer of *cookedness*.

It will also be observed that nothing in the definition of producer–product requires that the producer and the product be of different structural classes.

2.28. *Reproduction*: production by an object x_1 of class X of an object x_2 also of class X.

Thus oaks are reproducers: oaks produce acorns and acorns produce oaks. But production is a transitive relation — that is, if x produces y and y produces z, then x is a producer of z as well as of y.

A few auxiliary concepts will help us in the next step.

2.29.   *Actual producer:* an object x at time t_1 that has produced a member of a structural class Y prior to t_1.

2.30.   *Nonproducer:* an object x of class X in an environment $\bar{x}$ of class $\bar{X}$ at time t_1 is a *nonproducer* of another object y of class Y in an environment $\bar{y}$ of class $\bar{Y}$ at a later time t_2 if x in $\bar{x}$ at t_1 is not necessary for y in $\bar{y}$ at t_2.

2.31.   *Coproducers:* two or more objects, properties, and/or environments that are producers of the same product.

Since no producer is ever sufficient for its product, every producer has at least one coproducer. The set of all coproducers of a product y is the cause of y, since the set is sufficient as well as necessary for y.

In defining the formal image of producer–product relations, little attention has been given to the problem of adjusting observations to the image. This problem is engaged now by considering the meanings of *possible, potential,* and *probable* production.

2.32.   *Possible production:* members of a structural class of things are *possible producers* of another structural class of things if they are not actual producers of members of the second class, but there exist at least two class members of which one has and one neither has nor ever will have produced a member of the second class.

The need to observe at least one member as an actual producer is the reason that hens' eggs are not regarded as possible producers of oak trees. The occurrence of at least one acorn that does not produce an oak is the evidence that we are dealing with a producer–product relation, not a causal one. It should be borne in mind that this and the following definitions assume the schema previously defined. Thus an observed x can be defined as a possible y-producer only if it is observed to coexist in a natural system with an observed x that is an actual y-producer and an observed x that is an actual y-nonproducer. Coexistence in our schema is not restricted to the momentary space environment represented in our image of the natural environment.

2.33.   *Potential production:* all members of a structural class of things are *potential producers* of members of another structural class of things if *more than one* member of the first class has produced a member of the second class and at least one has actually failed to produce a member of the second class.

The meaning of this definition is clear, but one may wonder whether it is necessary. Could we not proceed directly from possible production to probable production? The justification for the category is simple. As long as we have only one producer x and one nonproducer x, it is possible that the difference in outcome was due to the difference that necessarily exists in their space-time coordinates. Observation of more than one producing x indicates a potential that resides in the class of x's despite the differences that exist in their locations in space-time.

2.34. *Probability of production:* (1) the probability that, within a time interval of specified duration *d*, an object *x* of class *X* in an environment $\bar{x}$ of class $\bar{X}$ will produce an object *y* of class *Y* in an environment $\bar{y}$ of class $\bar{Y}$ is the limiting relative frequency with which members of *X* in environments of class $\bar{X}$ produce members of *Y* in environments of class $\bar{Y}$ within time intervals of duration *d*; (2) the probability that, within a time interval of specified duration *d*, a particular object *x* in an environment $\bar{x}$ will produce an object *y* of class *Y* in an environment $\bar{y}$ of class $\bar{Y}$ is the limiting relative frequency with which *x* in environments of class $\bar{X}$ produces members of *Y* in environments of class $\bar{Y}$ within time intervals of duration *d*.

Therefore, the probability that an acorn in a particular type of environment will produce an oak is equal to the limiting relative frequency with which acorns in such environments produce an oak. The probability that a particular clock will strike twelve in a particular environment is the limiting relative frequency with which that clock strikes twelve at twelve o'clock in that environment.

The question about the probability that a *particular* thing will produce another arises only because of the uniqueness of that thing. If it were considered a member of a class, and hence not unique, its probability of production would be determined by virtue of its class membership. If the environment and the relevant properties of the particular thing (properties that affect its capability for production) remain constant over time, then that thing at different moments of time can be considered to be different things that form a class. Then the probability of that thing's production can be determined relative to that class. If these relevant properties change over time, however, it becomes more difficult to determine the thing's probability of production.

Consider a cigarette lighter that wears with use. In the first 100 tries it may light 100 times; in the second 100 tries it may light 90 times; in the third 100 tries it may light 80 times. If we know this sequence and want to estimate the lighter's probability of producing a flame on a try beyond the 300th try, common sense indicates 0.7; but this number is not its limiting relative frequency, which is approximately 0.0. Therefore, if the lighter's probability of producing a flame is a function of amount of previous use, we must take its previous use into account in determining this probability. If this lighter is not significantly different from others with the same amount of use, then we can revert to determination of its probability of production on the basis of class membership, which is based on usage.

If, however, it differs from other members of its class with respect to a relevant property, then the probability of production of class members can be used as a base; but this probability must be adjusted for the difference in probability produced by the difference in the relevant property. If this lighter contains a fuel different from other lighters with the same usage, then the probability of production of fire by members of the relevant class of lighters must be adjusted for the effect of the fuel. Therefore, we must conceptually construct a class of things similar to the unique one and infer the limiting relative frequency of its production from what we can observe about available things similar to the different lighter. Notice that inference is required even where we need not adjust observations, because the limiting relative frequency itself is never observed, but is inferred from a finite number of observations.

The concept of production is used extensively in the pure and applied physical sciences as well as in the behavioral sciences. For example, the reliability measures used in engineering are fundamentally probabilities of production or nonproduction. The reliability of a generator, for example, can be measured as the probability that turning it on under specified conditions will produce electric current.

Turning it on is an *act* that falls into a category not yet considered. The next set of definitions adds this category to the three we have already dealt with – objects and environments and their properties.

2.35. *Event:* a change in one or more structural properties of either an object, a system, an environment, or a relationship between them over a time period of specified duration.

Thus, for example, an event occurs when sugar dissolves in a liquid, because its structural properties change. Similarly, when a body falls an event occurs because at least its geometric properties change during the descent.

2.36. *Structural class of events:* a set of events that consists of similar changes of the same structural properties.

Note that the cause–effect and producer–product relations apply to events and to the concepts derived from them. This can be seen by substituting *event* for *object* in the relevant preceding definitions.

2.37. *Action of an individual or system (x):* an event occurring to x that is a potential producer of another event.

Thus an action is an *active* event, one capable of making something else happen to either x or its environment.

Two types of action are of particular importance.

2.38 *Reaction of an individual or system (x):* an event occurring to x that is *caused* by another event.

The causing event may be a change in either x or its environment.

2.39. *Response of an individual or system (x):* an event occurring to x that is *coproduced* by x and another event.

A man blown off the edge of a cliff *reacts* to the wind. He has no alternatives. If someone yells "Jump!" and he does so, or if he jumps to escape an attacking bear, he is *responding* to these environmental events. Alternatives were available to him. If he jumps because he wants to commit suicide (that is, an inner voice yells "Jump!") or because he wants to get to a lower level to rid himself of discomfort produced by the altitude, he responds to *inner* events. Although inner responses may be independent of any environmental event, they are not independent of the environment. The environment — not a change in it — coproduces the response.

2.40.   *Outcome:* the product of an individual's or system's action.

In other words, an outcome of an individual's or system's action is a change in that individual or system, or its environment, which is produced by that action.

We are now prepared to make another conceptual leap — from *producer-product* into *function* and beyond.

Functional Systems and Beyond

Function is a generic concept as *structure* is. It is not in any sense opposed to structure but is, as we have tried to show, completely compatible with it. A functional image of nature is completely compatible with one that is mechanistically and structurally oriented.

2.41.   *Functional class:* a set of structurally different individuals, systems or events, each of which is either a potential or actual producer of members (objects or events) of a specified class (*Y*) of any type.

The function of such a class is *Y*-production, and each member of the class can be said to have *Y*-production as its function. If an individual or system displays a type of structural behavior that is a member of a functional class of behavior displayed by other entities, then that individual or system can be said to have an *extrinsic function*. It is called extrinsic because the function is not one of its own but one it has by virtue of its membership in a class. The property that forms such a class is not structural but a common property of production. For example, a sundial, a water clock, a spring watch, and an electric clock — each differing structurally from the others — all coproduce time-telling and, hence, can be said to have time-telling as their extrinsic function. Similarly, automobiles, airplanes, ships, trains, and so on have the extrinsic function of transporting things.

A person who can telephone a store, write to it, visit it, or get another to visit it displays a set of actions (events) that constitute a functional class defined by, say, acquiring a new shirt. In this case the individual displays an *intrinsic function* because its function can be attributed to it on the basis of *its behavior alone.*

2.42.   *Functional environment:* the set of structural properties of a functional (*Y*-producing) individual's or system's environment that coproduce members of *Y*.

Going beyond functional classes and their environments, we can now construct a set of definitions to identify the members of a hierarchy of functional individuals or systems. This hierarchy is defined in terms of (1) structural characteristics of the individual's or system's actions and (2) the functional characteristics of their outcomes. First we need classifications of action-structure and outcome-function.

2.43.   *Uni-unistructural set of actions:* a set of actual and potential actions of an individual or system that can take place in structurally different environments and form one structural class.

2.44.   *Uni-multistructural set of actions:* a set of actual and potential set of actions of an individual or system that can take place in structurally different environments, which form two or more structural classes, but all the actions that take place in any one environment belong to only one of these structural classes.

Thus an individual who has such a set of actions available to him can display structurally different actions in different environments but not in the same environment.

2.45.   *Multi-multistructural set of actions:* a set of actual and potential actions of an individual or system that can take place in structurally different environments, which form two or more structural classes, and in at least one of these environments actions in two different structural classes can take place.

An individual with this capability can display structurally different behavior in one or in different environments.

A multi-uni set — one with different structures in one environment but the same structure in different environments — is not possible. If there are two or more structural classes in one environment, then all but one of these will be different from that class displayed in all other environments. Hence any entity that can display different classes of actions in one environment must be capable of displaying different classes in different environments.

Note that the three sets defined above are hierarchical because each has the capabilities of those that precede it.

Now outcomes can be similarly treated.

2.46.   *Uni-unifunctional set of outcomes:* a set of actual or potential outcomes of an individual's or system's actions — outcomes that can take place in structurally different environments and that form one functional class.

2.47.   *Uni-multifunctional set of outcomes:* a set of actual and potential outcomes of an individual's or system's actions — outcomes that can take place in structurally different environments, which form two or more functional classes, but all the outcomes that can occur in any one environment belong to only one of these functional classes.

2.48.   *Multi-multifunctional set of outcomes:* a set of actual and potential outcomes of an individual's or system's actions, outcomes that can take place in structurally different environments, which form two or more functional classes, and in at least one of these environments outcomes in two different functional classes can occur.

Using these two classificatory schemes, we construct Figure 2.2, which shows the possible classes of functional systems. Going from top to bottom and left to right in the table, additional properties are revealed. Each level possesses the properties of the levels to the left and above it.

Some of the cells in Figure 2.2 (1C and 2C) cannot be filled logically. Systems with only one structural type of action available to them in any one structurally defined environment can produce only one structural class of outcomes. Hence they cannot have a function based on what they do in any one environment. If they have an intrinsic function, it will be due to structural variations of outcomes over different environments. A function they have across a set of environments cannot vary within any environment in that set.

Now let us look at the various types of functional individuals and systems in more detail. Since our principal interest is in type 3 individuals and systems (multi-multistructural sets of actions), the others are treated lightly.

1A. *Passive functional individuals and systems* have available to them a uni-unistructural set of actions and a uni-unifunctional set of outcomes.

Such a system can do only one structural type of thing in any structurally defined environment. A clock just runs and a compass just points to the north. A clock can be said to have an extrinsic function (time-telling) because there is a class of structurally dissimilar objects (for example, sundials, water clocks, electric and spring watches, and so on) whose actions are structurally dissimilar but have a common function — time-telling. If these other time-tellers did not exist, a clock could not be said to have a function.

In general, meters are objects of this type. A thermometer can act in only one structural way in any environment. There is a structural correspondence between its reading and the temperature of the space it occupies.

Such systems can also have an intrinsic function. The same structural type of action can produce structurally different outcomes in structurally different environments, and these outcomes may form a functional class. Such a function would be a consequence of what the environment does to the action of the individual or system rather than what the action does to the environment. Such a function is therefore called *passive*. A factory may produce different amounts of air pollution in the area around it, depending on atmospheric conditions in that area, even though its emissions remain unchanged. The factory may thus have attributed to it the intrinsic function of polluting the atmosphere in the surrounding area.

1B. *Passive multifunctional individuals and systems* have available to them a uni-unistructural set of actions and a uni-multifunctional set of outcomes. Here, as in type 1A individuals and systems, any intrinsic function such a system can display is due to the structural variations in outcomes coproduced by the environment.

A simple example of such an entity is the chimney on the factory referred

FUNCTIONS OF OUTCOMES

STRUCTURE OF ACTIONS

	A. UNI-UNI One function in all environments	B. UNI-MULTI One function in any one environment, different functions in some different environments	C. MULTI-MULTI Different functions in same and different environments
1. UNI-UNI One structure in all environments	1A. PASSIVE FUNCTIONAL (meters)	1B. PASSIVE MULTIFUNCTIONAL (waste emitters)	
2. UNI-MULTI One structure in any one environment, different structures in some different environments	2A. REACTIVE FUNCTIONAL (servomechanisms)	2B. REACTIVE MULTIFUNCTIONAL (industrial robots)	
3. MULTI-MULTI Different structures in same and different environments	3A. ACTIVE FUNCTIONAL GOAL-SEEKING (single-program automata)	3B. ACTIVE MULTIFUNCTIONAL MULTI-GOAL-SEEKING (multiprogram automata)	3C. ACTIVE MULTIFUNCTIONAL AND ENVIRONMENTALLY INDEPENDENT PURPOSEFUL (people)

Figure 2.2. Classes of Functional Individuals and Systems

to above. It could be shown to have the extrinsic function of waste disposal and the intrinsic function of polluting the surrounding atmosphere.

2A. *Reactive functional individuals and systems* have available to them a multi-unistructural set of actions and a uni-unifunctional set of outcomes. Because they can display different structural behaviors in different environments but only one kind in any one environment, they *react* to environmental changes.

Servomechanisms and state-maintaining systems are a common type of reactive functional system. A heating system whose internal controller turns it on when the room temperature is below a desired level and turns it off when the temperature is above this level is state-maintaining. The state it maintains is a room temperature that falls within a small range around its setting. Note that the room temperature that affects the system's behavior can be conceptualized as either part of the system or part of its environment. Then the enlarged system would react to changes in the temperature of the external environment. In general, most stats (for example, thermostats and humidistats) are reactive functional systems.

Automatic pilots on ships and airplanes are also reactive functional systems. The structural events they react to are changing relationships between the system they control and their environments. Such systems can react in only one structural way to any particular kind of change. Their function is to keep on course the larger system of which they are a part.

2B. *Reactive multifunctional individuals and systems* are ones that have available to them uni-multistructural sets of actions and uni-multifunctional sets of outcomes. An automatic control system that keeps an airplane on course and level is a system of this type. Another example is an air-control system that maintains a desired temperature and humidity. Such systems are normally composites of reactive functional systems.

Systems that are reactive must be able to *discriminate* between different environments. Furthermore, such systems can adapt (see definition 8.1) to changes in environment, but unlike goal-seeking systems they are not capable of learning (definition 3.23) because they cannot choose their behavior. They cannot improve with experience.

2.49. *Goal-seeking individuals and systems* (3A): ones that can respond in structurally different ways to one or more structurally different (internal or external) events, and all their responses have the function of producing a particular outcome, which is its goal.

A goal-seeking individual or system is responsive, not reactive, because it has a choice (definition 3.1) of responses. (An event sufficient for — and thus deterministically causing — a reaction cannot cause different reactions in the same environment.) Such an individual or system may accomplish the same thing in different ways. If it has memory (definition 4.24), it can also increase its efficiency over time in producing the outcome that is its goal. Thus it can *learn* as well as *adapt*.

For example, an electronic maze-solving rat (a simple automata) is a goal-seeking system that, when it runs into a wall of a maze, moves in a programmed sequence of ways until it finds an open path. The sequence is such that it can solve at least some solvable mazes. If this rat has memory, it can also be programmed to take a *solution path* on subsequent trials in a familiar maze.

2.50. *Multi-goal-seeking individual or system:* one that is goal-seeking in each of two or more structurally different environments, and seeks different goals in at least two different environments.

Individuals and systems of this type can pursue different goals, but they do not determine the goal to be pursued – the environment does. However, such individuals and systems choose the means by which to pursue their goals.

A computer programmed to play more than one game (such as tic-tac-toe and checkers) is multi-goal-seeking. The game it plays is not a matter of its choice; it is usually determined by an instruction from an external source.

2.51. *Purposeful individual or system* (3C): one that can produce (1) the same functional type of outcome in different structural ways in the same structural environment and (2) can produce functionally different outcomes in the same and different structural environments.

Thus a purposeful system is one that can change its goals in constant environmental conditions; it selects goals as well as the means by which to pursue them. It thus displays *will*. Human beings are the most familiar examples of such systems.

The remainder of this book is concerned with purposeful systems. We begin to treat them in detail in Chapter 3. Ideal-seeking systems form an important subclass of purposeful systems – a subclass we consider briefly in Chapter 3 and at length in Chapter 14.

Up to this point we have concentrated on the behavior of functional entities to the exclusion of the *instruments* incorporated into this behavior. We now turn in this direction.

Instruments

2.52. *Instrument:* an object that coproduces the outcome of an individual's or system's action; the coproduction is itself produced by the individual or system.

Thus an instrument is a device used by a functional individual or system in its functional behavior. A hammer and the behavior of a carpenter coproduce the driving of a nail; the coproduction is produced by the carpenter. Hence the hammer is the carpenter's instrument.

The instrument employed by an individual or system operating at any functional level is always at a *lower* level than the level of the individual or system that uses it. If a purposeful individual (*A*) wants to use another purposeful individual (*B*) as an instrument, he can do so only by restricting the choices of *B* so that *B* acts at less than the level of purposefulness. A master thus uses his slave as goal-seeking or lower, not as purposeful. The master imposes his goals on the slave.

On the other hand, a goal-seeking system such as a volunteer fire department uses its equipment as instruments. These are not goal-seeking but of a lower functional type. The community that uses this department, however, is of a higher type — at least multi-goal-seeking.

A purposeful system (such as a person) can receive assistance from another such system if the second *cooperates* (definition 12.1) with the first. But in such interaction the second person is not an instrument of the first unless he is *malevolently exploited* (see definition 12.6) by the first. In such exploitation the options of one are reduced and those of the other are increased.

The parts of a system may, in some circumstances, be instruments of the system (as the parts of an automobile are to an automobile), or the parts may use the system as an instrument (as do the members of a democratic community). This aspect of system–part interaction is discussed at length in Chapter 13.

REFERENCES

Ackoff, R. L. *Scientific Method: Optimizing Applied Research Decisions.* New York: John Wiley & Sons, 1962.
Buckley, Walter. *Modern Systems Research for the Behavioral Scientist.* Chicago: Aldine Publishing Co., 1968
Mill, J. S. *A System of Logic.* 5th ed. London: Parker, Son, and Bourn, 1862.
Miller, G. A., E. Galanter, and K. Pribram. *Plans and the Structure of Behavior.* New York: Holt, Rinehart & Winston, 1960.
Rosenblueth, A., and N. Wiener. "Purposeful and Non-Purposeful Behavior." *Philosophy of Science* 17 (1950): 318–26.
Singer, E. A., Jr. *Experience and Reflection,* edited by C. W. Churchman. Philadelphia: University of Pennsylvania Press, 1959.
Somerhoff, G. "The Abstract Characteristics of Living Systems." In *Systems Thinking,* edited by F. E. Emery, pp. 147–204. Harmondsworth, England: Penguin, 1969.
Wiener, N. *Cybernetics.* 2nd ed. New York: John Wiley & Sons, 1961.

3

The Individuality of Psychological Systems

ME, *pro.* The objectionable case of I. The personal pronoun in English has three cases, the dominative, the objectionable and the oppressive. Each is all three.

The Devil's Dictionary

Introduction

If systems theory is to be of practical value, we must be able to proceed from general systems theory to the conceptual representation of individual systems. Our main concern will be with the representation of individual purposeful systems rather than with goal-seeking or multi-goal-seeking systems. We believe that only at this level can systems theory contribute to the core problems of psychology, sociology, and anthropology.

The concepts we will use as a basis for our analysis are those required to define a *purposive state* – that is, the behavioral state of a purposeful individual or system.

The kind of individual and system we have elected to analyze is psychological, but we believe our concepts are equally relevant to the analysis of social or cultural systems. (Such relevance is discussed in Chapter 13.)

Definitions of Personality

Psychologists have given a great deal of attention to the problem of defining the individuality of psychological systems – that is, with trying to define what is meant by *personality*. Some, like Angyal (1941, 1965), have consciously used systems concepts; some, like Lewin (1938) and Heider (1946), have recognized that the problem required a rigorous, even mathematical, solution. Despite the efforts that have been made, the situation today still justifies the conclusion of Hall and Lindzey (1957): "... it is our conviction that no substantive definition of personality can be *applied* with any generality" (p. 9, italics ours).

Churchman and Ackoff formulated a substantive definition in 1947, but, as Brand (1954) observed:

33

... it offers a proposal for the precise identification of personality within a general-behavior theory. A method is also suggested by which personality may be measured quantitatively. The disadvantage of the proposal is that it requires a methodology not familiar to current research practice in psychology, and still has to develop an experimental program (p. 16).

The program we will develop in this chapter is a progressive development and expansion of the 1947 proposal, and hopefully the wider range of concepts will lessen the disadvantages Brand refers to.

Although psychologists have as yet failed to agree on a definition of personality, there does emerge from their writings considerable agreement on what such a definition should do. It should (1) *capture the uniqueness of the individual* (Allport, 1957, p. 18), (2) *provide a very general concept under which all other psychological concepts can be subsumed* (Katz and Schanck, 1938, p. 391), and (3) *locate personality in the responses of an individual to his environment* (Cattell, 1966, p. 5).

We believe that no concept of personality can meet the criterion of uniqueness unless it represents the psychological individual as a purposeful individual and locates personality in the responses of an individual to his environment. If this can be done with sufficient generality and rigor, it may then be possible to subsume under it many, if not all, other psychological concepts. In Chapter 2 we provided a rigorous definition of purposeful individuals and systems. We shall now try to develop a definition of the state of a purposeful individual or system. This development leads to a definition of personality that satisfies the above criteria *and* provides a measure of it as well. A few preparatory definitions are necessary.

3.1. *Choice:* an individual's or system's production in a structural environment of one of two or more structurally different but functionally similar acts of which the individual or system is a potential producer in that environment.

Choice, thus defined, can be displayed only by type 3 individuals and systems (see Figure 2.2).

3.2. *Choice environment (S):* the functional environment of an individual or system that displays choice.

3.3. *Subject:* a purposeful individual or system.

3.4. *Behavior:* an actual or potential act of a subject.

3.5. *Courses of action* $(C_i; 1 \leq i \leq m)$: structurally different behaviors of a subject in a structurally defined environment; these behaviors have one or more common functions.

Thus a course of action is purposeful behavior of a purposeful individual or system.

Choice States of Purposeful Individuals and Systems

An essential characteristic of purposeful behavior is that it involves choice. The meaning of this characteristic is revealed by an analysis of the nature of a purposive state. Such a state has four types of *component:* (1) the subject that displays choice (A), (2) the choice environment (S), (3) the available courses of action (C_i), and (4) the outcomes possible in that environment (O_j).

The relevant relationships between these components are completely specified by three types of measures that are *parameters* of a purposive state. Their definitions follow.

3.6. *Probability of choice* (P_i): the probability that a subject A will produce a course of action C_i in a choice environment $S: P_i = P(C_i/A$ in $S)$.

This probability applies to a specific subject whose relevant properties may change over time. Because of learning, a subject's probability of choosing a particular course of action may increase or decrease. This change presents no great difficulty. In principle the change is no different than the effect of usage on the probability of a lighter's producing a flame. Adjustments for such changes are necessary, but awareness of the kinds of adjustment required can stimulate some very fruitful and fundamental research in the behavioral sciences.

3.7. *Efficiency of a course of action* (E_{ij}): the probability that a course of action C_i will produce a specified outcome O_j in a specified environment S if it is chosen by a specified subject $A: E_{ij} = P(O_j/A$ chooses C_i in $S)$.

The third parameter, *relative value* (V_j) *of an outcome* (O_j) to a subject, requires use of some concepts yet to be developed. (See definition 3.27.) For the time being the more familiar concept of *utility* can be substituted for relative value; the relationship and difference between them will be made explicit later in this chapter, where both are defined. We now examine more closely the four components and three parameters of a purposive state.

COURSES OF ACTION

A course of action is not to be construed as mechanistically conceived or physically defined action, but rather as morphologically defined action. Variations in an action with respect to certain of its physical characteristics may not change it. For example, *driving a car* may be designated as a course of action. There are many physically different ways of driving a car, but it is frequently useful to group these into one morphological class of actions. Despite the variations within the class, it can be distinguished from other morphological classes of action — for example, from *using a street car* or *walking.* The morphology of a course of action may be specified narrowly or broadly, depending on the purpose of the research. For one purpose (say, in testing drivers) it may be desirable to distinguish between automatic and manual shifting of gears. For another purpose (say, in planning an exercise program), it may be desirable to group the use of any self-powered vehicle into one course of action.

It should be noted that the problem of defining a course of action is essentially similar to that of defining a physical object. For one purpose an automobile may be considered as a unit; for another it is a composite of many other units (wheels, transmission, motor, body, and so on); for still another purpose it may be considered as part of a unit (a fleet of cars).

3.8.   *Available course of action* in a choice environment S: a course of action whose probability of being chosen in S by any subject is greater than zero.

3.9.   *Potential course of action* of a subject A in a choice environment S: a course of action whose probability of being chosen by A in S is greater than zero.

An available course of action may have no probability of being chosen by a particular subject, and hence is not a potential choice for him (it). On the other hand, every potential course of action is available. Furthermore, a course of action that is a potential choice for a subject in one environment may not be in another environment. For example, a person may use a bicycle sometimes in the country but never in the city. He may be aware of the availability of a bicycle in the city (in a sense to be considered in Chapter 4), and still it may not be a potential choice. For example, many are aware of the availability of narcotics but still never use them.

The relativity of courses of action and outcomes should be noted. Courses of action and outcomes are conceptual constructs of an observer of another's behavior; either may be converted into the other, depending on the observer's interests. For example, *chopping the trunk of a tree* may be considered to be a course of action and the *felling of that tree* to be its outcome. But felling a tree may also be considered to be a course of action that can coproduce the outcome *clearing a path*. Such relativity of concepts appears in all areas of science — for example, the effect of one cause may itself cause another effect — and hence does not present any unique methodological problem in this context.

Finally, it will be observed that courses of action are frequently called *means*, and outcomes are frequently called *ends*.

EFFICIENCY

Efficiency is commonly measured either as (1) units of input required to obtain a specified output, or (2) units of output obtained by a specified input. Neither type of measure is sufficiently general to be applied in all situations.

The input required for a fixed output and the output yielded by a fixed input are not constant but varied. For example, the number of units made by a machine per hour varies from hour to hour; the miles per gallon obtained by an automobile also varies. Hence, for a fixed input various possible outputs exist; to each of these a probability can be assigned. If an input is specified in the definition of a course of action, then the efficiency of that course of action for a specified outcome can be defined as the probability that the course of action will produce that outcome. This measure, unlike input and output measures, can always be applied to a purposeful state. In order to use probability of production as a measure of efficiency, courses of action that are alike in all respects except the amount of input they involve must be formulated as different courses of action.

This measure of efficiency of a course of action depends on the environment and the subject involved. Use of skis, for example, may be efficient for self-transportation down a snow-covered hill but not down an uncovered hill. Different individuals may ski with different efficiencies, and the efficiency of the same individual may change over time (for example, by learning). Consequently, in order to use this measure it is necessary to specify the relevant time period as well as the individual and relevant properties of the environment.

RELATIVE VALUE OF OUTCOMES

Like efficiency, there is no one generally accepted measure of the relative value or worth of an outcome. Fortunately, however, such agreement is not necessary for our purposes here. Nevertheless, it is convenient to use some kind of standard measure wherever possible. A dimensionless measure of *relative value* provides such a convenient standard. If all the values (v_j) assigned to the various outcomes are positive, a measure of relative value (V_j) for each outcome may be obtained by the conversion:

$$V_j = \frac{v_j}{\Sigma v_j}.$$

Then, since

$$\Sigma \frac{v_j}{\Sigma v_j} = 1.0,$$

it follows that

$$\Sigma V_j = 1.0.$$

The minimum relative value (0) occurs only when the absolute value (v_j) is equal to zero. The maximum relative value (1.0) occurs only when all but one outcome have zero value.

If some or all of the measures (V_j) are negative, one can add to each measure the amount required to raise the lowest value to zero, and can convert the resulting adjusted values to relative values. For example:

	Unadjusted Values	*Adjusted Values*	*Relative Values*
O_1	-100	0	0
O_2	-75	25	0.25
O_3	-25	75	0.75

In the discussion that follows, we shall use the concept of relative value and assume that $\Sigma V_j = 1.0$. All the results, however, are easily modified to cover either the use of absolute values or the case in which negative values are used.

In conceptualizing a purposeful state, it is convenient for the researcher to formulate the available courses of action and possible outcomes as exclusive and exhaustive sets. By use of a Boolean expansion, sets of courses of action and outcomes that are not exclusive and exhaustive can easily be transformed into sets that are. If we have a nonexclusive and/or nonexhaustive set of outcomes — o_1, o_2, o_3 — we can formulate the following exclusive and exhaustive set (see Figure 3.1).

$$O_1 = o_1 \text{ and not } o_2 \text{ or } o_3.$$
$$O_2 = o_2 \text{ and not } o_1 \text{ or } o_3.$$
$$O_3 = o_3 \text{ and not } o_1 \text{ or } o_2.$$
$$O_4 = o_1 \text{ and } o_2 \text{ and not } o_3.$$
$$O_5 = o_1 \text{ and } o_3 \text{ and not } o_2.$$
$$O_6 = o_2 \text{ and } o_3 \text{ and not } o_1.$$
$$O_7 = o_1 \text{ and } o_2 \text{ and } o_3.$$
$$O_8 = \text{not } o_1 \text{ and not } o_2 \text{ and not } o_3.$$

For an exclusive and exhaustive set of courses of action, the sum of the probabilities of choice must be equal to 1.0:

$$\sum_i P_i = 1.0;$$

and the sum of the efficiencies of each course of action over an exclusive and exhaustive set of outcomes must also equal to 1.0:

$$\sum_j E_{ij} = 1.0.$$

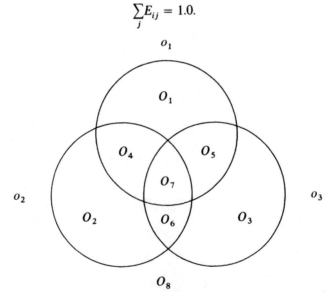

Figure 3.1.   Formulation of an Exclusive and Exhaustive Set of Outcomes

Unless otherwise specified, we will consider the sets of courses of action and outcomes to be defined so as to be exclusive and exhaustive.

Two special classes of outcomes will be of particular interest to us as we proceed.

3.10. *Possible outcome* for a subject A in a choice environment S in a time-period t_1-t_2: an outcome relative to which there is available to A in S at least one course of action that, if chosen by A, has an efficiency greater than zero for that outcome in t_1-t_2.

3.11. *Potential outcome* for a subject A in a choice environment S in a time-period t_1-t_2: a possible outcome for A in S in t_1-t_2, in which environment and time-period A's probability of choosing a course of action with some efficiency for that outcome is greater than zero.

Now we can define a purposive state of an individual or system.

3.12. *Purposive state* of a subject A: A in a choice environment S in which:
(1) There is at least one potential outcome O_1; the relative value of O_1 to A is not equal to that of another potential outcome O_2, and O_1 and O_2 are mutually exclusive in S: $V_1 \neq V_2$.
(2) There are at least two potential courses of action for A, C_1 and C_2: $P_1 > 0 \text{ and } P_2 > 0$.
(3) The efficiencies of C_1 and C_2 are such that

$$\sum_j E_{1j}V_j \neq \sum_j E_{2j}V_j.^1$$

This definition of a purposive state may be summarized less technically: a subject may be said to be in such a state if he (it) wants something and has unequally efficient alternative ways of trying to get it.

It will be noted that we have stated that the parameters of choice and efficiency may change their values during the period of choosing. The same is true of the relative value to the subject of the possible outcomes.

Definition of Personality (Individuality)

The analysis given above of a purposive state identifies the subject (A), the available courses of action $\{C_i\}$, the possible outcomes $\{O_j\}$, the environment (S_k), the subject's probabilities of choice $\{P_i\}$, the efficiencies of each available course of action for each possible outcome $\{E_{ij}\}$, and the relative values that the subject places on these outcomes $\{V_j\}$. The courses of action and outcomes are functions of both the environment and the subject. The probabilities of choice, efficiencies, and relative values depend on the subject but are not independent of the situation. Therefore, the individuality of the subject, his personality, must derive from the way his probabilities of choice, efficiencies, and relative values depend on the properties of the situation.

---

1. Thus Buridan's ass was *not* in a choice situation.

An individual's probabilities of choice, efficiencies, and relative values can each be expressed, in principle, as a function of the choice situation characteristics; that is, for a subject A the function shown in Table 3.1 can be formulated: In a sense, then, these three functions — f, g, and h — are the three *dimensions* of individuality. It would be desirable, however, if they could be combined into a single function. This can be done as follows.

Table 3.1. Components of the choice situation

Parameters of the choice situation	Available Courses of Action	Possible Outcomes	Environment	
Probability of choice	$P_i = f[\{C_i\},$	$\{O_j\},$	$S_k]$	(3.1)
Efficiency	$E_{ij} = g[\{C_i\},$	$\{O_j\},$	$S_k]$	(3.2)
Relative value	$V_j = h[\{C_i\},$	$\{O_j\},$	$S_k]$	(3.3)

The contribution of a purposeful individual to a choice situation must manifest itself by an effect on what happens in that situation — the outcome. Let $P(O_j)$ represent the probability that an outcome O_j will occur in a choice situation. If the probabilities of different outcomes in a choice situation were independent of the subject, then there would be no functional difference between different subjects in that situation. But it is just such a difference (that is, in outcome) that a difference in individuality must produce if it exists. Let us pursue this line a bit further.

If $P(O_j)$ represents the probability that an outcome O_j will occur in a particular choice situation, then

$$P(O_j) = \sum_i P_i E_{ij};$$ (3.4)

that is, the probability that O_j will occur is the sum of the products of the probability that each course of action will be selected and the probability that, if selected, it will produce the outcome O_j. For example, in the simple case where $P_1 = 0.6$, $P_2 = 0.4$, $E_{11} = 0.7$, $E_{12} = 0.3$, $E_{21} = 0.1$, and $E_{22} = 0.9$, then

$$P(O_1) = P_1 E_{11} + P_2 E_{21} = 0.6(0.7) + 0.4(0.1) = 0.46.$$
$$P(O_2) = P_1 E_{12} + P_2 E_{22} = 0.6(0.3) + 0.4(0.9) = 0.54.$$

Now the subject's probabilities of choice and the efficiencies of these choices depend on the properties of the situation: the available courses of action, the possible outcomes, and the environment. Therefore, $P(O_j)$ is a function of the choice situation. Hence we can write

$$P(O_j) = F[\{C_i\}, \{O_j\}, S_k].$$ (3.5)

What the individual contributes to a choice situation, then, is a transformation of situational properties into probabilities of choice, efficiencies, and relative values. So individuality must lie in this transformation. That is, if two individuals are placed in the same choice situation, the differences between them must be manifested in the difference in values of their probabilities of choice, efficiencies, and relative values. The sum of the products of these three parameters is equal to the subject's *expected relative value* (*EV*):

$$EV = \sum_i \sum_j P_i E_{ij} V_j. \tag{3.6}$$

But since the P_is, E_{ij}s, and V_js are functions of the choice situation, then so, too, is the expected relative value:

$$EV = \pi[\{C_i\}, \{O_j\}, S_k]. \tag{3.7}$$

Then we can define personality (individuality) as follows.

3.13. *Personality* (*individuality*) of a subject: a mathematical function π that relates his (its) expected relative value in any choice situation to the properties of the available courses of action, their possible outcomes, and the relevant environmental variables.

Hence, *personality* (*individuality*) *is not conceived here as an unobservable intervening variable that is invoked to explain choice, but as an observable function that describes how an individual or system converts a choice situation into an expected relative value for himself or itself.*

This definition of personality (individuality) is not as operational as it is programmatic; that is, it does not tell us how to find the function π, but it can be used to design a research program that will ultimately yield approximations to π. For example, to evaluate π we must develop appropriate and general quantitative ways of representing the available courses of action and possible outcomes, as well as a specification of a set of variables that are sufficient to characterize any choice environment. Such development requires considerable research. But the research can be divided into parts (types of research) that will enable us to move up on the individuality function by smaller steps than would otherwise be required. Each of these types of research and the concepts associated with them involves an aspect of individuality, a slice through the multidimensional individuality space. There are three such types of research; the essential characteristic of these is the variable that is treated as dependent — probability of choice, efficiency of choice, or relative value.

Studies involving probability of choice as the dependent variable will be referred to as *familiarity* studies; those involving efficiencies of choice, *knowledge* studies; and those involving relative values, *intention* studies.

Perhaps the relationship among these three aspects of psychological individuality is better understood in the following terms. All aspects require a measure of the probability of choice derived from observing what choices are actually made in a controlled situation. The differences lie in the situations when choice is observed. They are as follows.

(1) Measures of *familiarity* derive from the effect that different properties of courses of action have on probabilities of choice displayed in situations in which the course of action chosen has no effect on the outcome. Hence they are measures of means preferences.

(2) Measures of *knowledge* derive from the effect of different efficiencies of choice on probabilities of choice for whose outcomes the relative values remain constant. Hence they are measures of sensitivity to efficiency.

(3) Measures of *intention* derive from the effect that differences in outcome have on probabilities of choice, where each available course of action can produce only one possible outcome and each possible outcome can be obtained. Hence they are measures of ends preferences.

In measuring familiarity, knowledge and intention are held constant. In measuring knowledge, familiarity and intention are held constant. In measuring intention, familiarity and knowledge are held constant. Now let us consider each of these concepts and measures in more detail.

Probability of Choice: Familiarity

The objective here is to determine how an individual's probabilities of choice are influenced by properties of available courses of action and the choice environment — properties that do not affect the efficiencies of the alternatives. Hence we want to construct a choice situation in which possible influence of the relative efficiencies of choices has been removed. This can be done as follows.

3.14.   *Familiarity (choice) situation:* one in which (1) the possible outcomes are grouped into two exclusive and exhaustive classes, O_1 and O_2, where the subject prefers O_1 to O_2 (i.e., $V_1 > V_2$); and (2) each of the courses of action has an equal efficiency for each possible outcome. That is,

$$E_{11} = E_{21} = \ldots = E_{m1} = L(E_{i1})$$

and

$$E_{12} = E_{22} = \ldots = E_{m2} = L(E_{i2})$$

where $L(E_{ij})$ is the level of efficiency of courses of action for outcome O_j.
Note that

$$0 \leq L(E_{ij}) \leq 1, \text{ and } \sum_j L(E_{ij}) = 1.0.$$

In such an environment there is not a choice of outcome, only of a course of action. The relative values of the outcomes are kept constant for each set of observations used to establish probabilities of choice.

Consider a choice situation in which a subject wants to write a letter (O_1); hence, O_2 is not writing a letter. Suppose we have a set of ball-point pens identical in all respects except their color. Then the use of each is equally efficient for writing a letter. Choice in such a situation reflects the subject's preferences for color of ink.

Now we can identify an important measure and function that can be extracted from choices observed in familiarity situations.

3.15.   *Degree of familiarity:* A subject's degree of familiarity (DF_{ij}) with a course of action (C_i) relative to a preferred outcome (O_j) whose relative value (V_j) is equal to 1.0, and an available set of exclusively and exhaustively defined courses of action $\{C_i\}$ of which C_i is a member is the probability that he will select C_i in a familiarity situation where the level of efficiency for the preferred outcome, $L(E_{ij})$, is 1.0; that is,

$$DF_{ij} = [P_i \mid \{C_i\}, V_j = 1.0, L(E_{ij}) = 1.0].$$

Note that by setting the relative value equal to 1.0 we recognize the point made above about the effects this parameter might have on probability of choice. We also avoid the difficulty of transforming probabilities of choice obtained under different values of V_j into a measure that would enable us to compare individuals or the same individual in different states. The equation in the definition implies, for example, that in a study of food preferences it would be necessary to ensure that all subjects were really hungry ($V_j = 1.0$) and that the choices offered were equally capable of reducing their hunger.

By making the outcomes independent of choice in the familiarity environment, the courses of action are themselves converted into outcomes. Hence a subject's preferences among them may reflect their *intrinsic value* to him, not their instrumental or extrinsic value (that is, as a means to an end). In the ball-point pen situation described above if a subject most frequently selects the one with blue ink, then he may have a preference for this color in this context. Using blue ink may have a value in itself for him. On the other hand, he may select the blue ink because he (erroneously) believes it to be more efficient. (We shall consider such beliefs in Chapter 5.) In a familiarity situation the alternative courses of action are equally efficient for the desired outcome; if we additionally require that the subject *believes* them to be equally efficient, then the degrees of familiarity obtained are measures of the relative intrinsic values to him of the courses of action.

In definition 3.15 the relative value of the outcome and the level of efficiency are set at 1.0. Changes in either or both of these could affect the probabilities of choice. To describe how it does so would be to express the degree of familiarity as a *function* of them. Hence what has been defined as the degree of familiarity would be a value of this function.

3.16.   *Familiarity function:* A subject's familiarity function for a course of action (C_i) relative to an outcome (O_j) and an available set of courses of action $\{C_i\}$ is the mathematical function (f_F) that satisfies the equation

$$P_i = f_F[\{C_i\}, V_j, L(E_{ij})].$$

Very many aspects of the four components of the choice situation (that is, the individual, courses of action, outcomes, and the environment) may be varied to study their effects on degrees of familiarity or familiarity functions.

Variables whose effect on familiarity can be studied in this way can be classified as either *structural* or *functional*. Studies of familiarity involving structurally defined variables (such as color, shape, size, and texture) relate to what is called an individual's *taste* or *style*. Studies involving functionally defined variables relate to what psychologists have called *personality traits* (such as selfishness, generosity, bravery, cowardice, aggressiveness, introversion, cooperativeness). Only traits are considered further here.

In order to understand the behavior of an individual system (not just a psychological system), it is important to identify its traits — the characteristic ways it tends to respond to functional changes in itself or its choice environment. Given the definitions presented above, it is theoretically possible to measure degree of familiarity or the familiarity function for broad or narrow traits of the system by broadening or narrowing the stimulus or outcome that is considered. (How broad is simply a function of the purposes of the researcher.) This renders irrelevant the long-standing arguments in the psychological literature about surface traits versus depth traits, general versus specific, and enduring versus not-so-enduring traits. These arguments, admittedly, have just about vanished from the literature because there was no sign that anyone was getting anywhere with them and it became easier to extract factors, from factor analysis of specific concrete samples, than to generate theories. Much of that discussion, in any case, appears to have stemmed from structural notions of personality as some sort of self-determining entity, and hence of traits as neuropsychic dispositions or other such inherent attributes residing within the skin. The concept of personality we have derived from the producer–product relation excludes such a view of traits.

Without reproducing here our study of the relevant literature, let it suffice to remark that the trait measure we propose below encompasses the key notions that have emerged — that is, recurrent sequences of behavior (probability of choice of courses of action), response equivalence (the efficiencies of the alternative courses of action are equal), and stimulus equivalence (functionally defined stimuli). What we have avoided are the notions of structural determination that have traditionally haunted the concept of trait and have currently brought it into disrepute.[2]

In the study of traits as conceived here, the subject's possible responses (courses of action) are functionally classified, and traits are associated with the subject's characteristic response (relative to this classification) to a functionally defined stimulus.

---

2. We are criticizing a particular historical form of structural definition and are not suggesting that an adequate structural definition is impossible. See Chapter 15.

3.17.   *Trait:* Relative to a functionally defined stimulus in a familiarity situation, a degree of familiarity with one of the courses of action greater than any of the others is a trait. The degree of the trait is the degree of familiarity associated with the course of action most often selected.

Since the measure of a trait is a degree of familiarity, it is apparent that we can also formulate a trait function. Such a trait function might, for instance, show that for one individual empathy is a function of relative value of outcome to him; for another there may be no relation.

It may be helpful to show how this definition applies in the case of a specific trait. Furthermore, by developing a definition and measure of a specific trait we can also show how they can be used to design a trait test. We use the *ascendance–submission* trait for this purpose, because it has been one of the most widely discussed traits in the psychological literature. A trait test based on the definition and measure to be developed can yield information about the trait function as well as estimates of the degree of the trait in certain specified conditions.[3]

In the ascendant–submissive situation the subject is faced with the following set of conditions: an aggressive act has been committed, which decreases the efficiency of the subject's behavior with respect to his objective (that is, his preferred outcome). In other words, the stimulus is an aggressive act. The response we are interested in is the subject's attempt to retaliate on the aggressor — that is, to control rather than to be controlled by the aggressor. Thus we are interested in whether or not the subject responds to aggression and how he responds.

We can define ascendant–submissive behavior in terms of the following aspects of the subject's behavior:

(1) A response by the subject A to another purposeful individual's (B's) act, when B's act decreases the efficiency of A's behavior with respect to A's objective; that is, when B aggresses on A.

(2) An act by A that is a potential producer of a reduction in the efficiency of B's behavior relative to his (B's) objective.

In terms of these aspects of behavior, the following exclusive and exhaustive set of courses of action can be defined:

C_1: to exhibit both (1) and (2), an ascendant act.
C_2: to exhibit (1) but not (2), a submissive act.
C_3: to exhibit (2) but not (1), an aggressive (but not ascendant) act.
C_4: to exhibit neither (1) nor (2), neither an aggressive nor an ascendant nor a submissive act.

The degree of ascendance of an individual can be defined as the probability of his choosing behavior pattern C_1, and the degree of his submission can be defined as the probability of his choosing behavior pattern C_2. The sum of

3. For details on such a test, see Ackoff (1953), pp. 306–22.

these probabilities we can call his *degree of awareness* or *consciousness*[4] of the aggression.

From this observation we can immediately discern one loss involved in the use of verbal tests rather than overt behavior in the study of traits. In the verbal test we must ask the subject how often he tends to respond in a certain way when aggression occurs. Such a question will, at best, elicit information concerning his response to aggression when he is *conscious* of the aggression and his response to it. But many people respond to aggression without being fully conscious either of the aggressive act or of their response. Hence a verbal trait test will, at best, gather evidence on the subject's sensitivity to aggression when he is fully conscious of the aggression (in the sense that he can recall the aggression and his response to it). A more general measure of ascendance would depend on evidence other than the subject's verbal testimony or on a method of inferring from conscious responses to nonconscious ones.[5]

Efficiency of Choice: Knowledge

Another major aspect of the individuality of a system is its response capabilities or aptitudes. In considering psychological systems we use three terms in this connection – knowledge, understanding, and intelligence. The first two terms have received more attention from philosophers than from psychologists, but intelligence has been a major preoccupation of psychologists. The meanings of these concepts and the differences among them is far from clear in either ordinary or technical usage.

Knowledge, for example, is used in at least two different senses: (1) awareness or possession of a fact or state of affairs (such as in knowing that someone is at home or that water is made up of hydrogen and oxygen), and (2) possession of a practical skill. In the first sense knowledge consists of an individual's true beliefs or what he is aware of; that is, what an individual truly believes or whatever he is aware of, he *knows*. We shall pursue this sense of knowledge in Chapters 4 and 5, where the nature of awareness and belief is explored in detail. Here we concentrate on knowledge as a practical skill, on knowing *how* to do something rather than on knowing *about* or knowing *of* something. Abilities are relevant to knowing how, not to knowing about.

We shall consider knowledge of courses of action, and in this context knowledge is related to the efficiency with which an individual can use a course of action to obtain an objective. In this sense knowledge is clearly a capability.

Understanding implies something deeper than knowledge. For English and English (1958, p. 510) and G. W. Allport (1937, pp. 536–37) it involves

---

4. These concepts are treated in Chapter 4.
5. For a description of construction of an ascendant–submissive test that employs the concepts used here, see Ackoff (1953), pp. 306–24.

apprehending the meaning or significance of what is known. According to Dewey (1938):

> ... that which is observed, no matter how carefully and no matter how accurate the record, is capable of being understood only in terms of projected consequences or activities (p. 499).

This reflects Kohler's earlier observation (1929) that understanding implies *perception of causal connections* between what is understood and other things, or as F. H. Allport has put it (1955), "understanding is what one gets as a result of adequate explanation" (p. 11).

Following this lead we shall treat understanding as the ability to efficiently adjust one's behavior to changes in the conditions that affect its efficiency. This implies the ability to explain the effect of changes in one's environment on the efficiency of one's choices.

Know-how can be used in a general sense – to designate an individual's ability to obtain what he wants in a given situation by use of any means available to him.

We should like to delay discussion of intelligence until the concepts just considered are provided with adequate definitions.

KNOWLEDGE

As indicated in Chapter 2, courses of action are usually defined morphologically or functionally. Any functionally defined course of action can be broken down into a set of exclusive and exhaustive morphologically defined courses of action; and any morphologically defined course of action can be decomposed either into a similar set of physically defined courses of action or into a set of more finely defined morphological courses of action. If the course of action (C_i) is to use public transportation and the relevant outcome is to go from a to b in a specified time, the course of action may be decomposed as follows. Suppose there are only five possible ways $(w_1, w_2, \ldots, w_5)$ of going from a to b by public transportation. Then we can define an exclusive and exhaustive subset of actions.

$$c_{i1} = \text{to select } w_1.$$
$$c_{i2} = \text{to select } w_2.$$
$$c_{i3} = \text{to select } w_3.$$
$$c_{i4} = \text{to select } w_4.$$
$$c_{i5} = \text{to select } w_5.$$
$$c_{i6} = \text{to select any other way.}$$

Note that c_{i6} has no efficiency for going from a to b in the specified time. It is included to make the set exhaustive. Note also that the efficiencies of these subcourses of action for going from a to b in the specified time are independent of the subject. As far as the subject is concerned, the efficiencies are *determined*. As far as the researcher is concerned, they are *objective*. They may, of course, depend on the environment – for example, the efficiencies of the ways of going from a to b may depend on the weather.

3.18. *Knowledge situation*: a choice situation in an environment S in which a set of subcourses of action $\{c_{ik}\}$ is available – a set whose members are exclusive and that exhausts a morphologically or functionally defined course of action, C_i. The efficiency of each subcourse of action for a specified outcome (O_j) is independent of the subject who makes the choice.

Let e_{ikj} represent the efficiency of a subcourse of action (c_{ik}) for an outcome (O_j) in a knowledge situation, and let p_{ik} represent a subject's probabilities of selecting that subcourse of action. Then, using these concepts, we can reformulate the definition (3.7) of the efficiency of a course of action, C_i. The efficiency of C_i for O_j for a subject (A) in a knowledge situation is given by

$$E_{ij} = \sum_k p_{ik} e_{ikj}. \tag{3.8}$$

Now we can say what *knowing a course of action* means.

3.19. *Degree of knowledge* (DK_{ij}) that a subject (A) has of a course of action (C_i) relative to a preferred outcome (O_j) with relative value (V_j) equal to 1.0 in a choice environment (S) is

$$DK_{ij} = \left(\frac{E_{ij} - \min e_{ikj}}{\max e_{ikj} - \min e_{ikj}} \middle| S, V_j = 1.0 \right)$$

where $\min e_{ikj}$ represents the least (objective) efficiency associated with any of the C_is' subcourses of action, and $\max e_{ikj}$ represents the greatest such efficiency. These are the minimum and maximum possible efficiencies of C_i for O_j in S.

Note that when $\max e_{ikj} = 1.0$ and $\min e_{ikj} = 0$, $DK_{ij} = E_{ij}$. Also note that when $E_{ij} = \max e_{ikj}$, $DK_{ij} = 1.0$, and when $E_{ij} = \min e_{ikj}$, $DK_{ij} = 0$.

It can be seen that the degree of knowledge of a course of action relative to an objective in a specified environment is a measure of the amount of control a subject has over the outcome relative to the maximum amount of control known to be possible.

Suppose in the example that involves driving from a to b we have the following information for a subject (A):

	p_{ik}	e_{ikj}
c_{i1}	0.1	0.9
c_{i2}	0.3	0.8
c_{i3}	0.3	0.7
c_{i4}	0.2	0.6
c_{i5}	0.1	0.5
c_{i6}	0.0	0.0

Then A's efficiency would be

$$E_{ij} = 0.1(0.9) + 0.3(0.8) + 0.3(0.7) + 0.2(0.6) + 0.1(0.5) = 0.71.$$

A's degree of knowledge of C_i for O_j would be

$$\frac{0.71 - 0.50}{0.90 - 0.50} = \frac{0.21}{0.40} = 0.525.$$

If a subject were always to select that subcourse of action with maximum efficiency for outcome O_j, then his degree of knowledge of the relevant course of action (C_i) would be maximum and equal to 1.0. If he were always to select the least efficient subcourse of action, then his degree of knowledge would be minimum and equal to 0.0.

The degree of knowledge is a measure made relative to a particular set of environmental conditions (S) and a specific relative value of an outcome (V_j). Therefore, we can generalize as follows.

3.20. *The Knowledge function* of a subject (A) for a course of action (C_i) relative to an outcome (O_j) in an environment S is a mathematical function (f_k) that satisfies the equation

$$DK_{ij} = f_K(V_j|S)$$

A subject's degree of knowledge of a course of action may be independent of the relative value to him of the relevant outcome, but in general we would expect it to increase as V_j increases and to be maximum when $V_j = 1.0$. It could, however, decrease as V_j increases. The sensitivity of a subject's degree of knowledge of a course of action (C_i) for an outcome (O_j) to V_j can be measured by the derivative of the first with respect to the second:

$$\frac{d(DK_{ij}|S, V_j)}{d(V_j|S)}$$

If this derivative has a value of zero for all values of V_j, the subject's knowledge of C_i is insensitive to V_j. If it is positive, he is sensitive to V_j. If negative, he is also sensitive, but in a curious way: his knowledge decreases (increases) as the relative importance of the relevant outcome increases (decreases).

The knowledge function can be generalized further.

3.21. *The generalized knowledge function* of a subject (A) for a course of action (C_i) relative to an outcome (O_j) is a mathematical function (f^*_K) that satisfies the equation

$$DK_{ij} = f^*_K(S, V_j)$$

Recall that the choice environment (S) consists of a set of properties of the subject's physical environment that affect the outcome of his choice. Hence S may consist of more than one variable $(s_1, s_2, \dots)$. Therefore, the generalized knowledge function describes how the subject's efficiency depends on these variables and, hence, is an aspect of his personality function. For example, the efficiency of a subject's choice in going from one place to another may depend on the weather. How it does is an aspect of his knowledge and personality functions.

The concept of knowledge can be applied to instruments as well as to courses of action. Recall that in Chapter 2 (2.52) *instrument* was defined as an object that coproduces the outcome of a subject's behavior; the coproduction is itself produced by the subject. Oxygen in the air and a match may coproduce a fire, but oxygen is not an instrument as is the match. A purposeful individual must strike the match – hence produce its coproduction. The amount of oxygen in the air is not usually controlled by the subject, but the behavior of the match is.

Now if using a match is taken as a course of action, we can decompose it into subcourses of action, all involving use of a match. We can then define a subject's degree of knowledge of use of a match for the outcome, say, starting a fire. This would then be his degree of knowledge of the instrument relative to the outcome, starting a fire. By extension we can define his knowledge function and generalized knowledge function of use of a match.

Knowledge, as we have treated it, is an awareness of the efficiency of alternative subcourses of action when the relative efficiencies of the alternatives remain constant. Now we consider the effect of changes of these relative efficiencies on both his probabilities and efficiencies of choice – that is, on his probability of outcomes (equation 3.4).

Understanding

Understanding is responsiveness to whatever affects efficiency. If, for example, when a change occurs in the environment or the subject to reduce the efficiency of his behavior, he modifies his behavior so as to increase his efficiency; then he is said to understand what has happened. If when the car a person is driving begins to jerk and sputter, he stops and puts gasoline in its tank and then resumes normal driving, we say he understood what was happening to the car. Such a response may consist of either changing his course of action to another (modifying his P_is), or modifying his course of action without changing it to another (changing his E_{ij}s), or both. Thus understanding involves measures of probabilities of outcomes:

$$P(O_j) = \sum_i P_i E_{ij}.$$

In order to gain precision, imagine a set of environments or states $\{S\}$ of the subject that differ from each other with respect to one variable (s), which affects the efficiency of a course of action (C_i) relative to an outcome (O_j). Let $s_1, s_2, \ldots, s_n$ be an exclusive and exhaustive set of values of s over some relevant range of s-values. Let S' represent the set of state variables common to all members of the set $\{S\}$. Now we can define a set of subcourses of action that differ only with respect to values of s:

$$C_1{}^i : C_i \text{ under } s_1$$
$$C_2{}^i : C_i \text{ under } s_2$$
$$\cdot$$
$$\cdot$$
$$\cdot$$
$$C_n{}^i : C_i \text{ under } s_n$$

If these courses of action are made available to an individual (A) in a choice situation (S') his choice constitutes a selection of a sub-choice situation. Let $E_{ij}{}^i$ represent the subject's efficiency with $C_i{}^i$ in S' relative to outcome O_j. Then his overall efficiency for O_j is given by

$$P(O_j) = \sum_i P_i{}^i E_{ij}{}^i,$$

where $P_i{}^i$ is his probability of choosing $C_i{}^i$ in S'.

3.22. *Degree of understanding* (DU_{ij}) that a subject (A) has of a course of action (C_i) relative to an outcome (O_j) with relative value (V_j) equal to 1.0, with respect to a state variable (s) in a choice environment (S') is

$$DU_{ij} = \left(\frac{P(O_j) - \min E_{ij}{}^i}{\max E_{ij}{}^i - \min E_{ij}{}^i} \,\middle|\, s, S', V_j = 1.0 \right),$$

where $\min E_{ij}{}^i$ represents the efficiency of that $C_i{}^i$ in S' which is minimum and $\max E_{ij}{}^i$ represents that which is maximum.

Min $E_{ij}{}^i$ and max $E_{ij}{}^i$ represent the worst and best that the subject can do.

The degree of understanding has a maximum value of 1.0 and a minimum value of zero.

To take an example, the efficiency of the use of slides to convey information depends on the level of illumination in the room where they are projected. If we subclassify using slides by appending various levels of illumination, a test can be designed to determine how well a subject understands the effect of illumination on conveying information by use of slides.

The degree of understanding, like the degree of knowledge, can be generalized into an understanding function (f_U) where

$$DU_{ij} = f_U(V_j \,|\, s, S');$$

and a generalized understanding function ($f_U{}^*$) where

$$DU_{ij} = f_U{}^*(s, S', V_j).$$

Intelligence

The development of measures of knowledge and understanding enable us to consider a further derivative aspect of the functioning of systems — namely, *intelligence.* Many behaviors seem obviously, to an observer, more intelligent or more stupid than others; some individuals characteristically behave more intelligently or more stupidly than others.

Vast efforts have been poured into the development of measures of intelligence, largely to ensure that civil and military organizations can select the best individual components from those available for their needs. Rather less effort has gone into the definition of intelligence. We still lack any rigorous definition, and, not surprisingly, some uncertainty has begun to appear about what is actually being measured by so-called IQ tests. In the past decade research findings have increasingly led psychologists to believe that there is more than one kind of intelligence and that "the conventional IQ test tends toward the evaluation of those processes that have been called convergent, retentive and constructive" (Getzels and Jackson, 1962, p. 14).

In this situation we suggest that it is wise to return to the problem of defining intelligence in the hope that the definition arrived at will indicate how measures should be constructed. We have said above that "many behaviors seem obviously, to an observer, more intelligent or more stupid than others." What is it that is so obvious? Clearly the intelligent choice displays more knowledge or more understanding than the unintelligent choice. The difference we see is not, or at least we hope it is not, a difference of familiarity or of intention. However, the distinction sought between more or less intelligent systems goes beyond this.

The distinction between systems requires some measure of the probability of making intelligent choices when other conditions are held constant. The conditions to be held constant are, according to our model of the choice situation, familiarity, relative value (or intention), and existing knowledge or understanding. If initial knowledge and understanding were zero – a convenient control – then the system that most quickly arrived at the most knowledge or understanding would be judged to be the most intelligent system.

Intelligence clearly has to do with the rate at which a subject can learn.

3.23. *Learning:* an increase in degree of knowledge or understanding over time.

This definition suggests that there must be two measures of intelligence. The distinction we propose accords with the commonsense distinction between the kind of intelligence measured by most IQ tests and creative intelligence. It should be noted that the second measure incorporates aspects of environmental- and self-awareness. It therefore comes closest to the kind of intelligence that Chein (1945) defined as:

> *Intelligence is the apprehension of the relevant structure of the total behavioral field,* relevance being defined in terms of the immediate and presumptive future purposes of the actor (p. 115).

Time is normally used as the basis for measuring rate of change. But since different amounts of time are required to carry out different courses ог action, it may be preferable to use the number of trials (N_i) as a basis for measuring rate of change.

3.24 *K (knowledge) intelligence function* (I_K): A subject's K-intelligence function, relative to a course of action (C_i) for which his degree of knowledge is zero, and a preferred outcome (O_j) of relative value (V_j) equal to 1.0 in a choice environment S is

$$I_K = \frac{d(DK_{ij} \mid S, V_j = 1.0)}{dN_i}$$

3.25. *U (understanding) intelligence function* (I_U): A subject's U-intelligence function, relative to a course of action (C_i) for which his degree of understanding is zero, a preferred outcome (O_j) of relative value (V_j) equal to 1.0, and an environmental variable (s) in a choice environment (S') is

$$I_U = \frac{d(DU_{ij} \mid s, S', V_j = 1.0)}{dN_i}$$

These intelligence functions can be generalized to account for the effect of the given variables in each. Nevertheless they remain specific to a particular course of action.

In order to obtain a *general* intelligence function (of either type) of an individual, it would be necessary to use a set of courses of action. Standardization of such a sample is necessary if individuals are to be compared with respect to intelligence. Note, however, that the courses of action should be ones of which the subject has no knowledge or understanding before the test. In practice it may be possible to infer from rates of change of knowledge or understanding of a course of action for which there is some (but not complete) initial knowledge or understanding what would have been obtained had the ideal conditions been met. The more that is known about an individual's intelligence, the more likely it is that such extrapolations can be made.

Now we can see the difficulty of trying to represent intelligence by a single number. First, functions cannot be represented adequately by one number. Second, even if they could, it would be necessary to deal with distributions over sets of courses of action and choice environments. A completely general intelligence function is almost as complex as the personality function. Few have tried to represent personality by a single number; many have not shown equally sound judgment when it comes to intelligence.

Relative Value and Intention

Up to this point we have made extensive use of the concept *relative value* as it applies to outcomes, but it has yet to be defined. To do so we shall first consider a subject's degree of intention for an outcome, then its utility for him, and finally its relative value.

As in the case of familiarity and knowledge, it is necessary to construct an appropriate idealized standard situation.

3.26.   *Intention situation:* one in which (1) there are the same number (m) of available (exclusive and exhaustive) courses of action and outcomes, (2) each course of action has maximum efficiency for one outcome and hence no efficiency for any other, (3) each outcome has associated with it one course of action that has maximum efficiency for it, and (4) the alternative courses of action are equally familiar, known, and understood by the subject relative to the possible outcomes.

It is apparent that in such an environment the only objective basis for selecting a course of action is desire for the one outcome it is certain to yield.

3.27.   *Degree of intention* (DI_j) of a subject (A) for (or *Relative Value* to A of) an outcome (O_j) relative to an exclusive and exhaustive set of outcomes $\{O_j\}$ in an intention situation in a choice environment (S) is the probability that A selects the course of action that has maximum efficiency for O_j.

This measure, since it involves probability, has a maximum value of 1.0 and a minimum of O. Because it measures preference for an outcome relative to a specific set of outcomes, it is a relative measure.

The measure is also relative to the choice environment. Thus, a subject's degree of intention for an outcome (such as access to water) depends on the available alternatives (such as soft drinks, beer, liquor, milk) and the time and place.

If a subject can have any one, and only one, of a set of beverages, or none, by simply pushing an appropriate button or pushing none, then the relative frequency with which he selects each is his degree of intention for each.

The sum of the degrees of intention over an exclusive and exhaustive set of outcomes must be equal to 1.0. If the degree of intention for any outcome is greater than 0.5, it is necessarily preferred to any alternative, since this measure can exceed 0.5 for only one outcome in an exclusive and exhaustive set. That outcome in a set for which this measure is greatest is the subject's *preferred outcome.*

Degrees of intention are not necessarily additive. For example, suppose the following four outcomes are possible.

O_1: coffee and milk
O_2: coffee but no milk
O_3: milk but not coffee
O_4: neither

It is not necessary that $DI_1 = DI_2 + DI_3$. DI_1 may be either greater than or less than $DI_1 + DI_2$.

In the intention environment we control the efficiencies of the alternative courses of action $\{E_{ij}\}$; the degrees of familiarity $\{DF_{ij}\}$; knowledge $\{DK_{ij}\}$;

and understanding $\{DU_{ij}\}$. Therefore, we can formulate an intention function as follows.

3.28. *Intention (relative value) function:* A subject's intention function for an outcome (O_j) is the mathematical function (f_v) that satisfies the equation

$$v_j = f_v(\{E_{ij}\}, \{DF_{ij}\}, \{DK_{ij}\}, \{DU_{ij}\}|\{O_j\}, S).$$

3.29. *Generalized intention (relative value) function:* A subject's generalized intention function for outcome (O_j) is the mathematical function (f_v*) that satisfies the equation

$$v_j = f_v*(\{E_{ij}\}, \{DF_{ij}\}, \{DK_{ij}\}, \{DU_{ij}\}, S|\{O_j\}).$$

The relationship between the degree of intention for an outcome and its utility is revealed by examining what may be called a utility judgment. In the Case Institute Method of measuring utility (see Ackoff, 1962, pp. 91–93) the subject is confronted with a choice between two outcomes, O_1 and O_2 so that if he selects O_1 he is certain to obtain it (and hence $E_{11} = 1.0$), and if he selects O_2 he will obtain it with probability α (and hence $E_{22} = \alpha$). The researcher seeks a value of α such that the subject has no preference between O_1 with certainty and O_2 with probability α — that is, an α for which $P_1 = P_2$. Then the utility of O_1, U_1 is set equal to $E_{22} = \alpha$, and the utility of O_2 is set equal to $E_{11} = 1.0$.

This procedure, then, yields measures of utility that are equal to the efficiencies $(E_{11}$ and $E_{22})$ for which the degrees of intention for O_1 and O_2 are equal (that is, $DI_1 = DI_2$). This utility measure makes the same assumptions concerning familiarity, knowledge, and understanding as those that are made in obtaining the degree of intention. However, it makes an additional assumption: the subject attempts to maximize expected utility (that is, $E_{ij}U_j$).

Any of the various measures of utility that have been suggested can similarly be interpreted as a special case of what we have called the intention function. These measures and the degree of intention are all measures of the relative value of outcomes, but they need not yield equivalent results. For example, the utility of coffee may be 1.00 and of milk 0.25, which when normalized become 0.80 and 0.20, respectively. But the degree of intention for coffee may be 1.0 and for milk 0.

It is easier to obtain estimates of utility than of intention because of the simplifying assumptions made in measuring utility. For many purposes either may be used with equal efficiency. Both are measures of relative value. For our purposes here, however, relative value is used to refer to degree of intention. We will turn to defining types of outcome after considering one remaining aspect of intentions.

VACILLATION OF INTENTIONS

One aspect of the intention function is of particular interest. In the intention environment each outcome can be obtained with certainty; each course of action is perfectly efficient for its associated outcome. But suppose we were to reduce the efficiency of one course of action (C_i) for its associated outcome without affecting the others. How would this affect the probability of selection (P_i) of C_i, and hence the subject's intention for the associated outcome? If he were quick to give up an outcome as it becomes increasingly difficult to obtain, or if he is quick to take up its pursuit when it becomes easier to obtain, we would say that his intentions *vacillate*. One whose intentions do not vacillate with changes in the ease or difficulty of obtaining desired outcomes is said to have stick-to-itiveness or willpower. To have a strong will is not to be easily diverted from pursuit of a desired outcome by changes in the ease or difficulty of obtaining it.

A measure of the degree of vacillation of an individual relative to a particular outcome can be easily constructed by taking the derivative of his intention for it (the probability of his selecting the associated course of action) with respect to the efficiency of that course of action for that outcome. The greater the value of this derivative, the greater is his vacillation.

OUTCOMES

2.30.   *End* (an immediate intended outcome) of a subject A in a particular choice environment S in a (relatively short) time-period t_1–t_2: an outcome that (1) is a member of an exclusive and exhaustive set of available outcomes for A, and (2) has maximum relative value to A in S and t_1–t_2.

Thus an end is an outcome that a subject intends most strongly in a particular environment at a particular time and that is obtainable therein.

2.31.   *Goal* (an intermediate intended outcome) of a subject A over a set of choice environments and a time-period t_1–t_k: the last outcome O_k of a set of available outcomes $(O_1, O_2, ..., O_k)$, which are ordered so that $V_1 < V_2 < ... < V_k$ for A over t_1–t_k; if any outcome $O_j(j < k)$ of the set is obtained, the probability of obtaining O_{j+1} in t_1–t_k is increased.

A goal, therefore, is an outcome that a subject intends most strongly over a set of environments and a time interval, and that is obtainable in these conditions.

2.32.   *Objective* (a long-range intended outcome) of a subject A over a set of choice environments and a time-period t_1–t_m: the last outcome O_m of a set of outcomes $O_1, O_2, ..., O_m)$ (1) that are ordered so that $V_1 < V_2 < ... < V_m$ for A over t_1–t_m; and (2) O_m is not an available outcome for A in that set of environments over t_1–t_m; but (3) there is an outcome O_k ($1 < k < m$), which is A's goal over these environments and t_1–t_m and which, if obtained, increases the probability that A will obtain O_m at a later time $t_n(n > m)$.

Thus an objective is a desired outcome that is not obtainable in the time-period being considered, but progress toward it is possible during that time-period, and it is obtainable at a later time. For example, a college freshman's *objective* over the next four years may be to receive a Ph.D. His *goal* over this period may be to receive his bachelor's degree. His *end* this year may be to be promoted to his sophomore year. Ends, goals, and objectives are obviously relative concepts; they depend on how time is treated. If a period of one year is considered, the freshman's receipt of a bachelor's degree is an objective, promotion is a goal, and passing a particular examination may be his end.

2.33. *Ideal* (an ultimate intended outcome) of a subject A over a set of exclusive and exhaustive environments $\{S\}$ and a (relatively long) time-period t_1-t_n: the last outcome O_n of a set of outcomes $(O_1, O_2, ..., O_n)$ (1) that are ordered so that $V_1 < V_2 < ... < V_n$ for A over t_1-t_n; and (2) O_n is not a possible outcome for A in any possible environment in $\{S\}$ over t_1-t_n, but every not-yet-obtained outcome in the set possible for A at a time t_j ($1 \leq j < n$) is either an end, goal, or objective for A at t_j; and (3) at t_j there remain in the set of outcomes (O_1-O_n) available outcomes that A has not yet obtained.

An ideal, therefore, is an outcome that can never be obtained but can be approached without limit. In this sense we can say of some persons that their ideal is to move with infinite speed, or of some scientists that their ideal is to obtain errorless observations.

Even though an objective cannot be obtained in the time period of interest, and an ideal can never be obtained, we can speak meaningfully of their pursuit.

2.34. *Pursuit of a goal or objective* O_j by a subject A over a time-period t_1-t_m occurs if A's expected value relative to $O_j - \Sigma_i P_i E_{ij} V_j -$ increases monotonically over t_1-t_m.

2.35. *Pursuit of an ideal* O_n by a subject A over a time-period t_1-t_n occurs if A's expected value relative to the ordered set of outcomes $(O_1, O_2 ..., O_n) - \Sigma_i \Sigma_j P_i E_{ij} V_j -$ increases monotonically over t_1-t_n.

Increases in the relevant expected values that appear in these definitions constitute *progress* toward the goal, objective, or ideal.

Conclusion

The personality function developed here expresses an individual's expected relative value in a choice situation as a function of the available courses of action, the possible outcomes, and the relevant environmental variables. Expected relative value can also be expressed as a function of probabilities of choice, efficiencies of courses of action, and relative values of outcomes. Hence the personality function was decomposed into three functions:

1. The *familiarity* function, which relates probability of choice to other characteristics of the choice situation.
2. The *knowledge* function, which relates efficiency of choice to other characteristics of the choice situation.

3. The *intention* function, which relates the relative value of an outcome to other characteristics of a choice situation.

If these three functions were known, the personality function would be also.

In our definition of a purposive state we have, we think, avoided the limitations of the associationists' decision models — models that ignore the parameter of efficiency — and of the so-called decision theorists' models that ignore the parameter of familiarity (Jordan, 1968, pp. 126–29). Furthermore, we think we have provided a rigorous theoretical solution to a central problem of psychology — that of defining the life-space of an individual.

Perhaps the greatest advance in solving this problem was Heider's contribution in 1946. He identified the parameter we have called relative value. (He labeled it *L*, where *L* stands for liking, desiring, and so on.) He also identified a class of parameters that were concerned with cognitive aspects of the choice situation (labeled *U* for "cognitive unit formations"). He knew from his own work over the years that analysis of the choice situation required the specification of more than one kind of cognitive unit formation. However, his studies did not take him beyond a listing of such natural units as distance, familiarity, ownership, and perceived causality. (See Heider, 1959.)

Inspired by the initial promise of Heider's psychologics, many attempted unsuccessfully to by-pass the problem of defining an exhaustive and mutually exclusive set of *U*-relations (like Abelson and Rosenberg, 1958). The parameters we have defined — probability of choice (familiarity or psychological distance), probable efficiency (knowledge), and probable outcome (perceived causality) — are mutually exclusive, and we believe they exhaust all possible cognitive unit formations. By identifying a limited set of such relations it becomes possible to make further steps towards rigorous psychologics.

One further aspect of this chapter requires comment. The discussion in it has been directed toward providing the researcher with a conceptual framework within which to analyze a subject's choice. The subject's conceptualization of the choice situation, however, may differ widely from that of the researcher. (For example, see Figure 3.2.) We shall consider the subject's conception in detail in Chapter 5. Until then it is not possible to make explicit the nature of the expectations that are an output of the choice box shown in Figure 3.2. These expectations are fed into the outcome-evaluation function and play an important role in the subject's behavior subsequent to his taking action.

Several aspects of these expectations should be considered here. First, note that the term "expectation" is used in a psychological rather than in a statistical sense. Suppose the subject estimates the efficiency of the course of action he selects as 0.9 for an outcome whose relative value is 0.8, and 0.1 for an outcome whose relative value is 0.2. Then the statistically expected relative value is $0.9 \, (0.8) + 0.1 \, (0.2) = 0.74$. He will, in fact, obtain an outcome whose relative value is estimated at either 0.8 or 0.2. Psychologically his expectation is the 0.8 units of relative value, not 0.74. Therefore, if he does

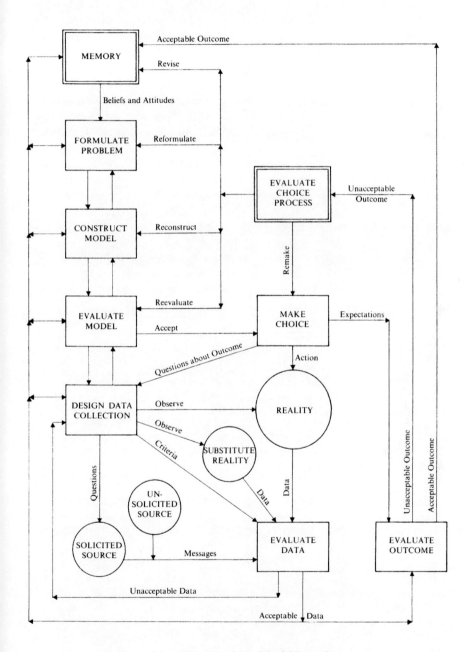

Figure 3.2.   Conceptual Model of Choice Process

not meet his psychological expectation (that is, he obtains only 0.2 units of relative value) he may consider the problem unsolved and reopen the choice situation, with the information on his failure as an input. That is, the psychological expectation involves what may be called a *satisficing* criterion: a relative value of outcome such that if the outcome that occurs is less valuable than this he reopens the problem, otherwise he closes it.

Say the subject's statistical expectation of earnings on a certain investment may be $500. He may, however, be dissatisfied with any return less than $750; should he obtain a return of anything less than $750, he will reexamine his choice.

In principle, the minimal acceptable level of outcome, the satisficing point, is a function of the subject's estimate of the cost (in a general sense, not necessarily monetary) of reopening the question and the potential returns from so doing. The satisficing point, then, is the minimal relative value of outcomes, improvement over which does not appear to the subject to justify the cost of reopening the question.

Satisfaction involves an intention not to change a situation; that is, an individual is satisfied with a situation if he has less intention to change it than to keep it as it is. Therefore, outcomes below the satisficing level are ones the individual intends to change if they occur. We shall consider satisfaction in more detail in Chapter 6.

REFERENCES

Abelson, R. P., and M. Rosenberg. "Symbolic Psycho-Logic: A Model of Attitudinal Cognition." *Behavioral Science* 3 (1958): 1–13.

Ackoff, R. L. *The Design of Social Research.* Chicago: University of Chicago Press, 1953.

———. *Scientific Method: Optimizing Applied Research Decisions.* New York: John Wiley & Sons, 1962.

Allport, F. H. *Theories of Perception and the Concept of Structure.* New York: John Wiley & Sons, 1955.

Allport, G. W. *Personality: A Psychological Interpretation.* New York: Henry Holt, 1937.

Angyal, A. *Foundations for a Science of Personality.* New York: Commonwealth Fund, 1941.

———. *Neurosis and Treatment.* New York: John Wiley & Sons, 1965.

Brand, H., ed. *The Study of Personality, A Book of Readings.* New York: John Wiley & Sons, 1954.

Cattell, R. B. *Scientific Analysis of Personality.* Chicago: Aldine Publishing Co., 1966.

Chein, Isadore. "On the Nature of Intelligence." *The Journal of General Psychology* 32 (1945): 111–26.

Churchman, C. W., and R. L. Ackoff. "An Experimental Definition of Personality." *Philosophy of Science* 14 (1947): 304–32.

Dewey, J. *Logic, The Theory of Inquiry.* New York: Holt, Rinehart & Winston, 1938.

English, H. G., and A. C. English. *A Comprehensive Dictionary of Psychological and Psychoanalytical Terms.* New York: David McKay, 1958.

Getzels, J. W., and P. W. Jackson. *Creativity and Intelligence.* New York: John Wiley & Sons, 1962.

Hall, C. S., and G. Lindzey. *Theories of Personality.* New York: John Wiley & Sons, 1957.

Heider, F. "Attitudes and Cognitive Organization." *Journal of Psychology* 21 (1946): 107–12.

———. *The Psychology of Interpersonal Relations.* New York: John Wiley & Sons, 1959.

Jordan, N. *Themes in Speculative Psychology.* London: Tavistock Publications, 1968.

Katz, D., and R. L. Schanck. *Social Psychology.* New York: John Wiley & Sons, 1938.

Kohler, W. *Gestalt Psychology,* New York: Liverwright, 1929.

Lewin, K. *Topological Psychology.* New York: McGraw-Hill Book Co., 1938.

II

The Process of Pursuing Purposes

In Part I the components and parameters of purposeful behavior were identified and defined. In Part II we consider the process that makes purposeful behavior possible. The steps in this process, the subprocesses, themselves constitute a system. Therefore our objective is to both identify and define the subprocesses and to show how they interrelate so as to form a system of purposeful behavior.

Chapter 4 is concerned with the processes by which information about or relevant to a situation is obtained from the environment, including others in it, and from oneself. The three basic processes involved are *perception*, *consciousness*, and *memory*. Together they provide a *description* (an *image*) and an *explanation* (a *conception*) of the situation, which generate a set of *beliefs* about the situation that are organized into a *model* or representation of it.

Chapter 5 details the types of beliefs required to represent a situation adequately and the measures appropriate to them.

In Chapter 6 we consider how the situation as modeled is evaluated — that is, whether it produces a state of *satisfaction* or *dissatisfaction* in the purposeful individual. Various types of satisfaction and dissatisfaction are identified with different *feelings* and *attitudes*. Choice situations in which dissatisfaction is produced in a purposeful individual in a state of doubt about what should be done constitute to that individual a *problem* situation in which a *decision* is required.

Chapter 7 deals with the various processes by which dissatisfaction can be removed from a problem situation — how it can be *dissolved, resolved,* or *solved.* The solution process itself is examined relative to different types of problem, and we discuss the role of experience, *intuition, thought,* and *feeling* in reaching a solution.

Purposeful systems are classified in Chapter 8 by use of two dimensions: (1) the extent to which their behavior is influenced by their immediate environment, and (2) the extent to which their behavior affects that environment. Division of these two scales into two regions yields a two-by-two or fourfold classification of purposeful systems. This classification is an extension and illumination of C. G. Jung's typology — *introversion–extroversion.*

4

Generation of Inputs: Perception, Consciousness, and Memory

SELF-EVIDENT, *adj.*   Evident to one's self and to nobody else.

The Devil's Dictionary

Introduction

In the preceding chapters we defined purposeful systems and constructed a set of measures of purposefulness. We have, however, taken for granted those processes that are prerequisite for purposeful behavior. Thus the familiarity, knowledge, and intentions that characterize a purposeful system in a given environment and affect its choice behavior presuppose certain inputs from that environment and previous experience. These are obtained through *perception* and *consciousness* of that environment and self, and usually some *memory* of previous situations. Thus the researcher needs to know of an individual purposeful system not only its characteristic responses (familiarity), its knowledge and understanding, and its intentions, but also whether and how these are likely to come into play in a given kind of situation.

This chapter seeks to identify what kinds of informational flows from the environment are getting through to the system and how these may be measured. The concepts that are introduced in the process are defined in producer–product terms and are consistent with the model presented so far.

Perception and Observation

The terms *observation, perception, sensation, awareness,* and *consciousness* are often used interchangeably in both ordinary and technical discussions. Most dictionaries define these concepts circularly. Nevertheless, we distinguish among them in a way we believe is both useful and in accord with the traditional core of meaning associated with these terms.

In considering an individual who observes something, *X*, we shall speak of *X* as the *stimulus* and of his *response* to it as a *perception*. Unfortunately, the terms stimulus and response have come into ill repute in psychology because they have usually been treated mechanistically – that is, as synonymous with deterministic cause and effect. Here, however, we treat these concepts functionally, as synonymous with producer and product.

4.1 *Stimulus–response:* A stimulus is a producer of a choice of a course of action by an individual in a purposive state. (The course of action produced is the response [definition 2.39].)

In dealing with these concepts it will be important to consider the *intensity* of both the stimulus and the response. We have done so briefly in the discussion of the ascendant-submissive trait in Chapter 3, but we amplify here.

4.2 *Intensity of a stimulus:* a measure of a property (of a stimulus) that produces a response.

The intensity of a stimulus may be treated either structurally (such as the brightness of a color or the size of an object) or functionally (for example, the decrease in efficiency of the behavior of the victim of an aggressive act). A stimulus may increase in intensity with respect to one of its properties (like the frequency of sound) and decrease with respect to another (like volume). Which property is used as a basis for measuring the intensity of the stimulus depends on the purposes of the observer. When the intensity of a stimulus is used as an independent variable in experimental work, values of the stimulus with respect to properties other than those used to define its intensity are usually held constant.

4.3. *Intensity of a response to a stimulus:* a measure of a property (of a response) that is produced by the stimulus of the response.

The property used to measure the intensity of a response may also be either structural (when frightened, the loudness of a scream, the distance of a withdrawal, or the speed with which action is taken), or functional (when aggressed on, the effect of the response on the efficiency of the aggressor's behavior, as in the ascendant–submissive situation).

PERCEPTION

The general class of responses with which we are first concerned may be called perceptions. Whereas all perceptions are responses to stimuli, not all responses to stimuli are perceptions.

4.4 *Perception:* a response to a stimulus that also produces a change in at least one structural property of the respondent.

Thus a perception is a two-stage production process, shown schematically in Figure 4.1. In perception there are two products of the producing stimulus (X). First, the stimulus produces structural changes (Y) in the respondent (A). We call this a *reaction* because this change in the respondent is not a choice. The tendency of the respondent to react to a stimulus is called his *sensitivity.* The reaction to a stimulus is its effect on the respondent's senses — sight, hearing, touch, taste, and smell. Such changes of structural properties

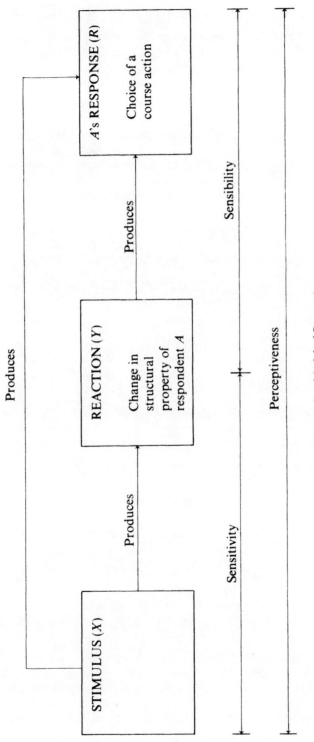

Figure 4.1.   Model of Perception

as the vibration of the ear drum, the formation of an image on the retina, and the associated changes in the nervous system and brain are reactions. These reactions are not under the respondent's control.

The subject's responsiveness to a change in one or more of his structural properties is his *sensibility*. A *sensation*, his response to the structural change, cannot occur unless there has first been a reaction; for example, a blind person cannot respond to a flash of light because he cannot react to it. Not every reaction is accompanied by a response. When among a large group of people, we may see (react to) someone but not notice (respond to) him. A sleeping person may react to a sound but not respond to it. Reflex actions are reactions, but not responses. Nonpurposeful entities can react, but only purposeful entities can respond. Photoelectric cells can display sensitivity (react) to light, but they cannot respond to it.

Now let us look at reactions and their related properties in more detail. The earlier definition of reaction (2.38) is adapted to our purposes here.

4.5   *Reaction to a stimulus* (X) by a subject (A) is a change in one or more of A's structural properties that is produced by X.

4.6.   *Intensity of reaction* to a stimulus (X) by a subject (A) is a measure of a structural property of the reaction produced by X.

4.7.   *Degree of sensitivity* to a stimulus (X) of specified intensity of a subject (A) in a structurally defined environment is the probability that A will react to X in that environment.

4.8.   *Sensitivity function* of a subject to a stimulus (X) is a mathematical function that relates his degree of sensitivity to X to its intensity and the structural properties of the environment.

Proceeding in parallel, corresponding concepts relating to sensation can also be defined as follows.

4.9.   *Sensation:* a response by a subject to a change in one of his structural properties.

The intensity of response has already been defined in 4.3.

4.10.   *Degree of sensibility* of a subject (A) to a change in one of his structural properties (Y) in a purposeful state is the probability that A will respond to Y in that state.

4.11.   *Sensibility function* of a subject to a change in one of his structural properties (Y) is a mathematical function that relates his degree of sensibility to Y to the intensity of Y and the properties of his purposeful state.

As we have treated the terms, a *sensation* is a response to a change in one's own (structural) properties, whereas a *perception* is a response to something that produces a change in one's own properties. In this way we have tried to capture the essence of the distinction made between these concepts in *Webster's Universal Dictionary* (1936):

Sensation is mere feeling without an object: *perception* is the mind's apprehension of some external object as occasioning that feeling.

Hence a perception involves a response to the producer–product relationship between stimulus and reaction; a sensation does not. One may feel (sense) cold without responding to what produced it. On the other hand, in sensing cold one may perceive a draft.

F. P. Kilpatrick (1961) observed that "A given physiological stimulus pattern may be produced by an infinity of different external conditions." (p. 443) Therefore, in mere sensation if the stimulus that produced a reaction were to change but the reaction did not, the sensation would remain unchanged; but this is not so for perception.

When a psychologist attempts to explain in psychological terms different responses by two persons to the same stimulus, he should first assure himself that they have had the same reactions. A color-blind person's response to a traffic light may be different from that of a person not color-blind because of the difference in their reactions. In studies of perception, however, it is not uncommon to assume that different subjects react similarly to the same stimulus.

The physiologist, rather than the psychologist, is concerned with an individual's reactions and sensitivity. The psychologist is primarily concerned with sensation and perception. The physiologist attempts to determine whether the subject receives the signal; the psychologist is primarily concerned with what the subject does with the signal once he has it. The psychologist is concerned with how an individual responds to what he can react to.

Measures analogous to those of sensitivity and sensibility are also applicable to perception.

4.12.   *Intensity of perception* of a stimulus (X) by a subject (A) is the intensity of A's response to the reaction produced by X.

4.13.   *Degree of perceptiveness* of a subject (A) to a stimulus (X) in a purposeful state is the probability that A will respond to X in that state.

4.14.   *Perceptiveness function* of a subject (A) to a stimulus (X) is a mathematical function that relates A's degree of perceptiveness of X to the intensity of X and the properties of his purposeful state.

Notice that the degree of perceptiveness of a subject is the product of the probability that he will react to the stimulus and the probability that he will respond if he reacts. The intensity of a perception is also a function of the intensities of reaction and response.

It is apparent from the measures defined above that we can study an individual's perceptions in different ways. First, we can attempt to determine how his degree of perceptiveness of a certain type of stimulus relates to the intensity of that stimulus. Second, we can attempt to determine how the intensity of his response to a stimulus relates to the intensity of the stimulus.

We can, in addition, combine these considerations. For example, for any intensity of stimulus we can record some function of the intensity of the response and the degree of perceptiveness of the subject: we can plot the average intensity of response or the variance of the intensity. We can also conduct research to determine how these response characteristics of a subject vary in different choice situations. An individual may be very perceptive of noise when he is pursuing an objective of high relative value, but not so when he pursues something of low relative value.

OBSERVATION

Perceptions may or may not be intended by the perceiver. For example, we see some things accidentally or by chance; others we look for deliberately. Instances of the second process form a particularly important class of perceptions, ones we call *observations*.

4.15.   *Observation:* a perception of a stimulus (X) by a subject who intended to perceive X.

Observations can be subdivided into a number of finer classes of perception. For example, when an individual observes something for the purpose of evaluating it relative to some purpose he has, he can be said to *inspect* it. If he looks for one or more specific properties of a stimulus, he can be said to *examine* it.

All types of perception, including observations, may be in error. The types of error they are susceptible to are discussed in Appendix I. Not all perceptions are *conscious*, but all observations are. Therefore, a complete understanding of the nature of observation requires an understanding of the nature of *consciousness*.

Consciousness

An individual may respond to a structural or functional property of an object or event without perceiving it. For instance, each of us has frequently responded to such properties of people whom we have never seen or heard, or of places where we have never been. We have done so because information about them has been communicated to us. (We shall explore this use of communication in depth in later chapters.) Those things a person has not perceived but responds to are ones he can be said to be *aware* of. But he can also be said to be aware of things he has perceived.

4.16.   *Awareness:* A subject is aware of something (X) if he responds to X.

A person may be aware of things he does not now perceive but once perceived if they are preserved in his memory (a subject to be discussed later in this chapter). Similarly, he may be aware of things he was informed about in the past. Hence to perceive something is to be aware of it, but to be aware of it is not necessarily to have perceived it. Therefore, perception is a special case of awareness.

Consciousness, on the other hand, is a special case of perception, a case we now turn to.

Few concepts have been as enigmatic to psychologists and philosophers as consciousness. One group of psychologists and philosophers has insisted vehemently that there is no such thing, that it is a useless, intervening variable. Another group has insisted that it is basic and its meaning is obvious. For example, Freud (1933) wrote, "What is meant by consciousness we need not discuss; it is beyond all doubt" (p. 99). J. G. Miller (1942) collected a large number of definitions of consciousness and showed the difficulty of finding a common ground among them. However, Singer (1929) performed a logico-historical analysis of uses of the term and found recent usage to be returning to its original meaning, *thinking with.*

Singer went on to analyze the meaning of consciousness in more detail. According to him, one observer (*B*) can observe a stimulus (*X*) and the response to it of an individual (*A*), and hence *B* can observe *A* perceiving *X*. In describing how this can be done

> . . . we must . . . have described all the stimulus-response relations any observer *C* would have to establish in order to convince himself experimentally that in *B*'s mind existed such knowledge or perception as might be called *B*'s perception of a sensation in the mind of *A*. In other words, one who has established the only conditions under which an observer *B* could know that yonder was an organism *A* possessed of the knowledge called a *sensation,* cannot *but* have defined the only conditions under which a second observer *C* could know that yonder was a first observer *B* possessed of the knowledge of a sensation in a third mind *A* (p. 565).

Singer then asked, "What should one call *B*'s perception of a sensation experienced by *A*?" He answered, "My suggestion would be that just this class of mental state be called *conscious*" (p. 566). Then Singer pointed out that it is quite possible for *B* to be conscious of states of mind in *A* of which *A* himself is unconscious. Furthermore, *B* and *A* may be the same person for

> It will be seen that nothing in this definition of a conscious moment *requires* the mental state which is to be the stimulus to lie in a mind other than the conscious mind itself; but neither is there anything to *exclude* this possibility (p. 566).

Singer's concept of consciousness is reflected in the writings of others. E. R. Guthrie (1938) wrote:

> In the inclusive sense of the words, consciousness and awareness are made up by our own secondary responses to our own movements. We may absently brush aside a tickling hair on our forehead, or ease our cramped position on a chair without being aware of it. Awareness of our own movements requires that the movement itself be responded to, be noticed. Noticing our own primary responses to an external situation is itself a secondary response (p. 357).

A similar view was expressed by Y. H. Krikorian (1938).

If to be conscious means a mental state knowing another mental state, the "another" can be either my prior mental state or my neighbor's mental state. . . . To be conscious means to respond cognitively to a stimulus which is itself a response (pp. 159–60).

Although Freud deliberately avoided defining consciousness, since he thought its meaning to be obvious, he referred to it as a "seat of awareness" that perceives some but not all mental states. It is like a sensory organ that senses other sensations (1933, p. 224). C. G. Jung (1924) vaguely suggested the same thing.

. . . by consciousness I understand the relatedness of psychic contents to the ego . . . insofar as they are sensed as such by the ego. Insofar as relations are not sensed as such by the ego, they are unconscious. Consciousness is a function or activity which maintains the relation of psychic contents with the ego (pp. 535–36).

It follows then that one individual (B) is conscious of another individual's (A's) sensation or perception of a stimulus (X) if B perceives A's sensation or perception of X. For him to be conscious of it, it is not sufficient for B to respond to A's response; he must respond to the producer–product relationship between the stimulus and the response, and hence to the fact that it is a response. While one of the authors was talking with a friend in his office recently, the friend rose, put on his topcoat, and sat down again. The author then arose and closed an open window in the room. His friend had perceived the cold because he had responded to it purposefully, putting on a coat. The author responded to his friend's behavior by shutting the window. The author was therefore aware of the cold and conscious of his perception of it. His friend had not perceived the open window and hence was surprised when the author closed it. Furthermore, the friend was not conscious of his response to the cold until he became conscious of the author's response to it.

Consciousness includes perception of another's perception, but it is not exhausted by such perception; it includes perception of any *mental state* of another. For example, one can be conscious of another's intentions, feelings, preferences, traits, beliefs, and so on. Hence in order to define consciousness it is first necessary to define a *mental state*.

4.17. *Mental state* of a subject (A) is any one or combination of functional properties of A's purposeful behavior.

Definition of mental states is the preoccupation of this book. In fact, it is concerned with the development of a methodology that facilitates one person's becoming conscious of another.

Now consciousness may be defined as follows.

4.18. *Consciousness:* One individual (B) is conscious of another individual's (A's) mental state if B perceives A's mental state.

Hence if B perceives any functional property of A's purposeful behavior, B is conscious of that property (mental state) of A.

4.19.   *Self-consciousness:* A subject (*A*) is self-conscious if he perceives one or more of his own mental states.

Peculiarly, there is considerably more agreement on the meaning of self-consciousness than there is concerning the meaning of consciousness. A. A. Roback (1933) summarized this general agreement as follows.

> To the philosopher and laboratory psychologist, particularly of the structural school, selfconsciousness means the act or condition of being (or the process of becoming) directly aware of the self or ego during any mental process, or in other words, awareness of what we experience as relating to a self as the subject of these experiences (pp. 1–2).

At first glance it may seem that once consciousness has been defined it should be relatively easy to define *unconsciousness*. But the meaning of the negative of a term depends on the universe of discourse to which the term applies. Although Miller (1942) observed that the term unconscious has often been applied to inanimate things (p. 22), most psychologists take a position like that taken many years ago by K. Koffka (1927). "The unconscious as a systematic concept is not synonymous with nonconscious . . . . The movements of a stone are not called unconscious, whereas those of an amoeba might be." (p. 43).

The problem of defining unconscious consists first of specifying the universe of discourse it applies to, and then dividing it into the two exclusive and exhaustive domains of consciousness and unconsciousness. The first requirement hinges on the question of whether unconsciousness refers to non-responses to stimuli or responses to stimuli that are not conscious. Miller (1942) argues for nonresponses:

> A person is unconscious . . . when he is one of the states in which the stimuli of the external environment are not affecting his behavior or in which he does not show normal reactions to or discrimination of the stimuli (p. 23).

When we speak of a person's being unconscious we sometimes seem to mean that he is in an unresponsive state—as when he has been knocked unconscious by a blow on the head. However, we also use unconscious in another sense, a psychoanalystic sense, which is quite different. In this sense, the unconscious is taken to contain experience that is suppressed or hidden in the dark recesses of the mind. But if there were no reactions or responses to a stimulus, there would be nothing to be hidden. Hence in the psycho-analytic sense unconsciousness involves receiving inputs that are not readily accessible to the receiver. One may either *receive* a stimulus (that is, react) but not respond to it, or he may respond but not respond to that response.

Both concepts described are important. We have chosen to label them as follows.

4.20.   *Unconsciousness:* A subject (*B*) is unconscious of another subject's (*A*'s) mental state if *B* perceives *A* but not *A*'s mental state.

If *B* perceive's *A* but not *A*'s perception of an *X*, *B* is unconscious of *A*'s perception of *X*.

4.21.   *Nonconsciousness:* A subject (*B*) is nonconscious of another subject (*A*) if *B* does not perceive *A*.

4.22.   *Unself-consciousness:* A subject is unself-conscious of his own mental state if he perceives himself but not his mental state.

If an individual perceives an *X* but does not perceive that he perceives *X*, he is unself-conscious of that perception.

4.23.   *Nonself-consciousness:* A subject is nonself-conscious if he does not perceive himself.

Hence if an individual perceives something he is not conscious of, he is unself-conscious of it. If he cannot perceive it, as when knocked out, he is nonself-conscious of it. Much of the activity of psychoanalysis can be viewed as bringing into consciousness functional properties of past responses of the subject and others — properties that previously were not responded to, previous perceptions of which the individual was not self-conscious, or has lost self-consciousness.

Memory

One's present observations and the conclusions drawn from them are always coproduced by one's past experiences. Past experiences, organized in various ways, come forth from one's memory in the form of beliefs and attitudes. Beliefs are inferences drawn from past and present perceptions, and attitudes are feelings about what was perceived. Beliefs and attitudes will be considered in the next chapter. Here we consider memory.

The storage and retrieval capabilities of the human brain have been under considerable investigation as a consequence of the development of information theory and computer memories. Such studies have made it abundantly clear that memory is more than reproduction of material to which an object has been previously exposed. The tape recorder, for example, can often reproduce information better than the human being, but it does not do so in a purposeful way. It does not use in a choice process what is reproduced. Reproduction in this sense is certainly not the essence of memory. A person may be able to remember something without being able to reproduce it structurally as a recorder can. Furthermore, the tape recorder does not have the human's ability to selectively forget or, perhaps, to selectively store in the first place. It is apparent that humans store only a small portion of the information they receive. Perhaps attempts to explain memory would benefit from increased attention to the loss of information — nonrecording and forgetting. It might also be fruitful to pursue experimentally the line of inquiry initiated clinically by Freud — study of the human's inability to recall, at least not consciously, what has been stored in his memory.

Recent research efforts have been devoted more to retrieval than to storage. Memory, however, involves more than storage and retrieval of past experience; it involves a purposeful response to what is retrieved. A computer that stores and retrieves (and even reproduces) information does not remember it unless it uses the information purposefully. If the computer's operations on the retrieved information does not involve choice, as is so in most programs, then the computer has not remembered. The use of memory in such a context is metaphorical at best, and misleading at worst.

A person who stores a letter in a file and later retrieves it does not necessarily remember its content. If he can reproduce its content without examining it, he is said to remember it because he is believed to be capable of using it in a choice process.

From this brief survey of what has been said about memory, and from what we have said about it, the following observations can be made.

1. Initially one might assert that unless something has been perceived, it cannot be remembered. It seems preferable however, to make a weaker statement: unless something has been reacted to (see definitions 4.4 and 4.5), it cannot be remembered. If one accepts the weaker statement, then perception is not necessary; that is, the response to the structural change (reaction) produced by a stimulus — the sensation part of perception — may come later when the reaction is recalled. For example, one may see something at time t_0 but not respond to it until a later time t_1.

2. One may remember a stimulus reacted to and/or the response to it. That is, we may not remember *all* of a perception. If a response is remembered, then, as a minimum, the individual must have reacted to his own response. When one responds to one's earlier response and, in addition, to the stimulus that produced it, the memory is self-conscious (see definition 4.19). Note, however, that response to a response need not be conscious — as when its stimulus is not responded to.

3. What is stored between an initial reaction and its recall is obviously not its stimulus or the response to it but a *representation* of these. The representation is a product of what is remembered and a producer of the act of remembering it. Since the representation (say, images or concepts) may not be accurate, recall may be in error. The representation must involve structural changes in the brain, because we know that damage to the brain can produce partial or complete loss of memory. Functional changes in an individual or his environment can also affect his ability to remember. An emotional shock can produce temporary or permanent loss of memory. An emotional experience may also produce remembering that would not otherwise have occurred.

4. Recall — a re-presentation of a previous experience and a response to it — does not just happen. It is produced by something in the *recall state*. That something may be either an internal or external event. If this were not the case, our consciousness would be inundated by irrelevant memories.

5. Recall, then, is itself a response to at least one stimulus that operates in the present. Recall of a past reaction ordinarily, but not necessarily, involves recognition that the reaction took place in the past. In hallucinations this may clearly not be so.

6. Recall is selective; it involves a search for the relevant. Otherwise everything stored would be recalled at once. Hence recall involves an association of something in the present to something in the past, and this association must be based on believed relevance — that is, on what the individual believes will enable him to make a better choice in the present.

7. An individual obviously cannot remember everything. He may not store something either because he believes it is irrelevant to choices he will have to make in the future or he believes he can retrieve it from some other source when necessary, as when he knows that it is recorded in an accessible place. This implies that committing something to memory is a matter of choice, even if an unconscious choice. To deny this requires either that we assert all things reacted to are committed to memory or that a selection is made nonfunctionally — that is, in a way an individual cannot control. For example, it has been argued that only strong (structurally intense) stimuli are remembered. But clearly we can remember whispers and forget shouts. A structural explanation of what is committed to memory seems infeasible. On the other hand, we know that a strongly motivated student remembers what he is taught, but one who is poorly motivated (he believes that what he is being taught is irrelevant or that it is not important to remember it, relevant or not) forgets.

We can now formulate a definition of memory that is compatible with these observations.

4.24. *Memory:* A subject who responds at time t_1 to a stimulus (X) to which he reacted at an earlier time, t_0, remembers X.

This concept of memory is a very general one. Since every stimulus precedes a response to it, all stimulus–response phenomena (including sensation, awareness, and consciousness) can be subsumed under it. Clearly, when the interval from t_0 to t_1 is very small (a moment) we do not usually associate memory with it, but it is clear that unless the stimulus is retained over even a short interval the response could not follow. In practice we apply memory only to situations in which the individual's exposure to the stimulus X is not continuous over the interval t_0–t_1.

The definition of memory formulated here does not require that the memory–response be a conscious one. It may be conscious, but is not necessarily so. For example, we can remember how to climb a set of stairs without being conscious of that act. Most of our habitual behavior displays unconscious memory; we frequently are not conscious of why we do things as we do. One of us wears his wrist watch face down on his left wrist for reasons he is not conscious of, but clearly the original stimulus is still operating on him as he puts on his watch each morning.

4.25. *Intensity of a memory:* the intensity of the response that defines it.

One may also speak of the durability of a memory as the length of time over which it persists.

4.26. *Correctness of a memory:* the efficiency of the memory response for the objective for which it is intended.

When a student takes an examination on material he has read, he remembers correctly if he wants a high grade and his responses are efficient in producing one.

What is remembered — the content of memory — is representable by statements in the same way that observations are. Hence the discussion in Appendix II of the form of statements is relevant here. Memories, it should be noted, are communications to oneself.

Conclusion

In this chapter we have considered the processes that provide the inputs to purposeful choices. The basic one is *perception*, a functional response to a stimulus. The second is *consciousness*, the perception of the mental state of another or oneself. The third is *memory*, which enables an individual to respond at one moment of time to something he has sensed earlier. It is through memory that experience can come into play at a later date.

A purposeful individual who perceives something (X) may respond to either its structural or its functional properties. The set of structural properties of the stimulus he responds to constitute his *image*[1] of the stimulus. The set of functional properties of the stimulus he responds to constitute his *conception* of the stimulus. Thus we can speak of both his image and his conception of the choice situation.

A purposeful individual's *model* of a choice situation is the set of structural *and* functional properties that he believes[2] the choice situation to have and that he believes affect his satisfaction[3] and dissatisfaction with the situation.

What an individual perceives in a situation is not merely a matter of what is *given* to him by the situation, because much more is *offered* by it than he can possible receive. Therefore, what he perceives is also a matter of what he *takes*. He enters such a situation with a set; the set is his model of the situation. It provides him with criteria of relevance and hence influences what he looks for.

This is not to say that an individual perceives only what he looks for. Some stimuli, by the sheer force of their impact on his senses, may impose themselves on him regardless of the criteria he employs. A person who is reading a book and intends to shut out the conversation around him may, nevertheless, hear a message shouted to him or to another. Unsolicited perceptions

---

1. *Image* and *concept* are defined in Chapter 9.
2. *Beliefs* are treated in Chapter 5.
3. *Satisfaction* and *dissatisfaction* are treated in Chapter 6.

may be relevant; the message he hears may be that the lights are about to be turned out.

What an individual perceives, is conscious of, and remembers in a choice situation and what he feels about it constitute the raw material from which his model of the situation is constructed. Therefore, his model influences what he takes from the situation, and what he takes from it influences his model. Thus, although we discuss models in Chapter 5, it should be borne in mind that perception, consciousness, remembering, and model construction go on simultaneously and interdependently.

REFERENCES

Freud, S. *New Introductory Lectures on Psychoanalysis.* New York: W. W. Norton & Co., 1933.

Guthrie, E. R. *The Psychology of Human Conduct.* New York: Harper and Bros., 1938.

Jung, C. G. *Psychological Types.* New York: Harcourt Brace & Co., 1924.

Kilpatrick, F. P. *Explorations in Transactional Psychology.* New York: New York University Press, 1961.

Koffka, K. "On the Structure of the Unconscious." In *The Unconsciousness, a Symposium,* edited by E. Drummer, pp. 43–68. New York: Alfred A. Knopf, 1927.

Krikorian, Y. H. "An Empirical Definition of Consciousness." *Journal of Philosophy* 35 (1938): 156–61.

Miller, J. G. *Unconsciousness.* New York: John Wiley & Sons, 1942.

Roback, A. A. *Self-Consciousness and Its Treatment.* Cambridge, Mass: Sci-Art Publishers, 1933.

Singer, E. A., Jr. "On the Conscious Mind." *Journal of Philosophy* 26 (1929): 561–75.

5

Modeling the Situation: Beliefs

FAITH, *n.* Belief without evidence in what is told by one who speaks without knowledge, of things without parallel.

The Devil's Dictionary

Introduction

In Chapter 3 we constructed a model of a purposeful state, one the researcher can use to represent a subject's choice situation. The subject's model of that situation may, of course, differ from the researcher's. The type of components and parameters will nevertheless be the same, with one exception. The researcher may be concerned with the probabilities of the subject's choice of each alternative course of action; the subject may be concerned with which course of action to choose.

We identified the available courses of action as an essential component of a model of a purposeful state. These are those courses of action that the researcher *believes* to be available. He may, of course, be in error. All the components and parameters in an individual's model are the ones *he* believes to be relevant. Hence a subject's model consists of his beliefs about the choice situation, and these may differ from the researcher's. These differences may help to explain the subject's behavior.

An individual's model of a choice situation is his representation of it. Models are used in such situations because they are easier to manipulate than is reality itself. In many cases it is clearly preferable to make one's trials and errors with a model rather than with reality. The relative ease of model manipulation derives both from their consisting of images and concepts that are usually easier to manipulate than is reality, and from their being usually simpler than reality. Every situation has an unlimited number of properties, but only comparatively few of these are relevant to a particular choice. Hence models of choice situations are selective. For example, in the physicist's model of a falling body he may relate its acceleration to such properties as mass, shape, and wind currents, but not to color, age, cost, and chemical composition. A model includes only those properties that either the individual believes have an effect on the outcomes of interest (and therefore

79

are relevant), or that he is doubtful about and wants to investigate further.

Neither the model nor the way it is used may be made explicit in a choice situation; in fact, the subject may be quite unconscious of both. By uncovering a subject's relevant beliefs, his implicit model can be revealed.

An individual's explicit formulation of his model — for example, a symbolic representation of his beliefs and assumptions — may not be an accurate representation of his implicit model. Hence we sometimes say to someone whose explicit model we can examine, "That is not what you really believe about this situation." In scientific research the investigator tries to make his model explicit, and to do so in such a way as to make it possible for others to evaluate it and use it as their own. In most of our everyday decisions, however, there is no pressure to do the same.

It is not at all uncommon to point out to another an assumption he has made unconsciously in reaching a conclusion. Consider the following problem. There is a block of cells occupied by fifteen prisoners (*P*'s) and a

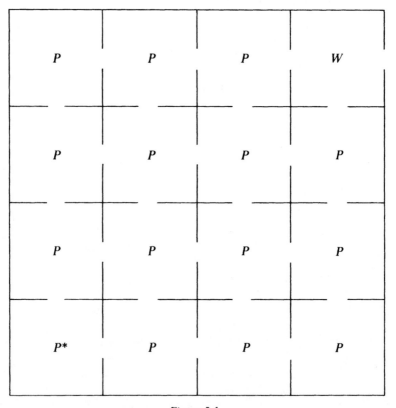

Figure 5.1

warden (*W*), as shown in Figure 5.1. Each cell is connected by a door to the cells adjacent to it. Only the warden's cell has an exit from the block. The prisoner, P^*, in the lower left-hand cell, is a homicidal maniac who is com-pelled to kill everyone he sees, but he cannot look at a person he has killed; if he does, he faints and remains unconscious for a very long time. One morning the maniac was found missing and the occupant of every cell other than the maniac's is dead in his cell. What path did the homicidal maniac take to escape? Try to solve this problem before going on.

Most people try to solve this problem by looking for a path from the cell occupied by P^* to W, which goes through every cell once and only once. There is no such path. Yet the problem is solvable. Of most persons whom we have observed trying to solve this problem we can assert that *they have assumed that P^* cannot return to any cell*. They frequently are not conscious of this assumption even though it restricts the alternatives they try. In fact, P^* can return to one cell, his own. Once this possibility becomes apparent the solution is easy to obtain.

Models of a choice situation must have a certain kind of structure if they are to represent the essential charateristics of such situations. Choice models must express a relationship (f) between the value of an outcome (V) to the subject and (1) those aspects of the situation over which the subject believes he has some control (X_i), and (2) those aspects over which he believes he has no control but which he nevertheless believes to have some effect on the outcome (Y_k). Therefore, the form of this part of a model – the *performance function* – can be represented symbolically as $V = f(X_i, Y_k)$. This relationship determines the believed efficiencies of the courses of action (defined by the X_i) for the possible outcomes in certain environmental conditions (defined by the Y_k).

The subject may be in doubt about what the environmental conditions actually are or will be at the time of choice. He may select a route to use in driving to work without knowing how congested it is. But he would usually have an estimate of the likelihood of the various possible relevant states of the route.

In many situations the subject has only limited control over one or more of the controllable variables. For example, the amount of time in a day that one allocates to a task cannot be less than zero nor more than twenty-four hours. The controlled variables (X_i) and the constraints on them define the alternative courses of action (C_i). For example, if X_i is the amount of time in hours to be spent on an activity in a day, then the courses of action are defined by the number of hours, from zero to twenty-four, spent on the activity.

The probability that a course of action will produce an outcome believed to be possible depends on the values of the uncontrolled variables (Y_k). That is, each believed E_{ij} can be conceived of as a function (g) of the Y_k. The believed relative value of an outcome O_i (V_j) may also be conceived as a function (h) of the uncontrolled variables (Y_k). Thus if the two functions (g and h) were known by the subject, he could determine for each course of action the probability that it would produce each possible outcome in the choice situation. The measure of performance of the choice must be some function of the relative value of the outcome and its probability of occurrence – for instance, the subject's expected relative value, $\Sigma_j E_{ij} V_j$. This is only one of the many possible performance criteria. If he seeks to maximize this function, then such maximization is his criterion of choice, *his personality function* in the choice situation.

To summarize, an individual's model of his choice situation consists of *what he believes to be:*

1. The courses of action available to him.
2. The possible outcomes of the available courses of action.
3. The possible states of the choice environment (possible values of the uncontrolled variables that can affect the outcomes of available courses of action).
4. The probability that each of the possible states of the choice environment is the true one.
5. The efficiency of each available course of action for each possible outcome in each possible state of the choice environment.
6. The relative value of each possible outcome.

In short, an individual's model of a choice situation must map, however inadequately, the components and parameters of the choice situation.

We shall consider each of the types of belief that go to make up such models, but first we examine certain basic types of belief in terms of which the six types listed above can be defined.

Beliefs about the choice environment

We begin by considering an individual's beliefs in the past, present, and future existence of objects, occurrence of events, and their properties in his perceived choice environment. These affect what courses of action he believes to be available and what efficiencies he believes them to have for the possible outcomes. (We will use the word "thing" in this discussion to represent either objects, events, their properties, or combinations of these.)

An individual believes in the existence of things only when he believes they make a difference in his pursuit of his goals. Hence any attempt to define what is meant by an individual's belief in the existence of a thing should make reference to the outcome that he seeks (to his purposeful state). This can be done by constructing an environment in which the individual has intention for only one end. Now in such an environment what does it mean to say that an individual has some degree of belief in the existence of a thing?

The simplest answer to this question would be that the individual is *acting as if the thing were present.* This is certainly the commonest characterization of belief to be found in the literature. Let us examine the feasibility of this suggestion. The literal translation would run somewhat as follows. When the thing is present, the individual practically always employs a certain course of action. For example, when his wife is home he always says Hello when returning from a day's work. When we observe the individual select such a course of action we *cannot* say that he believes the thing to exist, because he may select the course of action quite regularly when the thing is not present; he may always call out Hello when entering his house. Hence it appears that we must add a further stipulation to make the chosen course of action a critical case for inferring belief: when the thing is *not* present, the individual *never* employs the course of action. But this suggestion, although it does provide a clear-cut way of determining whether the individual takes the thing to be present, really defines belief out of existence except in the sense of *correct* belief. Since the individual would always act in a certain way when the thing is present, and would never act in this way when the thing is not present, he never displays an incorrect belief in the presence of the thing.

We can take care of this difficulty as follows. Suppose that *when an individual responds* to something relative to a certain objective he always (or almost always) displays a particular response. When a man perceives his wife on returning home and he wants her to know he is home, he always says Hello. Suppose further that when his wife is not at home and he is aware of it he never says Hello when entering the house. Now if he enters the house and does not observe his wife but is not aware of her absence and says Hello, an observer could conclude that he believes she is home, assuming, of course, that he wants her to know that he is home. In these conditions his belief may or may not be correct. Note that if he does not want his wife to know he is home, even when he observes her, he will not say Hello. Hence belief must always be determined relative to an intended outcome.

5.1.   *Belief in the presence (absence) of something:* An individual believes that something (X) is present (absent) in his environment of type S relative to an objective (O), if he displays a response (R) when the following conditions hold: (1) he does not perceive X (or its absence), (2) in other environments of type S in which he has perceived the presence (absence) of X and he intended O, he virtually always displayed R, and (3) when he was aware of the absence (presence) of X in environments of type S he virtually never displayed R.

Clearly our ability to establish an individual's beliefs depends on our ability to find characteristic belief responses $(R$'s) that can serve as belief indicators. Such responses may be defined either structurally or functionally. When one enters a room, his response on perceiving another person may not be to say Hello; it may be any greeting or just talking.

One can perceive something's absence as well as its presence. On returning home one can perceive that a familiar chair has been removed, or on arriving at his office that his secretary is not there.

Note that when an individual believes that something is present he also believes that selecting the course of action that is the belief indicator (R)

is efficient for accomplishing his objective. One may believe that calling out Hello when he returns home is an efficient way of letting his family know that he has arrived. Doing so has no efficiency for this end if no one is at home.

Now consider the following three response sequences. In the first, on returning home a man calls out Hello and receives no response. He then goes about other business whose efficiency does not depend on the presence of others. In the second, on returning home he calls out Hello and again receives no response, but this time he hides behind a door to scare one of his children whom he expects to come looking for him. In the third, after receiving no response to his Hello he starts to search the house, periodically calling out Hello. One would conclude that his belief in the presence of somebody was stronger in the second and third situations than in the first. In the third, however, he displayed more *doubt* than he had in the first and second.

Doubt seems to imply an intention to investigate the validity of a belief. The term is also used to connote a lack of decisiveness, a lack of belief one way or the other. In this second sense doubt is a redundant concept; hence we will use it in the first sense: *an intention to investigate*. In this sense one can doubt a strong belief as well as a weak one. For example, a scientist may strongly believe in the existence of a particle that he has not observed, but he may still want to prove it.

The *strength of a belief* seems to be related to the amount of evidence required to change it. If the belief that someone is at home is changed by one nonresponse to a Hello, it is weaker than a belief that requires several nonresponses to several Hellos. A very strong belief may not yield to any amount of contradictory evidence; the evidence is reinterpreted. If I believe strongly that someone is at home and get no response to my Hello, I may assume that I have not been heard; for example, someone is at home but is in the basement or out back.

5.2.   *Intensity of belief in the presence (absence) of something:* The intensity of an individual's belief in the presence (absence) of something (X) in his environment (S) relative to an objective (O) is one less than the number of times his belief response (R) must fail to produce O before his belief changes to one in the absence (presence) of X.

This number can range from zero to infinity. We subtract one from the number of failures because it is convenient for intensity to have a minimum value of zero.

Note that the intensity of a belief may change (usually decrease) with an increase in the number of failures of the belief response to produce the objective.

5.3.   *Degree of doubt of the presence (absence) of something.* An individual's degree of doubt of the presence (absence) of something (X) in his environment (S) relative to an objective (O) is his degree of intention to become aware of the presence (absence) of X.

A subject's degree of doubt may also decrease with an increase in the number of failures of the belief response to produce his objective. Eventually his doubt may be completely dispelled. Since the degree of intention can range from zero to one, the degree of doubt can also.

The strength of a belief should reflect both its intensity and the degree of doubt associated with it. It should increase as intensity increases and as the degree of doubt decreases. This suggests that the *strength of a belief* can be taken as the product:

$$\text{(Intensity of belief)} \times (1 - \text{Degree of doubt})$$

Repeated failures of the belief response to produce the subject's objective necessarily reduces the intensity of belief and may reduce his degree of doubt. Suppose that it takes four failures to change a belief. Then the intensity is $4 - 1 = 3$. But after the first failure only three are required to change the belief, and hence its intensity is reduced. *Faith*, it might be noted, is a strong belief in something that can neither be confirmed nor disconfirmed. Faith thus implies the absence of doubt.

Now let us consider something in an environment other than the one occupied by the subject.

5.4. *Belief in the presence (absence) of something in another environment:*[1] If a subject selects a course of action (C_i) when he wants an objective (O_j), and he is aware that C_i has no efficiency for O_j in his environment unless X is present (absent) in another environment, then he believes that X is present (absent) in that other environment.

For example, if one telephones a friend at his home in order to give him some information, he is aware that so doing is efficient only if his friend is at home. Therefore, when he telephones to give his friend information, he believes the friend is at home. Of course, he may telephone to determine whether his friend is at home. (Note that the objective has changed.) Hence telephoning when he wants to give his friend information shows belief in his presence there; but when he wants to find out where his friend is, telephoning indicates only belief in the efficiency of so doing for this purpose, not belief that his friend is at home.

If one telephones a friend and is not certain – does not believe strongly – that the friend is at home and he gets no answer, he hangs up and changes his belief to "the friend is not at home." If he is certain the friend is at home, he will assume something to be wrong in his dialing, or in the telephone, or even with his friend, and proceed to determine which of these is true. It is apparent then that *the amount of evidence one requires to change a belief depends on how strongly he holds that belief.* In the situation just described if one re-telephones his friend it indicates more doubt of the efficiency of his behavior than he has of his friend's presence at home.

1. Structurally defined.

Now suppose on calling at a friend's house one finds no one at home and leaves a note. From this one is likely to infer that he *expects* his friend to return at a later time; that is, he believes the friend *will* be present in that environment at a subsequent time. His leaving a note would have no efficiency for his desired outcome (to have the friend call him later) unless the friend were to return.

Consider another example. Suppose one puts on a raincoat on a clear morning when he is aware that it is not raining, because he wants to be dry when he returns home that evening. Then it can be asserted that he expects rain. If he had a different objective — say, to leave his coat at a cleaners — this conclusion could not be drawn; or if a raincoat is the only coat available, his wearing it would not show an expectation of rain. Examples such as these emphasize the importance of holding the objective constant in tests of belief.

5.5.   *Belief in a future event — expectation:* If an individual selects a course of action, C_i, at a time, t_0, when he pursues an objective, (O_j), at a later time, (t_j), and he is aware (1) that C_i at t_0 has no efficiency for O_j at t_1 unless X is present (absent) in the environment before t_1, and (2) X is absent (present) in the environment at t_0, then he can be said to *expect* (or believe that) X will be in that environment before or by t_1.

Belief in the past presence of something in an environment is not very different than belief in a future presence. When one goes out to the front of his house each morning to get the morning paper, he displays belief in the earlier presence of the delivery boy.

5.6.   *Belief in a past event:* If an individual selects a course of action, C_i, at a time, t_1, when he pursues an objective, O_j, and he is aware that C_i at t_1 has no efficiency for O_j unless X was present (absent) in the environment before t_1, then he can be said to believe that X was present (absent) in the environment before t_1.

Now that the basic types of belief have been taken care of, we can consider the six previously cited types of belief that are the elements out of which an individual's model of a choice situation is constructed.

Belief in availability of a course of action

A course of action is something that an individual does; hence it is an event — a change in one or more of his properties. It may involve use of an instrument (a car or a telephone), or it may not (in walking). An individual believes a course of action is available if he believes he is capable of doing what is necessary and any required instruments or environmental conditions are present. For example, he believes he can use a telephone if he believes (1) *a telephone is available*, (2) *it is functioning*, and (3) *he knows how and is capable of using it*. Note that the required beliefs are beliefs in the presence of properties of the environment and himself, and of required instruments if any. This kind of belief had already been defined (see 5.1). Therefore, the remaining task is to determine what environmental and personal properties and instruments a subject believes must be present (are necessary) if he is to carry out a course of action.

5.7.   *Belief in necessity:* A subject believes something (X) in environment S_1 at time t_1 is necessary for something else (Y) in environment S_2 at a later time t_2 if he believes (1) whenever Y occurs in S_2 at t_2, X was present in S_1 at t_1; and (2) if X is not present in S_1 at t_1, Y will not be present in S_2 at t_2.

The environments S_1 and S_2 may be the same.

5.8.   *Belief in the availability of a course of action:* An individual believes a course of action (C_1) is available to him in a choice environment (S) if he believes all the properties of S and himself and any instruments he believes necessary to take C_1 are present in S.

Belief in response capabilities and outcomes

An individual's model of a choice situation contains uncontrolled variables, properties of the state which he believes affect the outcome of his choice. Determination of what properties of a state an individual believes to be relevant is closely related to determining what courses of action he believes are available.

5.9.   *Belief in sufficiency:* A subject believes something (X) in environment S_1 at time t_1 is sufficient for something else (Y) in environment S_2 at a later time t_2 if he believes that whenever X occurs in S_1 and t_1, Y will occur in S_2 at t_2.

5.10.   *Belief in producer–product:* A subject believes something (X) in environment S_1 at time t_1 is a producer of something Y in environment S_2 at a later time t_2 if he believes that X in S_1 at t_1 is a necessary but not a sufficient condition for Y to occur in S_2 at t_2.

5.11.   *Belief in control of a property of the choice situation:* An individual believes he can control a property of his choice environment if he believes that choice at time t_1 of one of the courses of action believed to be available to him will produce a change in that property at a later time t_2.

For example, if an individual believes that manipulation of a thermostat will produce a change in room temperature, then he believes room temperature is a controllable variable. If, on the other hand, he believes that he can do nothing to affect the weather and that weather will affect the outcome of what he does, then he believes weather is an uncontrollable variable.

5.12.   *Belief in relevant uncontrolled properties of the choice situation:* An individual believes that a property of a choice situation is a relevant uncontrolled property of that situation if he believes (1) he cannot produce a change of that property and (2) that property is a (co)producer of the outcome of one or more of the courses of action he believes to be available to him.

Note that these are the properties of a choice situation about which an individual may want information. Furthermore, his expectations of what outcomes his behavior will produce are based on his beliefs about what are the relevant uncontrolled variables and their values.

An outcome of a course of action in a choice situation is the set of changes in the properties of the subject and his environment that are produced by that course of action.

5.13.   *Believed outcomes:* An individual believes an outcome (O_j) is possible in a choice environment (S) if he believes that one or more of the courses of action he believes to be available can produce O_j in S.

HYPOTHESES AND ASSUMPTIONS

Up to this point we have considered only how to determine that an individual believes that something, X, is or is not, will be or will not be, was or was not present in an environment. The X's can be objects, events, courses of action, or properties of these.

Now we turn our attention to belief in the presence or existence of things that have not been perceived and that, indeed, may not be perceivable — such as living things on Mars, the ether, and God. In such cases we clearly cannot determine how an individual responds to such things when he perceives them. Hence the previously described test of belief does not apply here. The X's involved in such beliefs — be they objects, events, or properties — can be called *hypothetical.*

5.14.   *Hypothesis:* a belief (which has some doubt associated with it) in the past, present, or future existence of something that has never been perceived.

How can we determine an individual's belief in an object that either has not or cannot be perceived. The answer is that we must determine how the individual *would* behave if X did exist and he perceived it. To do so does not raise any unique experimental problem in principle.

The determination of what properties an individual actually has in this environment is no more *direct* an investigation than the determination of what properties an individual would have in any specified environment. This should be clear from all that has been said above. To determine what an individual intends or knows in *this* environment requires our developing a concept of a model (controlled standard) environment and determining what the individual would do in that environment. Therefore, the determination of what properties an individual has always depends on the determination of what an individual would do *if.* Even if our task is to determine whether or not an individual selects a specified course of action in this environment, we must employ the producer–product model in an idealized environment and relate *this* environment to it. The selection of a course of action is not determined by so-called direct observation any more than is knowledge of it. The process of determining what *is* and what *would be* are methodologically similar; the *would* presents no unique problems.

If we know how an individual responds to various climates, we can find techniques for inferring how he would respond to a climate he may never have been in. If we know how an individual responds to various forms of authority, we can infer how he would behave in response to the presence of so complete an authority as God is defined to be. These problems are analogous to determining how a body would fall *in a vacuum* on the basis of observations made in something that is never quite a vacuum.

Once we have determined how an individual would respond to a hypothetical *X*, then the procedure for determining whether he believes that *X* to be present corresponds exactly to the general description given in definition 5.1 for determining belief in real things. For example, with respect to the end of saving his soul, we could determine how an individual would respond to the existence of God. On the level of common sense, at least, we would say that prayer is a type of behavior that indicates a belief in God. Also we would say in most cases that if the individual did not believe in God he would not pray. Hence in this environment we can perhaps take prayer to be an indication of belief in God. Similarly we can determine how a scientist would respond to the presence of ether if he observed it, and infer from this whether he believes it to exist.

We sometimes use *assume* and *believe* synonymously, but this is careless. Clearly an individual may assume something he does not believe as well as something he does believe, or he may assume something he neither believes nor disbelieves. In assuming *X* one acts as he would if he believed it, but with an important additional condition: he does so for the purpose of determining the consequences (outcomes) of the belief. This purpose may or may not be conscious. If not conscious, it is referred to as an *implicit* assumption. If conscious, it is *explicit* and frequently takes the form of an axiom or postulate, which are linguistic representations of assumptions.

5.15. *Assumption:* An individual (*A*) assumes something (*X*) in a choice situation (*S*) if (1) a belief in *X* in *S* would produce different behavior of *A* in *S* than would nonbelief, (2) *A* behaves as he would if he believed *X* in *S*, and (3) he intends to determine (perceive) the consequences of this belief (what outcomes such belief behavior produces).

To *pretend* something is true is not quite the same as to assume it is true; furthermore, to *believe* and to *make believe* are not equivalent. We distinguish, for example, between the psychotic who believes he is Napoleon and the actor or masquerader who pretends or makes believe he is Napoleon. In ordinary language we would characterize make believe as acting as though *X* were so, but really knowing better. It is the "but really knowing better" that provides the clue for making the distinction between believe and make believe more precise.

First, it is to be noted that the behavior of the individual who makes believe could be interpreted as belief were we to ignore certain aspects of it. The actor who moves heavy furniture about on the stage that he occupies before an audience makes believe that no one else is present to aid him. If his intention were *only* to move the furniture (O_1), we would say that he believes no one else to be present; that is, relative to O_1 his behavior could be interpreted as belief in the absence of other people. However, we know his intention is to entertain the audience (O_2), and that his behavior has some efficiency for this second outcome. In addition we know that relative to O_2 the actor senses the presence of other people; that is, relative to O_2 he behaves efficiently in his response to the presence of the audience. He is aware, in addition, that his behavior can be interpreted as belief in the absence of people, and it is precisely for this reason that he so behaves, since such interpretation on the part of the audience is necessary for the actor's attainment of O_2.

5.16. *To make believe or pretend:* An individual (A) makes believe or pretends that he believes something (X) in a choice environment (S) if (1) he does not believe X in S, (2) he behaves as he would if he believed X in S, and (3) he believes that such behavior will produce a response in one or more individuals that he (A) intends to produce.

This definition appears to be self-contradictory: How can an individual display a characteristic belief response and not believe what is indicated? The answer is R, which is a belief response when the subject's objective is O_1, may not be a belief response when his objective is O_2. In make believe he pretends to have objective O_1 but doesn't. An actor may pretend to want to harm another actor without actually wanting to do so.

It seems appropriate to bring this section to a close with an illusion.

5.17. *Illusion:* An individual has an illusion of something (X) in a choice environment (S) if he does not perceive X in S but believes he does.

Beliefs in Efficiency

In many situations an individual has very high intention for an outcome and yet does not select the most efficient course of action for pursuing it. We sometimes explain such a choice by saying he believed that the course of action he did select was the most efficient available.

If we observe an individual putting on a raincoat on a cold clear day, we do not necessarily conclude that he believes wearing a raincoat to be the most efficient way of keeping warm. He may, in fact, believe that wearing a raincoat has a very low efficiency for this purpose, but he may want to take his overcoat (concering which he has a higher opinion) to the tailor for cleaning, or he may merely want to take the raincoat to be repaired. As long as there is the possibility that the individual in this environment is pursuing many different ends, we cannot use his behavior directly as evidence of what efficiency he believes a course of action to have with respect to any one outcome, for we do not know with respect to which outcome his behavior can be taken as an indicator of such belief.

To determine an individual's belief in the efficiency of a course of action for any outcome, it is necessary for us to isolate the outcome so that his choices cannot be taken to be serving any other objectives. If we know that an individual wants to keep warm, and has no other conflicting objectives, and further that when he wants to keep warm he almost always wears a raincoat, we would then take his behavior as indicating a belief in the efficiency of wearing the raincoat for that purpose.

The first condition, then, to be incorporated in the definition of a belief environment is that the individual have intention for one and only one outcome. But where the individual is interested only in, say, keeping dry, that he repeatedly wears a raincoat may not indicate that he believes the act to be the most efficient possible. First, he may have no other course of action available that he believes to be more efficient. He may, in fact, believe a woolen overcoat to be much more efficient, but such a coat may not be available to him. Then the repeated choice of wearing a raincoat in such an environment can at best indicate a belief in its *relative efficiency* – that is, a belief that wearing a raincoat is the most efficient *available* means for keeping warm in that environment.

An individual who is faced with the problem of making a difficult calculation may repeatedly use a slide rule, even when a calculating machine is available, and yet we might consider him to believe that use of a calculator is more efficient than use of a slide rule. He may be unfamiliar with the machine and not know how to use it, and thus refrain. It is necessary, therefore, to distinguish between his and someone else's use of the instrument. The repeated choice of a behavior pattern in the belief environment can only be taken to indicate belief in the relative efficiency of his use of a course of action in that environment.

Suppose now that an individual has only one intended outcome – obtaining an answer to a complicated mathematical problem – and further that he has only two potential courses of action in the environment – use of pencil and paper, and use of a slide rule. Then we can take the relative frequency with which he selected each course of action as an indication of his degree of belief in its *maximum relative efficiency* (to be designated hereafter as MRE). If he always selected the slide rule in this situation, we would say that he believes with certainty in the MRE of the use of the slide rule relative to his objective in that environment, and that he has absolutely no belief in the MRE of the pencil and paper calculations. If, on the other hand, his probability of choice of the slide rule is 0.75, and his probability of choice of the other course of action is 0.25, then we would not take him to be absolutely sure of the MRE of the use of the slide rule for that end. He would be surer, however, of the efficiency of the slide rule than of the efficiency of using pencil and paper. Where probabilities of choice are equal, his degrees of belief in the MRE's of both are equal.

Unless we are careful, belief in the MRE of a course of action can be confused with familiarity with it. It is necessary, therefore, to construct the belief environment so that the intrinsic values of the courses of action studied are not compounded with beliefs in MRE's. This is done by requiring that the subject places equal relative value on each alternative when they are treated as ends.

5.18. *Degree of belief in maximum relative efficiency of a course of action:* This measure of an individual (A) with respect to a course of action (C_1), an objective (O_j), and a set of alternative courses of action that A believes to be available and for each of which and C_i he has the same degree of intention in the choice environment (S) is the probability of A's choosing C_i in S when his degree of intention for O_j is 1.0.

If the course of action in the available set for which the subject has maximum degree of belief in its MRE actually has Maximum Relative Efficiency, we would be inclined to say that the individual's belief is *true* and that he *knows* the MRE of that course of action. The relationship between belief and knowledge was commented on by J. S. Mill (1865) as follows.

> We do not know a truth and believe it besides, the belief *is* knowledge. Belief altogether, is a genus which includes knowledge; according to the usage of language, we believe whatever we assent to; but some of our beliefs are knowledge, others only belief. The first requisite, which, by universal admission, a belief must possess, to constitute it knowledge, is that it be true (p. 80 fn.).

The degree of belief in the MRE of a course of action is not equivalent to the degree of knowledge of the MRE of that action, but they are related. Just how becomes apparent in the following definition.

5.19. *Degree of knowledge of MRE:* An individual's degree of knowledge of the MRE of a course of action (C_i) relative to an objective (O_j) in a choice environment (S) is his degree of belief in its MRE when C_i actually is the most efficient course of action for O_j in S.

Therefore, an individual's degrees of belief and knowledge in the MRE of a course of action are equivalent when the course of action involved is the most efficient available. If it is not, then the degree of belief is false and hence does not constitute knowledge.

An individual's degree of belief in the MRE of a course of action relative to an objective is different from the intensity of his belief in its MRE.

5.20. *Intensity of belief in MRE.* An individual's intensity of belief in the MRE of a course of action (C_i) for an objective (O_j) relative to a set of courses of action which he believes to be available in a choice environment (S) is one less than the number of failures of C_i to produce O_j in S, which are required to change his degree of belief in the MRE of C_i to zero.

The individual's degree of doubt of the MRE of a course of action is another matter.

5.21. *Degree of doubt of relative efficiency:* An individual's degree of doubt about the relative efficiency of a course of action (C_i) relative to an objective (O_j) in a choice environment (S) is his degree of intention to become aware of that relative efficiency.

An adequate measure of the strength of a belief in the MRE of a course of action should be a function of its degree, intensity, and the degree of doubt associated with it. It should increase with increases in the first two and decrease with increases in the last. It should be zero when either of the first two measures are at their minimums (zero) or the last is at its maximum (one). A measure that would satisfy these conditions is

(*Degree of Belief*) × (*Intensity of Belief*) × (1-*Degree of Doubt*).

This measure of belief can range between zero and infinity.

Believed Relative and Absolute Efficiencies

It is to be noted that the probability of choice in the belief environment provides a measure of the degree of belief in the MRE and does not indicate *how* efficient (in the absolute sense) the individual believes the courses of action to be. Nor does the probability of choice of each of the alternative courses of action indicate how the individual ranks their efficiencies; it merely indicates which course the individual most believes to have the MRE.

We can move up one notch now and consider how to determine what relative efficiency an individual believes courses of action to have relative to an outcome, O, in a state, S. By relative efficiency of courses of action we mean the *ratios* of their efficiencies. Therefore, if one course of action has an efficiency of 0.08 and another an efficiency of 0.04 for an outcome, then 2 and 1 or 1.0 and 0.50 represent their relative efficiencies. For convenience we express relative efficiency as the ratio to the highest efficiency of the set, thereby yielding a scale between 0 and 1.0.

Suppose an individual in S has a degree of intention of 1.0 for a specific outcome, O. This is the same situation we used to determine the degree of belief in the MRE of the available courses of action. In this situation we assume the subject *could* select any course of action; that is, the selection and occurrence of each course of action is the same. Now suppose we separate them by having him indicate which course of action he wants to select. Then we can control the probability that the course of action will occur if he selects it. If one course of action is to use the telephone, we can arrange for the telephone to be dead a specified proportion of the time. Let $a_i, a_2, ..., a_m$ represent the probabilities of occurrence that we attach to $C_1, C_2, ..., C_m$. The subject is made aware of these. We then seek a set of values of $a_1, a_2, ..., a_m$ such that the probabilities of choice are equal:

$$P_1 = P_2 = \cdots = P_m = \frac{1}{m}.$$

These values of the a's give us the values of the relative efficiencies that the subject believes the courses of action to have. If $a_1 = 1.0$ and $a_2 = 0.4$, we conclude that the subject believes C_2 to be $1.0/0.4 = 2.5$ times as efficient as C_1, or C_1 to be $0.4/1.0 = 0.4$ times as efficient as C_2.

Note that when the courses of action and outcomes available in a state are defined so as to form exclusive and exhaustive sets although

$$\sum_{j=1}^{n} E_{ij} = 1.0,$$

$$\sum_{i=1}^{m} E_{ij}$$

may take on any value from O to m. For this reason we cannot translate the believed relative efficiencies directly into believed (absolute) efficiencies.

If the number of exclusive or exhaustive courses of action (m) is equal to or greater than the number of exclusive and exhaustive outcomes (n), then the believed absolute efficiencies can be determined. This is so because we can form m equations in n unknowns.

Suppose there are two courses of action, C_1 and C_2, and two exclusive and exhaustive outcomes, O_1 and O_2. Let a_1 and a_2 represent values associated with C_1 and C_2 relative to O_1 (when intention for it is equal to 1.0), which make the probabilities of their choice equal ($P_1 = P_2$); and b_1 and b_2 represent the corresponding values with respect to O_2 (when intention for it is equal to 1.0). Let these values be as follows:

	O_1	O_2
C_1	$a_1 = 0.5$	$b_1 = 1.0$
C_2	$a_2 = 1.0$	$b_2 = 0.33$

Now we can formulate the following equations:

$$a_1 E_{11} = a_2 E_{21} \tag{5.1}$$

$$b_1 E_{12} = b_2 E_{22} \tag{5.2}$$

$$E_{11} + E_{12} = 1.0 \tag{5.3}$$

$$E_{21} + E_{22} = 1.0. \tag{5.4}$$

Then from (5.1) and (5.2) we get

$$E_{11} = \frac{a_2}{a_1} E_{21} \tag{5.5}$$

$$E_{12} = \frac{b_2}{b_1} E_{22}. \tag{5.6}$$

Substituting in (5.3) yields

$$\frac{a_2}{a_1} E_{21} + \frac{b_2}{b_1} E_{22} = 2E_{21} + 0.33 E_{22} = 1.0. \tag{5.7}$$

Multiplying (5.4) by 2, we get

$$2E_{21} + 2E_{22} = 2.0. \tag{5.8}$$

Subtracting (5.7) from (5.8) yields

$$\frac{5}{3} E_{22} = 1.0 \tag{5.9}$$

or

$$E_{22} = 0.6. \tag{5.10}$$

Then, from (5.4) $E_{21} = 0.4$, and from (5.1) and (5.2) $E_{11} = 0.8$ and $E_{12} = 0.2$.

Therefore, in formulating a model of the subject's choice situation if we do so in such a way that $m \geq n$ we can determine what are the subject's believed efficiencies of each course of action for each outcome. These believed values are sometimes called subjective efficiencies.

This discussion can be summarized in an awkward and lengthy definition.

5.22. *Belief in efficiencies:* In a choice environment in which a subject (A) believes
(1) n exclusive and exhaustive outcomes are possible (O_j, where $j = 1, 2, ..., n$),
(2) $m(m \geq n)$ exclusive and exhaustive courses of action are available (C_i, where $i = 1, 2, ..., m$), when his intention for O_j is 1.0, then for a set of probabilities $\{\alpha_{ij}\}$ associated with $C_1, C_2, ..., C_m$ respectively so that $P_1 = P_2 = \cdots = P_m$;

the believed efficiencies of the C_i's for the O_j's are those values of E_{ij}, which satisfy the following set of equations:

$$\alpha_{11}E_{11} = \alpha_{21}E_{21} = \cdots = \alpha_{m1}E_{m1}$$
$$\alpha_{12}E_{12} = \alpha_{22}E_{22} = \cdots = \alpha_{m2}E_{m2}$$
$$.$$
$$.$$
$$.$$
$$\alpha_{1n}E_{1n} = \alpha_{2n}E_{2n} = \cdots = \alpha_{mn}E_{mn}$$
$$\sum_j E_{ij} = 1.0.$$

Belief in Probabilities

Suppose an individual (A) believes that two states are possible—S_1 and S_2 (it will or it won't rain today). Relative to an objective (O_j) for which his degree of intention is 1.0, suppose he believes the efficiency of a course of action, C_1, is 1.0 if S_1 pertains and 0 if S_2 pertains. Correspondingly he believes the efficiency of C_2 is 0 if S_1 pertains and 1.0 if S_2 pertains. No other courses of action are available. Now we construct a choice situation in which probabilities α_1 and α_2 ($\alpha_1 + \alpha_2 = 1.0$) are associated with C_1 and C_2, respectively, so that (1) if A selects C_1 he will be able to carry it out α_1 portion of the time, with C_2 occurring ($1 - \alpha_1 = \alpha_2$) portion of the time; and (2) if he selects C_2 it will materialize α_2 portion of the time, with C_1 occurring ($1 - \alpha_2 = \alpha_1$) portion of the time. Then we find the values of α_1 and α_2 for which A's probabilities of selecting C_1 and C_2 are equal ($P_1 = P_2 = 0.5$). Where this is so, $\alpha_1 C_1$ and $\alpha_2 C_2$ are equally preferable to A.

Now we can determine what he believes to be the probabilities of S_1 occurring (p_1) and S_2 (p_2). Suppose $\alpha_1 = 0.4$ and $\alpha_2 = 0.6$. Then since $P_1 = P_2$,

$$0.4p_1 = 0.6p_2. \tag{5.11}$$

Solving, we get

$$0.4\, p_1 = 0.6\,(1 - p_1) \tag{5.12}$$
$$p_1 = 0.6 \tag{5.13}$$
$$p_2 = 1 - 0.6 = 0.4. \tag{5.14}$$

A corresponding procedure can be used when more than two possible states are involved. For example, consider three states (S_1, S_2, and S_3) for which we have found that when $\alpha_1 = 0.5$, $\alpha_2 = 0.3$, and $\alpha_3 = 0.2$; $P_1 = P_2 = P_3 = 0.33$. Then

$$0.5\, p_1 = 0.3\, p_2 = 0.2\, p_3 \tag{5.15}$$
$$p_3 = (1 - p_1 - p_2) \tag{5.16}$$
$$0.5\, p_1 = 0.2(1 - p_1 - p_2) \tag{5.17}$$
$$0.7\, p_1 + 0.2\, p_2 = 0.2. \tag{5.18}$$

Multiplying through by 3/2 yields

$$1.05\, p_1 + 0.3\, p_2 = 0.3. \tag{5.19}$$

Adding

$$0.5\, p_1 - 0.3\, p_2 = 0 \tag{5.20}$$

yields

$$1.55\, p_1 = 0.3$$
$$p_1 = 0.19. \tag{5.21}$$

Then, from

$$0.5\,(0.19) = 0.3\, p_2 = 0.2\, p_3 \tag{5.22}$$

we set

$$p_2 = 0.32 \text{ and } p_3 = 0.48. \tag{5.23}$$

Note that the values of the α's essentially reflect the odds that the subject is willing to set for each course of action to yield fair bets.

This discussion, like the last, may also be summarized in a rather awkward and lengthy definition as follows.

5.23. *Belief in probability of states:* In a choice environment in which
(1) a subject (A) believes n states are possible ($S_1, S_2, ..., S_n$),
(2) A believes there are n exclusive and exhaustive courses of action available (C_1, C_2, C_n) such that
(3) relative to an objective (O_j) for which A's degree of intention is 1.0,
(4) he believes

$$E_{ij}\,|\,S_1 = 1.0,\ E_{ij}\,|\,S_k(k \neq 1) = 0;$$
$$E_{2j}\,|\,S_2 = 1.0,\ E_{2j}\,|\,S_k(k \neq 2) = 0$$
$$\vdots\ ...;$$
$$E_{nj}\,|\,S_n = 1.0,\ E_{nj}\,|\,S_k(k \neq nn) = 0$$

then, for a set of probabilities $[(\alpha_1, \alpha_2, ..., \alpha_n) \text{ where } \alpha_1 + \alpha_2 + \cdots + \alpha_n = 1.0]$ associated respectively with $C_1, C_2, ..., C_n$, for which $P_1 = P_2 = \cdots = P_n = 1/n$; the believed probabilities of $S_1, S_2, ..., S_n$ ($p_1, p_2, ..., p_n$) are those values for which

$$\alpha_1 p_1 = \alpha_2 p_2 = \cdots = \alpha_n p_n$$

where

$$p_1 + p_2 + \cdots + p_n = 1.0.$$

Believed probabilities are frequently referred to as *subjective* probabilities.

Note that when an individual is *asked* what probability he believes X to have he may reply with a two-place decimal — for example, 0.25. But in his behavior he may not discriminate between values from, say, 0.10 to 0.40. Therefore, verbal testimony must be treated with care.

Beliefs in Intentions and Utilities

The only aspect of an individual's model of a problem situation that remains to be considered involves the values he places on the outcomes he believes are possible.

Many would argue that what an individual *thinks* (believes) he wants and what he wants are the same thing. Such an argument must either be based on fact or on a tautology; that is, what an individual believes he wants and what he wants are defined to be the same thing. To define them as equivalent is to ignore a commonly made distinction between the two. Most would agree that what one individual, *A*, wants and what another individual, *B*, believes *A* wants are not necessarily the same thing. We certainly do not want to equate these by definition. If our definition allows them to differ and is general enough to allow *A* and *B* to be the same individual, then it becomes a question of fact whether what an individual wants and what he believes he wants are the same.

A parent who believes his child wants to learn how to play the piano behaves differently from one who doesn't. The desire to play the piano – a high degree of intention to do so or a high utility placed on doing so – is a property of the child. To determine whether or not a parent believes the child to have such a property is the same as determining whether he believes the child to have any other type of property, particularly a functional property. Once the belief indicators have been identified, we would proceed as described above in the discussion of belief in the presence of objects, events, and properties of either (5.1).

One should proceed in the same way to determine what properties an individual believes he has. We often say of another that he believes he knows more than he does, or he is less or more generous than he thinks he is, and so on. Of course, an individual may be as smart or generous as he believes he is. The point is that we commonly distinguish between what properties an individual believes himself to have and those he actually has.

Therefore, to determine what relative value or utility an individual believes an outcome, *O*, has for him in a state, *S*, we must find a type of behavior he displays almost invariably when he is aware of this utility and that he almost never displays otherwise.

An individual may not be aware that he has a certain illness, physical or psychological – such as paranoia. If paranoic, he may not believe he is. If not paranoic, he may believe he is. A doctor can make a person aware of an illness he was previously unaware of. An individual can become aware of his own relative values or utilities either by observing himself in appropriate conditions or by being informed by someone who has so observed him.

Suppose that when an individual, *A*, is aware (relative to an outcome that he intends, O_1) that another individual, *B*, has a high intention for an outcome O_2, he displays a characteristic response *R*, which he virtually never displays when he is aware that *B* has low intention for O_2. Then if *A* is not aware of *B*'s intentions and *A* has high intention for O_1 and displays *R*, he can be said to *believe* that *B* has a high intention for O_2.

For example, when a person (*A*) wants to please his wife (O_1) and he is aware that she (*B*) wants a particular household appliance (O_2), he buys it for her. He never does so when he is aware that she does not want that particular appliance. Then if he is observed buying an appliance to please her when he is not aware of her desires, he can be said to believe that she wants it.

5.24.　*Belief in relative values of outcomes:* If when an individual (*A*) is aware (relative to an objective, O_1) that another individual (B, who may or may not be the same as A) has intention for another outcome (O_2, where O_1 and O_2 need not be exclusive) he displays a characteristic response (R), which he virtually never displays when he is aware that B has low intention for O_2, then if when A has high intention for O_1 and he is not aware of B's intentions for O_2 he displays R, he believes that B has high intentions for O_2.

Suppose that when an individual wants to relax (O_1) and is aware that he also wants to see a movie (O_2) he virtually always goes to a motion picture theater (R) and virtually never does so otherwise. Then when he wants to relax and does not know (is not sure) whether or not he wants to see a movie, he can be said to believe he wants to see a movie if he goes to a theater. An observer, noting his restlessness during the movie, may conclude that his belief is in error; that he does, in fact, not want to watch a movie. Indeed, the individual himself may become aware of this by observing his own restlessness.

The discussion up to this point has been concerned only with two levels of intention, above and below 0.5. It is possible, however, to divide the intention scale into smaller intervals and obtain characteristic responses for each. This would enable one to determine which of smaller ranges of intention an individual believes another or himself to have.

Conclusion

The beliefs of a purposeful system can be categorized as beliefs about the components of the model of a purposeful state — courses of action, outcomes, relevant state variables, efficiencies, relative values, and so on. If the individual has doubts about any of these, it will be reflected in his evaluation of his model and possibly in the design of data acquisition and evaluation. The intensity of these beliefs affect the amount of data he requires to confirm or disconfirm his beliefs.

6

Evaluating the Situation: Feelings and Attitudes

EMOTION, *n*. A prostrating disease caused by a determination of the
heart to the head. It is sometimes accompanied by a copious discharge
of hydrated chloride of sodium from the eyes.

The Devil's Dictionary

Introduction

When part or all of a situation is observed, it is susceptible to evaluation by
the observer. If the situation observed is a product of the observer's earlier
action, then the outcome of that action can be evaluated. The essential
characteristic of such evaluations is the decision to change or retain the
situation and/or the observer's relation to it. Hence the value placed on what
is observed is the *intention to change or retain it*.

Evaluations are intentions. Intentions produced by what is observed —
that is, intention responses — are *feelings*. Therefore, when we study intentions
from the point of view of what produced them, we study feelings. Feelings
are about something, they are about what produced them, what they are
responses to.

The purpose in this discussion is to show that feelings can be adequately
treated in a system of objective teleological concepts. All possible feelings
cannot be dealt with here. More than a thousand of them have been identified
by Orth (in Reymert, 1928, p. 375), but several are dealt with to show how they
can be treated within the system. The particular connotations attributed to
them here are clearly debatable, because there is little agreement and precision
in discussions on the nature of specific feelings. We cannot hope to resolve
wide differences of opinion on what a particular feeling connotes. However,
by formulating at least one possible connotation of each of several particular
feelings we do hope to show how a range of feeling connotations can be treated.
To assist the reader in these exercises, we will quote definitions drawn from
the fifth edition of *Webster's Collegiate Dictionary*.

We have already mentioned the dependence of the concept of feeling on
that of intention. It will also become apparent that the concept of belief,

100

particularly expectation, plays a very important role in defining certain feelings. Intention was discussed in Chapter 3 and belief in Chapter 5.

Feeling, Emotion and Satisfaction

According to *Webster's* to disappoint is "to fail to come up to the expectation of." Using the concepts previously developed we can construct the following definition.

6.1. *Disappoint:* An individual (*A*) is disappointed if an object, event, or situation (*X*) desired by *A*, which he believed would be present or occur at time *t*, does not appear or occur at *t*.

An individual (*A*) is disappointed *with* another entity (*B*) if *A* believed *B* was capable of producing and would produce the desired *X* by time *t*, and *A* believes that *B* did not do so.

Whether or not a subject is also *dissatisfied* by the nonoccurrence of *X* at *t* depends on what he intends to do about the failure of *X* to occur.

According to *Webster's*, to satisfy is "to fill up the measure of a want of (a person or thing); hence to gratify fully the desire of . . ." Attainment of a desired outcome brings satisfaction. To be completely satisfied is to want nothing other than what one has; to be completely dissatisfied is to want nothing that one has.

6.2. *Satisfaction:* An individual's degree of satisfaction with an object, event, property or properties of either, or a state, *X*, is his degree of intention to produce a nonchange in *X*.

For example, if an individual is in a particular environment, *S*, and he is presented with two exclusive and exhaustive classes of courses of action — members of one will change the environment and members of the other will not — and the other conditions of an intention environment are met, then the probability that he will select a course of action that will not change *S* is his degree of satisfaction with *S*. The probability that he will select the course of action that will change the environment is his degree of dissatisfaction with *S*. If the first probability is greater than the second, he is said to be *satisfied*. If the second is the greater, he is *dissatisfied*. If these are equal, he is *indifferent* to the situation and can be said to have no feelings about it.

6.3. *Feeling:* To have a feeling is to be in a state of satisfaction or dissatisfaction.

A feeling is a functional property of an individual. It is an intention to change or retain something, an intention produced by that something.

Particular feelings (say, fear) may frequently be accompanied by certain changes in the individual's structural properties (say, accelerated heart beat, perspiration, trembling). Those structural changes that occur in association with a feeling can be called *emotions*. It is in this sense that some have said emotions fall in the domain of physiology, whereas feelings fall in the domain of psychology. C. Lange put it this way more than a century ago:

If from one terrified the accompanying bodily symptoms are removed, the pulse permitted to beat quietly, the glance to become firm, the color natural, the movements rapid and secure, the speech strong, the thoughts clear, —what is there left of his terror? (*Om Sindsbevaegelser,* Kobenhavn, 1855, trans. from thẹ German translation of H. Kurella by B. Rand in *The Classical Psychologists,* London, 1912, p. 675).

Many concepts of the relationship between feeling and emotion different from the concept suggested here have been proposed. (These have been extensively surveyed and analyzed by Hillman, 1964.) However, there is an attractive symmetry in the treatment of feeling as a *functional* response to a situation and emotion as an associated *structural* response. Hence feeling and emotion are the head and tail of the same coin—two different ways of looking at the same thing.

When an individual is confronted with a situation, whether it is a product of his previous choice or not, and he is dissatisfied with it, he intends to change it. Whether he *tries* to do so depends on his appraisal of other aspects of the situation—for example, the availability of means for so doing. To say he intends to change the situation is to make an assertion, not about what he does, but about what he would do in certain idealized conditions of choice required in an intention environment (discussed in Chapter 3). He may not act in accordance with his intentions because of the deviations of the actual situation from the intention environment.

SOME SPECIFIC FEELINGS

When an individual selects a course of action, he may believe that a certain outcome will occur (his expectation). As indicated above, if this outcome is desired and it does not occur, he is disappointed. His feelings, however, may go beyond this.

6.4. *Regret:* An individual regrets his earlier choice (or lack of choice) of a course of action if he believes that it was a producer of an unintended outcome with which he is dissatisfied.

Put another way, regret is dissatisfaction with a previous choice, or failure to act. This reflects *Webster's* definition of regret: "To have distress of mind or misgivings concerning; . . . as, to *regret* one's past mistakes."

One can obtain a measure of an individual's regret as a function of (1) the measure of his belief that his choice produced the unintended outcome and the degree of his dissatisfaction with that outcome. If either or both of these measures (both of which range from 0 to 1) are at zero, he has no regret; if both are at their maximum value, 1, he has maximum regret. Therefore, the measure of regret can be taken to be the product of the relevant measure of belief and degree of dissatisfaction.

Curiously, there does not seem to be a term uniquely applicable to the contrary of regret: belief that a previous choice was a producer of an intended outcome that brings satisfaction. This is a type of self-satisfaction, but self-satisfaction connotes more than this.

Whereas regret refers to dissatisfaction with things past, hopelessness and despair refer to dissatisfaction with things anticipated. Hope, according to *Webster's*, is "desire with expectation of obtaining what is desired...."

6.5.   *Hope:* An individual is hopeful if he is satisfied with what he believes will occur. If he is dissatisfied with his expectation, he feels *hopelessness* or *despair*.

The measure of hope can be defined as the product of the measure of belief in the future occurrence of a desired state and the degree of satisfaction with that state. Correspondingly, the measure of hopelessness is the measure of belief that a desired state will not occur and the dissatisfaction with what is expected. Hence either measure is one minus the other.

An individual who, in general, tends to be hopeful rather than hopeless is referred to as an *optimist*; one who tends to be hopeless rather than hopeful is referred to as a *pessimist*. Optimism and pessimism, as we shall see, are *attitudes* toward the future. Attitudes are discussed below.

Confronted with the possibility of a desired or an undesired outcome, an individual may have no basis for expecting one rather than the other; that is, he doesn't know what will happen and believes he can do nothing to affect it. Then he may be *anxious*, which, according to *Webster's*, is to be "concerned, or solicitous as to something future or unknown."

6.6.   *Anxiety:* dissatisfaction with a future state that the individual believes is possible and over the occurrence or nonoccurrence of which he believes he has no control.

The measure of anxiety, therefore, is the measure of dissatisfaction with a state in which the measures of belief associated with the possible outcomes are virtually equal (and possibly are all zero). As belief increases in any one outcome, anxiety converts to hope or despair.

Hope, despair, and anxiety are a trilogy of feelings that reflect an individual's intention response to what he believes or does not believe about the future. If an individual believes he can prevent an undesirable outcome, he has some hope; if not, he may be frustrated.

6.7.   *Frustration:* When an individual has no hope of obtaining a desired outcome, and he believes it is possible to produce that outcome but that he cannot do so, he feels frustrated.

Hence frustration involves both despair and dissatisfaction with oneself—holding oneself responsible for an undesirable expectation, at least in part.

Fear has been one of the most discussed and least agreed on feelings. This is reflected in the fact that most dictionaries define it by use of such synonyms as dread and disquiet. It seems to us that fear involves dissatisfaction with expected harm to oneself, physical or psychological—that is, reduction of one's capabilities for pursuing one's objectives in the future.

6.8.   *Fear:* Dissatisfaction with something that the individual believes will produce a reduction in his ability to pursue his objectives in the future.

The harm anticipated may restrict either his ability to choose efficient courses of action or his ability to desire. Expectation of harm is not sufficient for fear. Witness the masochist. Dissatisfaction is also required.

6.9.   *Inhibition:* When fear of one or more expected consequences of a course of action, other expected consequences of which are desired, produce a nonchoice of that course of action in an individual, he feels inhibited.

Thus inhibition is a felt constraint on choice produced by fear of undesirable consequences. The choice may or may not be made. If it is, the fear, though not the inhibition, may remain.

We hope we have gone far enough into these few feelings to show how they can be incorporated into a system of objective teleological concepts.

Now we consider an important class of feelings – *attitudes.*

Attitudes

Webster's defines an attitude as a "position or bearing as indicating action, feeling, or mood; as, keep a firm *attitude;* the feeling or mood itself; as, a kindly *attitude.*" In 1929 Thurstone and Chave offered the following often cited definition of an attitude: "the sum-total of a man's inclinations and feelings, prejudice or bias, preconceived notions, ideas, fears, threats, and convictions about any topic" (pp. 6–7).

In an earlier book Ackoff (1953) showed some of the consequences of taking this definition literally.

> First it would be necessary to define the relevant sets (populations) of *(a)* inclinations, *(b)* feelings, *(c)* prejudices or biases, *(d)* preconceived notions, *(e)* ideas, *(f)* fears, *(g)* threats, and *(h)* convictions. Then either a complete count of each population or a probability sample would be required. An estimate of the "sum" of these would have to be made assuming the research obtained comparable measures which could be summed. As a matter of fact, none of this is done or tried, and for obvious reasons. For example, the test items are actually selected because they *seem* pertinent and not because they can be demonstrated to be so on the basis of the definition. Furthermore, the items provide no identifiable measure. In the test for "measuring" attitudes toward the church (Thurstone and Chave, 1930) for example, such items as the following can be found:
>   "I regard the church as a monument to human ignorance."
>   "I feel the church is the greatest agency for uplift of the world."
> The subject is instructed to check those statements with which he fully agrees. Such a check or lack of it may *seem* to provide information concerning an attitude as defined above, but no demonstration that this is the case has been provided. The definition does not make it easy to do so (pp. 305–6).

A very extensive examination and analysis of psychological definitions of attitude, including that of Thurstone and Chave, was made by Sherif and

Cantril (1945). This effort yielded four properties that, they asserted, a definition of attitude should reflect.

(1) Attitudes are always related to defined stimuli or stimulus situations (p. 301).
(2) Attitudes are formed (p. 301).
(3) Established attitudes are charged with affective or value properties in varying degrees (p. 302).
(4) Attitudes are more or less enduring states of readiness [for action] (p. 303).

The definition developed here satisfies these conditions.

6.10.   *Attitude:* An attitude is a feeling about something that persists over time and a variety of environments.

6.11.   *Mood:* A mood is a relatively short-lived feeling that includes everything or most things experienced during that period.

Thus an attitude is a directed feeling, one that is produced by its object, such as an attitude toward a particular person, organization, or event. Hence one individual can have a hostile attitude toward another, and it will persist over time and manifest itself in different environments. On the other hand, a person who is in a hostile mood directs this feeling at all or most persons with whom he interacts during the life of the mood.

An attitude is an intention set, a feeling posture toward its object. It is a characteristic intention response pattern to a specific stimulus. Hence, attitude is to intention what trait is to familiarity. Both are patterns of response to stimuli. One would hardly extract this relationship from an examination of the previously quoted definition of attitude given by Thurstone and Chave, and that of a trait given by G. Allport (1937): "a generalized and focalized neuropsychic system (peculiar to the individual), with the capacity to render many stimuli functionally equivalent, and to initiate and guide consistent (equivalent) forms of adaptive and expressive behavior" (p. 295). Nevertheless, the similarity between traits and attitudes has been recognized often, and results in their frequent association in the psychological literature.

Since an attitude is a feeling, it involves satisfaction or dissatisfaction, and hence lends itself to such dichotomous characterization as favorable-unfavorable, for-against, like-dislike. These dichotomies sometimes obscure the fact that there is an underlying scale of satisfaction (of intention) that ranges from 0 to 1.

Now let us examine some of the items on the Thurstone-Chave (1930) test for attitudes toward the church in the light of this discussion. There are forty-five items in this test. The subjects are instructed to check those items with which they "fully agree."

An examination of these items reveals that "church" is used ambiguously throughout. In some of the items the individual is asked to respond to *religion* in the most general sense, and in others to a specific denomination or even a *specific building*. For example, church is used in a very general sense in the following items.

4. I regard the church as a monument to human ignorance.
5. I believe that the church is losing ground as education advances.
6. I feel the church is trying to adjust itself to a scientific world and deserves support.

Some items in which church is used in a much narrower sense are:

21. My church is the primary guiding influence of my life.
31. There is much wrong in my church, but I feel it is so important that it is my duty to help improve it.
36. In the church I find my best companions and express my best self.

Because of the ambiguous treatment of church in the test, it is not at all clear what it measures an attitude toward—a specific congregation, a denomination, a religion, or religion in the general sense.

There are other difficulties. Consider item 39: "It seems absurd to me for a thinking man to be interested in the church" is a statement that specifies only a certain aspect of intention relating to the church. Considered as an agent of emotional uplift, or as a center of social activity, rather than an agent of thinking, preservation of the church might be an end of high intention. A religious man may deny this statement because he does not find the church interfering with his thought and it provides him with religious uplift. On the other hand, a sociologist who is an ardent atheist may agree with the statement because he considers the church as a social institution rather than a religious one, for he finds it cannot be ignored by a thinking man who would completely understand a culture. Is "interested in" meant to imply "participate in"?

Many of the items in the test do not seem to be designed to elicit the same expression of belief in intention over a variety of people. For example, consider 34: "I feel that church attendance is a good index of the nation's morality." If a person felt that the nation was immoral and church attendance was low, then he might very well agree with Thurstone. However, a person who feels the church is immoral (as Lenin did) and that the nation's morality is low would also agree with this item. Clearly the attitudes of the two persons would not be the same.

It should be noted that a verbal test of an attitude does not tell us what a person wants, only what he *says* he wants. These are not necessarily the same thing. Hence unless a verbal test of an attitude is validated experimentally against relevant behavior, its basic assumption of the equivalence of what a person feels and what he says he feels is not justified.

Finally, it is not at all apparent, even if we assume the identity of what a person says and feels, that answers to *these* items are evidence from which intentions can be inferred. No explicit criterion of relevance of these items was used in selecting them; all that was required was agreement among independent judges who were given no criterion to use in their judgments.

Conclusion

A choice situation in which (1) an individual is dissatisfied with that situation as he has modeled it and (2) he has doubts about which course of action to select is a *problem* situation to that individual. If there is no dissatisfaction in a choice situation, then there is no need for a choice. If there is dissatisfaction but no doubt over what to do about it, there is no problem because the choice is apparent. Thus a problem consists of a situation in which an individual wants to determine how to remove his dissatisfaction. In Chapter 7 we consider the process by which choices are formulated and evaluated in problem situations.

REFERENCES

Ackoff, R. L. *The Design of Social Research*. Chicago: University of Chicago Press, 1953.

Allport, G. W. *Personality: A Psychological Interpretation*. New York: Henry Holt & Co., 1937.

Hillman, James. *Emotion*. Evanston, Ill.: Northwestern University Press, 1964.

Reymert, M. (ed.). *The Wittenburgh Symposium*. Worcester, Mass.: Clark University, 1928.

Sherif, M., and H. Cantril. "The Psychology of Attitudes." *Psychological Review* 52 (1945): 301–4.

Thurstone, L. L., and E. J. Chave. *The Measurement of Attitudes*. Chicago: University of Chicago Press, 1929.

_____. *A Scale for Measuring Attitudes toward the Church*. Chicago: University of Chicago Press, 1930.

7

Formulation and Evaluation of Choices: Thought and Intuition

INDECISION, *n.* The chief element of success; "for whereas," saith Sir Thomas Brewbold, "there is but one way to do nothing and divers ways to do something, whereof, to a surety, only one is the right way, it followeth that he who from indecision standeth still hath not so many chances of going astray as he who pusheth forwards" . . .

The Devil's Dictionary

Introduction

A problem, it will be recalled, is a special type of purposeful state. Previous discussion of its characteristics can be summarized in the following definition.

7.1. *Problem:* A purposeful state that a purposeful individual is dissatisfied with, and in which he is doubtful about which of the available courses of action will change that state to a satisfactory one.

A purposeful individual has three different ways of disposing of a problem: *dissolution, resolution,* and *solution.* We will consider each of these in turn, and then consider problem-solving in more detail, particularly with respect to formulating and evaluating alternative courses of action.

Ways of Disposing of Problems

An individual who has a problem can change his intentions so that his dissatisfaction *dissolves.* For example, a child may find that a toy he wants to play with is out of his reach. He can either use a chair to reach it or call on his mother for help. He may decide, however, that getting the toy is not worth the trouble and shift his interest to another activity. He no longer wants to play with the toy, and thus his dissatisfaction over not being able to reach it is dispelled and the problem is disposed of. So a person whose intentions easily vacillate may often dissolve his problems.

7.2. *Dissolution of a problem:* the removal (production of the subsequent absence) of a problem situation by a purposeful individual who is in it, by a change in that individual's intentions.

One person can dissolve another's problem. If the child, referred to above, calls his mother for help and she too cannot easily reach the toy, she may

108

try to divert his interests to another toy that is accessible. Thus she attempts to dissolve the child's problem.

A problem situation can also be made to disappear by making a choice *arbitrarily*. A person confronted by a menu in a foreign language may select an item from it by guessing, tossing a coin, or use of random numbers. A choice so made, however, rids one of the problem only if the course of action selected removes the state of dissatisfaction.

7.3. *Arbitrary choice:* selection of one of a set of available courses of action by a purposeful individual who has equal strength of belief in the maximum relative efficiency of each course of action for removing his dissatisfaction.

7.4. *Resolution of a problem:* the removal of a problem situation by a purposeful individual who is in it, by an arbitrary choice.

The last possibility is that the individual in a problem situation conducts *inquiry* to find out which of the available courses of action serves his purposes, thus dispelling his doubt and finding what becomes a *solution* to his problem.

7.5. *Inquiry:* a course (or courses) of action that produces a strengthening of belief in the efficiency of another course (or other courses) of action relative to some outcome(s).

7.6. *Solving a problem:* selecting one of a set of available courses of action that, as a result of inquiry, the individual believes in as the most likely to produce a state of satisfaction in him, and that does produce a state of satisfaction.

Solving a problem involves answering two questions: (1) What alternatives are available? (2) Which one is best or good enough? Any alternative that replaces dissatisfaction with satisfaction is a *satisficing* solution to the problem. An available solution that produces *as much or more* satisfaction than can any other solution not only satisfices but *optimizes*.

Formulating and Evaluating Courses of Action

Identification of possible courses of action is an essential part of constructing a model of a choice situation. Most breakthroughs in problem-solving are the result of finding either a new way of accomplishing an old objective or a new outcome obtainable by use of a familiar course of action. The newness of these discovered alternatives implies that a creative act has occurred. In a sense, then, we are going to examine creativity in formulating models of choice situations.

Consider the following problem. An overly generous housewife returning from a shopping trip with a bag of apples meets a friend and gives her half of the apples plus half an apple. She later meets a second friend and gives her half of the remaining apples plus half an apple. The process continues through four friends; after the last no apples are left. With how many apples did she start out?

A fairly obvious way of solving this problem (to those who know algebra) is as follows. Let X represent the initial number of apples. Then the amounts she gave to each friend in succession were:

$$a_1 = 1/2X + 1/2$$
$$a_2 = 1/2(X - a_1) + 1/2$$
$$a_3 = 1/2(X - a_1 - a_2) + 1/2)$$
$$a_4 = 1/2(X - a_1 - a_2 - a_3) + 1/2$$

Then

$$X - a_1 - a_2 - a_3 - a_4 = 0.$$

One can proceed by substitution, and obtain a cumbersome equation in terms of X and solve it.

Most who are given this problem proceed in the way described. Some, however, see the problem in a different way. They start at the other end. If the woman gave her last friend half of her apples plus half an apple and had nothing left, she must have had only one apple left after meeting her third friend. Then she must have had three apples left after her second friend, and have given two to the third. She must have had seven apples after her first friend, four of which she gave to her second friend; and fifteen to start with, eight of which she gave to her first friend. This second procedure is one most people do not see, even though it is there.

The perception of a new potential course of action is frequently attributed to the mental function called *intuition*, which is defined as follows by *Webster's Collegiate Dictionary* (1937):

Immediate apprehension or cognition; the power of knowing or the knowledge obtained without recourse to inference or reasoning; insight, familiarity, a quick or ready apprehension.

Many observers of intuition have noted that the process itself is not immediate, but consciousness of its output occurs suddenly. Poincaré and others have noted that they have lived with problems for long periods before having an insight that made possible their solution. An unconscious process may well have been going on for an extended period of time.

Webster's definition also asserts that intuition is *not* an inferential process such as is reasoning or thinking. Our own reasoning leads to a different conclusion.

First let us consider thought and intuition in a discursive way. When, by intuition, one perceives a possible course of action (such as a possible solution to a problem) it is not necessarily a good one. The output of either intuition or thought may be wrong. Therefore, the quality of the outputs of thought and intuition does not differentiate between them. Furthermore, since both thought and intuition produce belief in the efficiencies of courses of action, there is no difference in the nature of their products. The difference lies in the processes, not in the nature or quality of their outputs.

Next observe that once a suggestion has been put forth by intuition, it can often then be extracted by thought from what one knows about the situation. For example, when a theorem is suggested to a mathematician by his intuition, he can usually go back and derive it or show that it is not derivable from his premises. Thus intuition may produce belief that a theorem follows from certain axioms and postulates, and thought may prove that it does or does not. In this sense intuition is a kind of elliptical thought process; it appears to jump steps and proceeds from premises to conclusion without *consciously* going through the intermediate steps that thought goes through. Intuition does not consciously relate conclusions to premises; thought does.

Intuition usually produces a strong belief in the validity of the suggestions it yields. This belief may persist even when the suggestion is demonstrated to be inconsistent with one's accepted premises. In such cases it requires a reexamination of one's premises and may eventually lead to their modification. Thought can reveal which premises must be changed to make the intuitive suggestion derivable, but intuition usually provides the motivation.

It is through this process that intuition suggests new ways of thinking about a situation. By calling assumptions – particularly those that are implicit – into question, it opens up new possibilities for thought. It is for this reason that intuition is so commonly associated with creativity. Its output, however, may not be superior to what it proposes to replace.

Consider the following problem. Nine dots are placed on a piece of paper to form a square. (See Figure 7.1.) The problem is to draw four straight lines without lifting one's pencil or pen from the paper, and to pass through all the points. Most people have great difficulty with this problem because they implicitly assume the lines must be contained within the square formed by

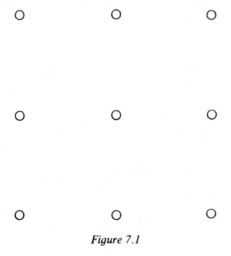

Figure 7.1

the eight points on the perimeter. Occasionally a person goes through a sudden "aha" experience in which it occurs to him that he is not so constrained. Once this possibility is opened he is likely to find the solution shown in Figure 7.2. The breaking of an implicit assumption here (as in the homicidal prisoner problem discussed in Chapter 6) is usually an intuitive act. It could be done consciously and thoughtfully by systematically formulating one's assumptions, evaluating them, and exploring the consequences of their denial.

One can also use thought to develop new ways of thinking about a choice situation and, therefore, of revealing previously unperceived courses of action. For example, one can systematically deny or omit any of the postulates of Euclidean geometry and thus develop new geometries. This is precisely what Lobacevskii and Riemann did.

We have observed, then, that intuition may draw a conclusion from a set of premises without apparently going through the steps that link the conclusion to the premises. It may also perceive a conclusion that can be drawn only if the premises are modified.

In this discussion of thought and intuition we have been talking about the process of *inference*, which according to Webster's is "the act of passing from one judgment to another, or from a belief or cognition to a judgment," or it is "a logical conclusion from given data or premises."

Inference is a process in which new beliefs are produced by old ones.

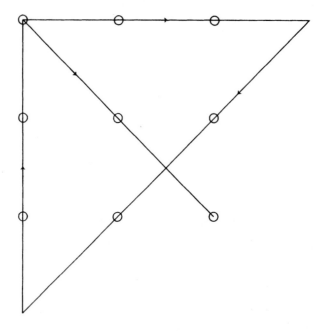

Figure 7.2

If a man believes

B_1:   his wife is at home,

B_2:   the phone at home is operating,

then he believes

B_3:   he can reach his wife at home by phone.

Note that beliefs B_1 and B_2 are each necessary, but neither is sufficient, for B_3. Hence B_1 and B_2 are producers of B_3.

7.7.   *Inference*: the production of one or more beliefs or assumptions by one or more other beliefs or assumptions.

An inferential process is always about something—some class of objects, events, or situations, or combinations of these. An inference about choice involves the *elements* we have already identified—controlled variables, uncontrolled variables, constraints, outcomes, and so on. These are the class of things an individual believes are relevant to his choice. (Another individual may perceive a different set of elements in the same situation.) Therefore, the first part of a formalized inferential system is a set of *elements* the subject believes are relevant—that is, objects, events, or combinations of these that the subject believes are producers of his future feelings, or signs or symbols[1] of these.

The second part of a formalized inferential process is a set of beliefs concerning the form in which relevant beliefs can be represented—that is, the relevant form of predicational and relational statements[2] composed only of elements of the system. These beliefs constitute a set of *belief-formation rules* or representations of these.

Next, there is a set of beliefs and assumptions that the subject is willing initially to accept as true. These beliefs and assumptions contain only elements of the system and are expressible consistently with the formation rules. These rules constitute the *premises* of the system. In a deductive system these premises may be axioms or postulates; in an inductive system they may be a set of accepted facts or observations.

Finally there is a set of beliefs concerning how acceptable beliefs (other than those contained in the premises) may be derived from accepted ones. These beliefs can be called *transformation rules*. For example, "If A is included in B, and B is included in C, then A is included in C" in such a rule. Applying this rule to accepted beliefs of the form "Cleveland is in Ohio, and Ohio is in the United States" one can conclude "Cleveland is in the United States."

Formation and transformation rules are regularities in a subject's behavior that an observer can attribute to him, even though the subject himself may not be aware of them. These rules are, in effect, the subject's *program* for deriving new beliefs from old. Such a program is functionally oriented; it is part of the subject's purposeful activity.

1. *Signs* and *symbols* are defined in Chapter 9.
2. These forms are identified and discussed in Appendix II.

The inferential process may be either *deductive* or *inductive*. In a deductive process the premises are believed by the subject to be more general than the consequences derived from them. In an inductive process the premises are believed to be less general than the consequences. Therefore, inferences from what one believes to be laws to facts are deductive, and inferences from what are believed to be facts to laws or theory are inductive. Since beliefs in generality may differ, what appears to be deductive to one person may appear to be inductive to another.

Now let us return to the difference between thought and intuition. Intuition appears to be a mental leap over an inferential gap, whereas thought is associated with an orderly and logical construction of a bridge across that gap.

7.8.   *Thought* is conscious inference.

That is, if an individual employs an inferential process and is conscious of its parts — the elements, the formation rules, the premises, and the transformation rules and the way they are used — he can be said to be *thinking*.

Thought can be used to evaluate courses of action in a systematic way. Using the model of a situation as a set of premises, one can often deduce the consequences of a course of action taken in that situation. (The model manipulation involved in this inferential process is facilitated by dealing with an explicit model.)

Recall that the results of thought, like those of intuition, may be false. Intuition, like thought, is a belief-producing process, but the process is not carried out consciously.

7.9.   *Intuition* is unconscious inference.

A subject may be unconscious of any part or all of the inferential process employed. Thus thinking–intuition represent regions on the scale of consciousness involved in an inferential process. Few if any inferences are either pure thought or pure intuition. For example, the premises or rules in a rigorous and conscious deduction may be suggested by an intuitive process. On the other hand, intuition is based on at least some premises that are consciously held. Little wonder, then, that one man can intuit what another has reached by thought, or that one may reach by thought a result that another has intuited.

Intuition supplies may possible beliefs — hunches, conjectures, suggestions, and so on — that thought can be used to *evaluate* systematically. Thought is an evaluative process in which the values involved are based on the true–false scale. Intuition does not evaluate, it *proposes*. Thought *proves*.

It might seem more reasonable to conceptualize intuition not only as unconscious but also as unprogrammable. We have not done so for several reasons. First, we want to distinguish between intuition and *guessing*. A guess seems to us to be obtained both unconsciously and in an unprogrammed way. Second, intuition often brings with it a degree of belief that a guess does not. That is, an intuitively arrived-at conclusion is often one we believe we can prove to be correct. Such conviction seldom accompanies a guess. It seems reasonable to assume that this difference results because intuition is a programmable process. Nevertheless, there are no serious consequences for this conceptual system if intuition is taken as unconscious and unprogrammable. Thought is conscious and programmable; intuition is unconscious and programmable; guessing is unconscious and unprogrammed. The remaining type of process — a conscious but unprogrammed one — appears to be one that is *random*. In such processes the user is usually motivated by a desire to avoid any implicit or explicit bias in selection. Thus randomized selection is used when we want to give each alternative an equal chance of being selected.

If a thought process is applied to a conclusion that was arrived at intuitively, and this is done with the intention of justifying the conclusion rather than determining whether it is justified, the process is that of *rationalization*. In thought one determines whether or not a specified conclusion is justified by the premises and the rules. In rationalization the validity of the conclusion is accepted and an inferential system that justifies it is sought. Hence rationalization may involve the search for premises or for rules that yield the desired outcome.

No Solution Available

If a purposeful individual in a problem situation believes that none of the available courses of action of which he is aware can work, he still has two alternatives available to him. First, he can *search* for another alternative which is available but of which he is not initially aware. Secondly, he can *develop* a new instrument and course of action that is associated with it.

7.10. *Search:* one or more observations whose intended outcome is awareness of a course of action that the observer was not aware of before making the observations.

For example, if none of the keys given to a man by a friend will open the front door to the friend's house, he may look for another door or a window that is unlocked. A search is always conditioned by the searcher's model of the situation; the model affects what kinds of possibilities he looks for. How best to conduct a search may itself be a problem — a *methodological* problem because its goal is to produce a better solution to another problem.

The man who wants to get into the house may have observed that the back entrance is blocked only by a screen door that is locked by a hook and eye on the inside. He may then look for a thin piece of pliable wire that he can shape appropriately, insert through the screen, and use to unlock the door. Then he has *developed* a course of action that was not possible until he made the wire instrument.

7.11. *Develop an instrument:* to produce an instrument in an environment which makes possible a course of action that was not previously available in that environment.

Thus, through search or development, a purposeful individual can convert a state of dissatisfaction that he initially has no control over into one he does control. The extension of its control over its environment is a characteristic objective of a purposeful system. In such an extension lies the meaning of *progress*, which E. A. Singer, Jr. (1923) defined as "The measure of man's cooperation with man in the conquest of nature . . . " (p. 89).

Conclusion

A purposeful individual can derive (infer) courses of action from his model of a problem situation; that is, the beliefs incorporated into his model can produce a belief about which courses of action are possible and which of these will produce a state of satisfaction. The derivation may be conscious and thus be obtained through thought, or it may be unconscious and hence be obtained by intuition. On the other hand, a course of action may be selected by a guess or be chosen arbitrarily (as by a random choice). In guessing and arbitrary choice, inference is not involved.

Inference is a procedure by which a set of beliefs or assumptions in the form of premises, formation rules, and transformation rules produces another set of beliefs or assumptions. The process is deductive if it proceeds from the general to the specific, and inductive if it proceeds from the specific to the general. An individual's inferential process is his logic. The components of an individual's logic have been so defined here as to make it possible to study such a logic behaviorally. Logic is discussed in more detail in Chapter 14.

REFERENCES

Singer, E. A., Jr. *On the Contented Life*. New York: Henry Holt & Co., 1923.

8

Purposeful Systems and their Environments

INCOMPATIBILITY, *n.* In matrimony a similarity of tastes, particularly the taste for domination . . .

The Devil's Dictionary

Introduction

In Chapter 3 we defined individuality, and hence personality, as a mathematical function π (definition 3.1). We also noted that although this definition was not so operational as it is programmatic, it should be possible to move up on the individuality function by focusing research on the different aspects of the multidimensional individuality space. In Chapters 4–7 we have been concerned with just these aspects. Now we want to see how far we can go toward research that will yield approximations of π itself.

Naturally this chapter must be more speculative than the preceding ones. We include the chapter, however, because it suggests what is possible and it reflects a possibility that initiated the authors' active collaboration in 1964. In our mutual concern to understand the purposes for drinking alcohol we found a remarkable convergence between the theoretical work Churchman and Ackoff had done in systematizing C. G. Jung's theory of extroversion-introversion (1921) and the types that had emerged from Emery's empirical study of alcohol users (1959). To overcome the incompleteness of Jung's theory and avoid the oversimplification of Eysenck (1947), we have started again from the beginnings made possible by our conceptualization of purposeful systems.

Our starting point is that *personality is not conceived here as an unobservable intervening variable that is invoked to explain choice but as an observable function that describes how an individual converts a choice situation into an expected relative value for himself.*

We are concerned with trying to characterize the personality of an individual in terms of the two relations that can exist between him and his environment:

1. The extent to which his environment affects him (environmental responsiveness).

117

2. The extent to which he affects his environment (environmental effectiveness).

It will be convenient (but not necessary) in this discussion to assume that courses of action are defined narrowly (structurally rather than functionally). Then the efficiency of each course of action relative to each possible outcome cannot be affected by the subject, only by the environment. The environment, to repeat, is the set of properties of objects or events that, with the subject's choice, coproduce the outcome. Each environmental property is a potential stimulus to the subject, and hence a change in any of these properties is also a potential stimulus; for example, both the weather and a change in the weather may affect his behavior. A response to such a stimulus must consist of either a change in the subject's probabilities of choice (P_is) or his relative values (V_js).

Intensities of environmental stimuli are normally measured along physical scales, as in measuring the intensity of light or sound. Different scales are used for different stimuli. As a result we cannot compare the intensities of different kinds of stimulus (such as light and sound). Yet it is necessary to be able to do so if we want to characterize an individual's responsiveness to a wide variety of stimuli. We can compare intensities as follows.

Since an environmental property is a coproducer of the outcome of a subject's choice, it affects the efficiency of his choice and hence his expected relative value. Therefore we can define the intensity of a stimulus functionally as *the difference in expected value produced by its presence as compared with its absence.* If a radio is playing in a room where a person is trying to read, the intensity of the stimulus (radio playing) is the difference in expected relative value to the subject between the environment in which the radio is playing and one in which it is not. Symbolically the intensity of the stimulus I_s is $|(EV \mid p) - (EV \mid p')|$, where p represents the presence of property p, and p' represents its absence, all other properties remaining the same. The absolute value of the difference is used because we are interested in the magnitude of the effect, not its direction. The intensity of a stimulus, so defined, can range between 0 and 1.0.

Note that a change from radio not playing to radio playing is a stimulus of the same intensity as a change from radio playing to radio not playing.

Similarly, the response of an individual to a subjective or objective stimulus may or may not have an effect on his environment. His course of action has a significant effect on his environment only if it changes the efficiency of one or more of the available courses of action for one or more of the possible outcomes. A person who wants to read in a room where a radio is playing loudly can turn the radio off and hence increase the efficiency of his reading. Turning on a light to read by is also a way of increasing one's efficiency by modifying the environment.

Here, too, we want a standardized measure of the intensity of effect on the environment. One is provided by the ratio $|\Delta EV/EV|$ where EV is the expected relative value *before* the subject acts, and ΔEV is the change in expected value produced by his action.

We have now initiated measures applicable in particular choice situations; the next step is to develop measures of the individual's *environmental response function* and his *environmental effect function.*

Generalized Measures of the Two Dimensions

First, we are interested in the probability of a subject's responding to environmental properties or changes in them as a function of their intensity. His environmental response function is the mathematical function that relates his probability of responding to environmental stimuli (P_s) to the intensities of the stimuli (I_s); that is, we are interested in f where $P_s = f(I_s)$.

This function can be plotted graphically as is done in Figure 8.1.

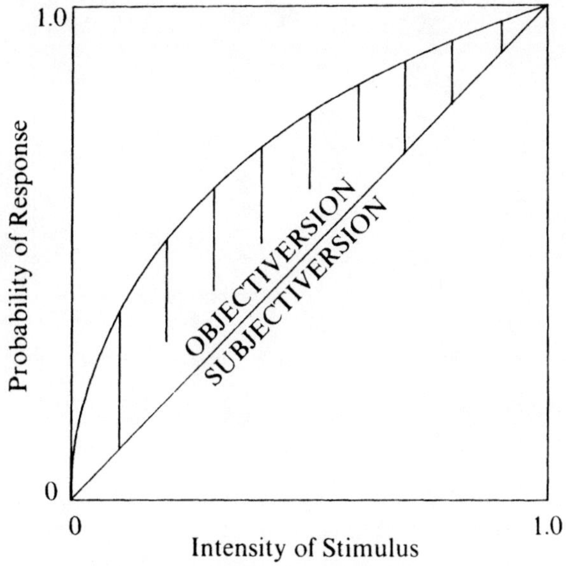

Figure 8.1. An Illustrative Environmental Response Function

The *environmental response space* can be divided into two equal areas by a diagonal from lower left to upper right. The upper area (*objectiversion*) is one of relatively high responsiveness to the environment; the lower area (*subjectiversion*) is one of relatively low responsiveness. The space can also be divided by a horizontal line drawn at the midpoint of the ordinate. We chose to use the diagonal because, in general, subjects are more likely to respond more frequently to more intense stimuli. Therefore even a very environmentally insensitive person is very likely to respond to a very strong stimulus.

Clearly objectiversion is extroversion and subjectiversion is introversion on the input (stimulus) side. These tendencies of an individual can be measured in the following way. The ratio of the cross-hatched area in Figure 8.1 to the area above the diagonal (which is equal to 1/2 since the area of the space is equal to 1.0) is the measure of objectiversion. This measure has a maximum of 1.0 and a minimum of 0, and the same holds for the measure of subjectiversion; but it would be convenient if it were to have a negative value. If the

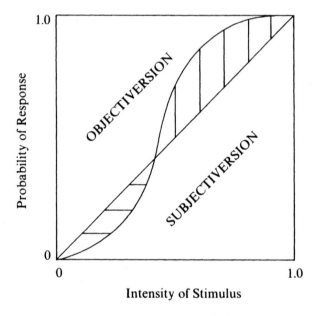

Figure 8.2.   Another Environmental Response Function

environmental response function crosses the diagonal as is shown in Figure 8.2, the difference in areas would be used. More generally and precisely, the measure is

$$2\left[\int_0^{1.0} f(I_s)dI_s - 0.5\right].\tag{8.1}$$

The value of this measure can range from -1.0 to $+1.0$. Negative values indicate subjectiversion, and positive values indicate objectiversion.

An *objectivert*, then, is one who is responsive to his environment; a *subjectivert* is not. Hence the objectivert is more likely to be aware of what is going on around him and to be influenced by it. The subjectivert is more likely to be influenced by his own thoughts and feelings than by his environment. The objectivert is objectively moved and motivated, whereas the subjectivert is subjectively moved and motivated.

Objectiversion and subjectiversion are tendencies, not rigid commitments. Hence an objectivert may act like a subjectivert in some circumstances and vice versa. The less extreme a person's position in this space is, the more likely he is to respond to both external and internal stimuli. In some circumstances (for example, at a social gathering) a subjectivert is likely to behave more like an objectivert than he usually does. On the other hand, an objectivert working in his study may look like a subjectivert.

The objectivert is sensitive and responsive to what is going on around him and thus is more likely to be sensitive to others than is the subjectivert. The subjectivert is more inclined to introspection and hence is more likely to understand himself, even if he is less likely to understand others. The difference is reflected in the difference between a realistic painter who tries to faithfully capture that part of his visual environment to which he responds, and the surrealistic painter who tries to capture his internal images. We can turn now to the other dimension.

An individual's *environmental effect function* is a mathematical function (F) that relates his cumulative probability of choosing an available course of action (CP_e) to the intensity of the effect of that course of action on his environment (I_e); that is, $CP_e = F(I_e)$. The environmental effect *space* and an illustrative function are shown in Figure 8.3.

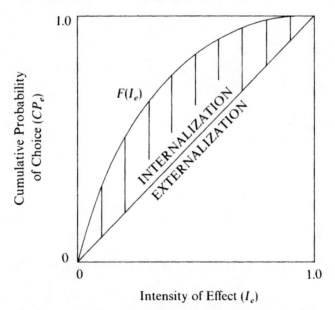

Figure 8.3. Environmental Effect Space and an Illustrative Function

The diagonal from lower left to upper right represents indifference to intensity of effect. Again the difference between the ratios of the areas between the function that are above and below the diagonal and 1/2 yields a measure of *internalization* and *externalization*, depending on which area is the larger. More precisely, the measure is

$$2\left[\int_0^{1.0} F(I_e)dI_e - 0.5\right]. \tag{8.2}$$

An externalizer is one who tends to change his environment to suit his needs. The internalizer adapts himself to his environment. If someone enters an externalizer's environment and annoys or distracts him, he is likely to try to stop the intrusive behavior. An internalizer in the same situation is more likely to try to ignore the intruder or move to another place. The externalizer will try to organize a group of which he is a part, to lead it; the internalizer is more likely to be a follower. If cold in a house, the externalizer will try to turn up the heat; the internalizer is more likely to add clothing.

Personality Types

By combining the two classifications, four personality types result as are shown in Figure 8.4. The location of a person in this space is at a point determined by his two measures — (1) and (2).

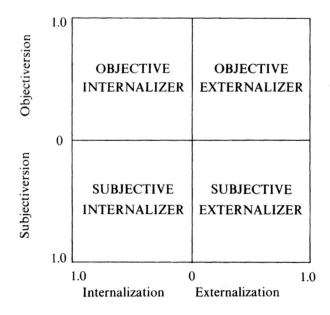

Figure 8.4. Personality Types

In practice, measurement of the relevant variables is very difficult. We are still working on development of instruments that will simplify the process.

In the meantime we have been using clinical interviews and the judgments of five independent observers applied to them to obtain estimates of the subjects' positions in the personality space. The judges have produced very consistent estimates. The results referred to in this chapter are based on data obtained in this way from approximately 100 couples, husbands and wives.

The fourfold, two-dimensional typology shows why use of the dichotomy introvert–extrovert is difficult to apply in many cases; that is, to the mixed types – subjective externalizers and objective internalizers. Jung's classes cannot be applied to them. Furthermore, the data we have indicates that most people fall into these mixed classes. This, we believe, is not accidental because we theorize that these types are more stable than are the pure types.

The pure types live almost entirely inside or outside themselves, like Koestler's *The Yogi and the Commissar,* but both the mixed types maintain some contact with both their psychic reality and their environment, although in different ways. For reasons that we shall explore later, the pure types have more difficulty than do the mixed types in adjusting either to themselves or to their environments, particularly to others in their environment.

We hypothesized that those who are pure introverts or extroverts, when confronted with problems that require self-adjustment, tend to modify themselves out toward the edges of the personality space (the Yogi becomes more of a Yogi and the Commissar more of a Commissar). We also hypothesized that the mixed types tend to move themselves toward the center of the space, toward the point of *centraversion,* as we called it (following Neumann, 1954). Our data indicate, for example, that consumption of alcohol produces just these effects in the short run. The pure types are more likely to drink to an excess and become high or drunk and move out in the personality space with increasing dependence on alcohol. The mixed types drink moderately as a whole and tend to move in when under the influence; over time their drinking habits tend to be self-corrective. Our data also indicate that as the pure types mature and grow older their personalities tend to move out, while the mixed types tend to move in.

A special point must be made about the concept of centraversion. The closer an individual approaches to this, the more he is responding to and seeking to modify an integrated reality of his psychic world and his environment. This we believe is what constitutes psychological maturity and strength.

The Types and Adaptation

The four types of psychological individual that have been identified have an important correspondence to the ways in which a functional individual or system can *adapt.*

8.1. *Adaptive:* an individual or a system is adaptive if, when there is a change in its environmental and/or internal state that has reduced its efficiency in performing its function(s), it reacts or responds by changing its own state and/or that of its environment so as to increase its efficiency with respect to its function(s).

Thus adaptiveness is the ability of an individual or system to modify itself or its environment, when either has changed to the individual's or system's disadvantage, so as to regain at least some of its lost efficiency.

The definition of adaptive implies four types of adaptation.

8.2. *Other-other adaptation:* an individual's or system's reacting or responding to an external change by modifying the environment.

Example: a person turns on an air conditioner in a room that has become too warm for him to continue to work in. Such adaptation is typical of the *objective externalizer*.

8.3 *Other-self adaptation:* an individual's or system's reacting or responding to an external change by modifying itself.

Example: the person in a room that has become too warm for him to continue to work moves to another and cooler room. Such adaptation is typical of the *objective internalizer*.

8.4 *Self-other adaptation:* an individual's or system's reacting or responding to an internal change by modifying its environment.

Example: a person who has chills because of a cold turns up the heat. Such adaptation is typical of the *subjective externalizer*.

8.5 *Self-self adaptation:* an individual's or system's reacting or responding to an internal change by modifying itself.

Example: a person who has chills because of a cold takes medication to suppress the chills. Such adaptation is typical of the *Subjective internalizer*.

Other-self adaptation is the most commonly considered because it was only this type that Darwin considered in his studies of biological species as systems.

Interpersonal Relations and Personality Change

Consider two persons, *A* and *B*, who are located in the personality space as shown in Figure 8.5. The relationship between them can be characterized by two measures.

1. *Imbalance* ($|AO - BO|$). This measures the difference in their distance from *O*, the point of centraversion. If both are equidistant from *O*, then they can be said to be in balance. Note that if two people are located at the same point they are in balance.

2. *Asymmetry* (θ), the included angle between *AO* (extended) and *BO*. If *A* and *B* are at the same point, this angle is taken to be 180 degrees.

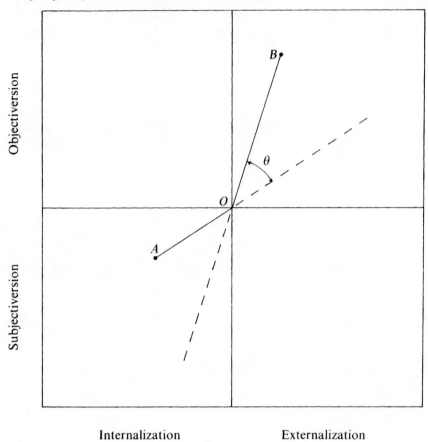

Figure 8.5.   *Two Individuals in the Personality Space*

We hypothesized that as the imbalance between two individuals increases they will have increasing difficulty in adapting to each other. The more centraverted, mature partner will tend to guide and influence the less centraverted. This will tend to happen regardless of traditional roles that may have to be kept up for appearance sake.

We also hypothesized that as asymmetry increases from 0 to 90 degrees the distortion of the perceptions of each of the other increases, but the distortion decreases as the angle increases from 90 to 180 degrees. By perception we mean the location that each believes the other to occupy in this personality space. These perceptions coproduce the expectations each has of the other, and if the perceptions are distorted, these expectations constitute a set of mutual pressures to reduce asymmetry. Beyond 90 degrees partners start to give up hope of inducing change.

Looked at another way each individual's personality can be considered to be a force of magnitude proportional to its distance from the point of centraversion. Using this notion we can characterize a pair of individuals as an entity with typology equal to half the resultant force. (Dividing by two keeps the resultant within the space. If two individuals were located at adjacent corners, the resultant would fall outside the space, but half of it falls on the boundary.) The resultant can also be found by constructing a parallelogram based on *AO* and *BO* – that is. *AOBD* (see Figure 8.6). Then the pair is representable as a force at the midpoint of *OD*, or the intersection

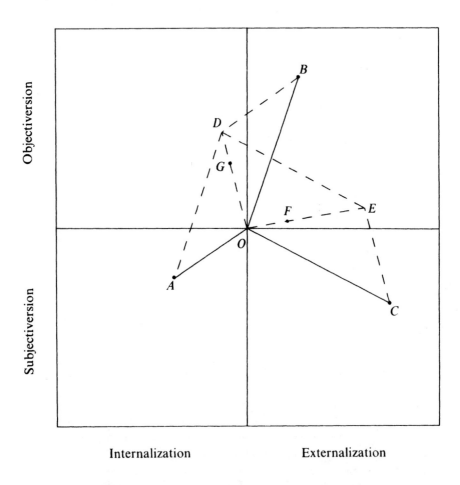

Figure 8.6.   Location of a Trio in the Personality Space

of *AB* and *OD. G* is used to represent the pair. As we shall see, this procedure can be extended to represent a group of any size by a point in the space.

Note that a pair will always be located closer to the point of centraversion than at least one of its members, except when both are at the same point. Then the pair is located at the same point as are its members. If a pair is symmetrical and balanced, it will fall on the point of centraversion and thus be in a state of equilibrium.

We hypothesized that the further the pair-point is from the point of centraversion, the less successful it is likely to be. We first tested this hypothesis by comparing the locations of successful and unsuccessful collaborators in research and academic pursuits. The results obtained were supportive. A stronger test was then designed. Clinical psychologists who were unfamiliar with our theory were asked to classify sixty married couples of varied ages as successful, unsuccessful, or do not know. Successful was defined as "would remarry each other if their marriage were annulled and all external bonds and obligations were removed." Other researchers independently classified the subjects by evaluating clinical interviews of them. The results strongly supported this hypothesis.

The reasoning behind this hypothesis was as follows. A pair at or near the point of centraversion can divide its psychological labors effectively and cooperate with respect to their functions. The further from centraversion a pair is, the more competition there is for performing the same psychological function or functions. For example, a pair consisting of an internalizer and an externalizer will not compete for manipulation of the environment. One wants to do it, and the other wants him to.

Since each of the members of a pair of mixed types on the diagonal — a subjective externalizer and an objective internalizer — move toward centraversion as they mature, the pair itself moves toward centraversion as it matures. In a pair that consists of the pure types — subjective internalizer and objective externalizer — each member will tend out to the borders with the passage of time. The pair may remain at or close to equilibrium, even though its members grow further apart. In any of the possible mixed pairs — one of mixed type and the other a pure type — one will move toward centraversion and the other away from it. This means that the pair will move toward the personality of the pure type, and hence become less stable. A pair that consists of two of the same pure type will move away from centraversion as its two members do, and hence become less and less stable over time. Finally, a pair of two in the same mixed type will move toward centraversion as its two members do, and hence become more stable over time as it approaches centraversion.

Let us examine each pair in more detail.

PAIRS IN DIAGONAL CELLS

1. *Objective internalizer and subjective externalizer (OI-SE).* If there is a problem between them, the *OI* is likely to be aware of its effect on the *SE* rather than on him(her)self. The *SE* is likely to be aware of the same thing.

Both the *SE* and the *OI* will try to change the *OI* so as to solve the problem as perceived. If a change in the environment is required, the *OI* is likely to perceive it and so inform the *SE*, who is likely to modify it. Thus there is complete psychological cooperation between them — no conflict of functions.

2. *Subjective internalizer and objective externalizer (SI-OE).* If there is a problem between them, the *OE* is more likely to be aware of its effect on the *SI* than on himself. The *SI* is likely to be aware of the same thing. The *SI* is inclined to modify himself to solve the problem, and the *OE* is inclined to change the *SI* as a method of solution. The *SI*, however, is likely to be insensitive and unresponsive to the *OE*'s efforts, but will nevertheless change himself for internal reasons. The *SI* will allow the *OE* to handle the environment and use the *OE* as a shield against it. The natural tendency of the *SI* to withdraw from the environment and the tendency of the *OE* to bury himself in it are augmented by their interactions. Thus, as a pair, these two unstable individuals can attain a stability.

PAIRS IN CONTIGUOUS CELLS

3. *Objective externalizer and subjective externalizer (OE-SE).* Both are likely to be aware of the effect of an interpersonal problem on the *SE*. The *OE* and *SE* are likely to try to change each other to solve it, but only the *OE* is likely to be sensitive to such efforts; however, he will not be responsive to them. They will compete with each other for manipulation of their environments as a problem-solving method. As a pair they will be nonadaptive to their environment but appear to be aggressively oriented toward it, and to others in it they may appear overbearing.

4. *Objective internalizer and subjective internalizer (OI-SI).* Both will perceive their problems through its effects on the *SI*, but each will try to change him(her)self to solve it. Personal sacrifices will constantly be required of the *OI*, but the *SI* will be unaware of them and hence is likely to show little appreciation. As a pair they have no ability to change the environment in ways that will ease their problems. They will thus appear to be a passive couple that does very little.

5. *Objective internalizer and objective externalizer (OI-OE).* Both are likely to be aware of the effect of interpersonal problems on the other. The *OI* will respond by trying to change himself, and the *OE* will try to change the *OI*. The *OI* is likely to be sensitive to and responsive to such efforts. But they are likely to perceive the problems differently since each sees it in the other.

6. *Subjective internalizer and subjective externalizer (SI-SE).* Neither will be very aware of or responsive to each other. The *SE* will try to manipulate the *SI* for his own purposes, but the *SI* will not be sensitive to or responsive to such efforts. Hence these efforts are likely to diminish over time and the two move further apart.

PAIRS IN SAME CELL

7. *Both subjective externalizers (SE-SE).* Each will see their joint problems in their effect on themselves, and each will try to manipulate the other to solve it. But each will be insensitive and unresponsive to the other. They are thus likely to be argumentative and unaware of their effect on others; yet they will compete for control of social situations that each will try to manipulate for his own purposes.

8. *Both objective internalizers (OI-OI).* Each will see their joint problems through its effect on the other, and each will try to adapt himself to solve it. Thus their perception of problems and their efforts to solve them are likely to be independent of each other. As a couple they will be aware of what is going on around them but will make no effort to change it. Thus they will be an aware but passive couple.

9. *Both subjective internalizers (SI-SI).* Neither will be sensitive or responsive to the other. They will live together but with little interaction. Each will leave the other alone and want to be left alone. As a pair they will be out of contact with their environment and completely passive with respect to it.

10. *Both objective externalizers (OE-OE).* Each will be sensitive to the other and try to modify the other to solve their joint problems. But neither will be responsive to such efforts. Both will be driven to modifying their environment to find solutions, and will compete in these efforts as well as in their interpretations of what the problem is. The couple will have no inner life.

Trios and Families

The position of a trio in the personality space can be found by determining the resultant of the three forces. An example is shown in Figure 8.6, where the resultant of *A*, *B*, and *C* is at *F*. In this case one-third of the diagonal *OE* is taken because three persons are involved. In general $1/n$th of the resultant is taken when *n* persons are involved. It should be apparent, and it can be proved, that even for randomly selected points, as *n* increases, the location of the group will approach the point of centraversion. Hence larger groups tend to be more stable than smaller ones. This appears to be true for families as well as for other types of groups. If nothing else, in larger groups subgroups can be formed that are relatively stable. Thus psychological coalitions can be formed by selection processes within groups.

A pair that is having trouble in interpersonal relations can improve the situation by adding a third or more parties to it (Greco, 1950). This, of course, occurs in families through the addition of children. One would expect, therefore, that the first child would be under pressure to form a personality that brings his parents closer to equilibrium. We have found this to be so.

In this sense a child can socialize his parents' problems. Note that the child is likely to be closer to the parent that is closest to centraversion and will himself be closer to centraversion the more stable the pair is. If the parents are at or near adjacent corners of the personality space, addition of a third person can make the trio more stable than the pair but cannot put it into equilibrium, but addition of two persons can. The adjustment required to bring a trio to equilibrium may be quite different than that required to bring the original pair to equilibrium. This may explain why successive children (1) tend to have quite different personalities, and (2) tend to come closer to centraversion. (Our data indicate this to be so.) It also raises the tantalizing prospect of a personality genetics; certain combinations of parents create certain kinds of children who, in turn, tend to seek certain types of partners.

A family that, as a unit, is objective internalizing is likely to be sensitive to the needs of its members, and its members are likely to adapt to each other's needs. There will be collective sacrifices for the benefit of those who require most assistance. There will be little activity of the family as a whole. Activity of members will tend to be independent. Privacy will be valued and provided to each of the family members. The unit is likely to be entertained by others more than it entertains others. It will not engage in a great deal of social activity. What social activity it has is likely to be confined to a relatively small group of friends. There will be a lot of reading, watching TV, and general exposure to media, because the family will be interested in what is going on around it, but will not intervene in external events and try to direct them.

A family that is subjective externalizing will be less sensitive to its members' needs, and its members will be more inclined to manipulate each other. The members are likely to be more independent of each other; yet they will engage in more collective activity. It is a family that does things together. It will have more social activity, and is likely to entertain more than it is entertained. Its social activities are likely to involve a relatively large number of different people, many of whom are acquaintances. There is likely to be a good deal of organized recreational activity of an active sort—such as swimming, boating, and picnicing.

A family that is subject internalizing will have many characteristics in common with a monastery or nunnery. The home will be a castle with a moat around it. The unit will be withdrawn from its environment and will be an escape from it. Its members will have little interaction; each will want privacy and will respect such a desire on the part of the others. It will have few visitors and its members will visit others infrequently.

A family that is objective externalizing will have many characteristics in common with an army unit that occupies a barracks. There will be little privacy and little desire for it. There will be a lot of conversation, interaction, and group activities. It will be an effusive and overbearing unit, frequently spilling out into its environment and bringing its environment into it. It will have gang-like properties. It will take up causes and be active in community affairs.

Cultures

The logical extension of the small group whose characteristics we have been discussing is to the culture that contains it. The typology and concepts developed here seem as applicable to societies as they are to individuals or small groups. We have asked many people who have been exposed to the typology to locate nations in the personality space, and they have no difficulty in doing so. The agreement among them is considerable. The nations that have most frequently been identified with each type are the following:

Objective internalizer: England
Subjective externalizer: United States
Subjective internalizer: France and India
Objective externalizer: Russia

Most have been quick to point out that nations have changed their personalities over history. Empire-building Britain was not objective internalizing but subjective externalizing.

Many manifestations of the characteristics associated with the types may be seen in the behavior of the nations listed above. It is clear, for example, that the U.S. and U.S.S.R. do more manipulating of other nations and intervene in others' affairs more than do the internalizing nations. On the other hand, examination of their aid programs show that the U.K. and U.S.S.R. tend to be more perceptive of the needs and wants of the nations they aid than do the United States or France.

It is particularly interesting to examine these nations with respect to their attitudes toward the use of alcohol. In those nations that seem to fall into the objective internalizer and subjective externalizer cells (the stable ones), alcoholic beverage drinking is institutionalized. There is a special kind of establishment whose principal function it is to provide a place to drink. In the United Kingdom it is the *pub*; in the United States it is the *cocktail lounge* and *bar*. Of course alcoholic beverages are consumed in additional places in these nations, but they provide places especially meant for drinking. In nations that are in the subjective internalizer or objective externalizer cells, such establishments do not exist or are not prevalent, but drinking takes place everywhere or is prohibited (and hence takes place everywhere).

In objective internalizer nations the drinking institution (such as the pub in the United Kingdom) functions to permit objective internalizers to become more like subjective externalizers, and hence to draw them toward centraversion. The pub is a socializing institution, one in which objective internalizers are induced to externalize and to become more introspective by talking about themselves.

In subjective externalizer nations the drinking institutions (say, the cocktail lounge in the United States) functions to permit subjective externalizers to receive from one or two others and to reflect on these inputs — that is, to be more like objective internalizers. Hence subjective externalizers are drawn toward centraversion by such lounges. They separate their occupants into small isolated groups in darkened surroundings rather than bring them together into large groups in well-lighted surroundings, as in the pub. The neighborhood tavern in the United States sometimes resembles a pub, just as some private clubs in the United Kingdom provide facilities like cocktail lounges. Even the minorities in these nations have minority drinking institutions.

In subjective internalizer and objective externalizer nations, drinking tends to move people away from centraversion toward introverted withdrawal or extroverted orgies.

Conclusion

It is a risky venture at this stage to try to design research that will yield approximations to the personality function π. Relying on our model of purposeful systems, we identified two fundamental dimensions corresponding to the ways an individual can relate to his environment. It was possible to formulate general measures for these dimensions. The combination of these measures enabled the identification of four major types of personality and a more general tendency toward or away from centraversion. Even with the simplifying assumption that the personality space can be treated as a Euclidean space, our treatment not only clarifies issues raised by Jung many decades ago but it also has yielded a number of fruitful hypotheses for our joint research into alcohol usage. The personality space that is defined by these measures gives some first insights into the way the individuality of systems can change through their interaction. In Part III we will consider the specific forms of interaction that occur between purposeful systems.

REFERENCES

Emery, F. E. *Social and Psychological Functions of Alcohol Usage*. London: Tavistock Institute of Human Relations Document Number 548, 1959.
————. "The Next Thirty Years: Concepts, Methods and Anticipations." *Human Relations* 20 (1967): 199–235.
Eysenk, H. J. *Dimensions of Personality*. London: Routledge and Kegan Paul, 1947.
Greco, M. C. *Group Life*. New York: Philosophical Library, 1950.
Jung, C. G. *Psychological Types*. London: Routledge, 1921.
Koestler, Arthur. *The Yogi and the Commissar*. New York: Macmillan Co., 1945.
Neumann, E. von. *The Origins and History of Consciousness*. London: Routledge and Kegan Paul, 1954.

Conclusion to Part II: A Paradigm for Inquiry

Once a model is accepted, a choice of a course of action can be made. The process of selection was considered in Chapter 7, but now we can focus more clearly on one aspect of it by use of the concepts that have been developed in Part II. *Intuition* suggests possible courses of action that can be evaluated by use of the choice model and the process of *thought*. The model itself is the product of past and present *observations* or, more generally, *perceptions*. The consequences predicted are evaluated by *feeling*. A course of action that is predicted to yield satisfaction is selected.

It is apparent that *thought, intuition, perception,* and *feeling* all are involved in choice. The manner in which they are involved suggests the pattern of inquiry followed by purposeful systems.[1]

1. A choice situation is a necessary antecedent of a problem. A choice situation becomes a problem situation only if the situation produces a state of dissatisfaction in the subject (a feeling) and he is doubtful about what to do. The existential situation is never known in all its detail by either the subject or the one who observes him. Different subjects and different observers may, and usually do, see the situation differently.

2. Unless the subject responds to the possibility of choice, and he is *aware* of it, a problem cannot arise. This awareness as well as a state of doubt and dissatisfaction is necessary before an individual can be said to have a problem.

3. The role of perception is to provide information. This affects possible choices. The contributions of the senses, present and past, when believed or assumed become the raw material from which a model of the choice situation is constructed.

A solution is a course of action, and a course of action can be defined by a set of values of the controlled variables. The perception of a possible course

1. The influence on this discussion of the work of C. G. Jung (1923) and John Dewey (1938) will be apparent to those familiar with their respective discussions of mental functions and the pattern of inquiry.

of action, when it just pops up, is a product of intuition. Not all suggestions, however, are intuitive; they can also be the result of thinking over the situation, derived from what is known or believed about the situation.

4. A suggestion becomes an idea only when it is evaluated by a thought process that employs the inputs of perception and feeling. Evaluation here means predicting whether or not a suggested course of action will produce a desired outcome in the situation involved.

Possible courses of action can be evaluated either by predicting their consequences by using what is believed about the situation (a thought process), or by trying them and observing the consequences and evaluating them (feeling). These are not exclusive processes. Every evaluation of a possible course of action involves all of these functions, but the one that dominates may differ from evaluation to evaluation, or from evaluator to evaluator, depending on the individuality of the system.

Thinking is an operation, and what it operates on are concepts, images, and signs of these. Meanings are contained in beliefs about consequences of courses of action that can be taken, and beliefs are expressible in sign complexes that are statements or propositions. Thus thought presupposes at least a private (if not a public) language. *Thought involves the manipulation of signs.* Hence it is only by communication with himself that a subject can think, let alone solve a problem. Thinking involves a conversation with oneself. Therefore, *not only do we need to understand choice to understand communication, but we also need to understand communication in order to understand choice.*

Thought relates concepts, images, and beliefs. The product of the process is either a conclusion that is believed and hence becomes a basis for selecting a course of action, or a conclusion that can be tested (tried, observed, and evaluated).

5. The choice process has no fixed sequence of a fixed number of steps. One choice (and problem) situation arises out of another in a continuing stream. Several problems may coexist and interact. Hence the process of choice is very rich; it can be infinitely varied. It is a process in which each step can feed back to every other.

Little wonder, then, that inquiry is so seldom carried out in a completely efficient manner or that we do not know what is the most efficient manner. Nevertheless, the combined efforts of scientists and philosophers have made it possible for us to become more efficient in making choices. The compilation of our knowledge on this subject constitutes the field we have come to call *methodology.* Methodology is inquiry into the process of inquiry, the process of making choice, the purposeful pursuit of objectives.[2]

Choice, as we have indicated, involves not only obtaining information

---

2. For discussion of how the inquirer's values enter into every decision made in an inquiry as well as in his ultimate choice, see Churchman (1961), Ackoff (1962), and Churchman and Emery (1966).

about and from the environment (which may include other purposeful systems) but also communicating with oneself (in thought). Hence Part III is concerned with the interactions of purposeful systems in general and communication between them in particular.

REFERENCES

Ackoff, R. L. *Scientific Method: Optimizing Applied Research Decisions.* New York: John Wiley & Sons, 1962.

Churchman, C. W. *Prediction and Optimal Decisions.* Prentice-Hall: Englewood Cliffs, N.J., 1961.

Churchman, C. W., and F. E. Emery. "On Various Approaches to the Study of Organizations," in *Operations Research and the Social Sciences,* edited by J. R. Lawrence. London: Tavistock Publications, 1966.

Dewey, John. *Logic: The Theory of Inquiry.* New York: Henry Holt, 1938.

Jung, C. G. *Psychological Types.* Translated by H. G. Baynes. New York: Pantheon Books, 1923.

III

Interactions of Purposeful Systems

Up to this point we have considered the internal processes of purposeful systems, even though we have attempted to externalize them by defining them so that they are observable by other purposeful systems. Now we turn to what may be called external processes, in particular the interactions of purposeful systems.

In Chapters 9–11, after a brief discussion of *interpersonal feelings*, we consider what *communication* between purposeful individuals is and how it is carried out.

Chapter 12 is concerned with the way purposeful individuals affect one another's purposeful pursuits — *cooperation*, *conflict*, and *competition*.

Finally, Chapter 13 examines collections of individual purposeful systems as systems — *social systems*.

9

Feelings and Communication

TALK, *v.t.* To commit an indiscretion without temptation, from an impulse without purpose.

The Devil's Dictionary

Introduction

One of the most important properties of the environment of a purposeful individual or system is whether or not it contains one or more other purposeful systems.[1] We are concerned here with the potential effects of each system on the others and how such effects are brought about.

We have already defined what it means for a purposeful system to sense, perceive, and observe its environment. It is now necessary to examine what is meant by *mutual* sensing, perceiving, and observing between systems that are capable of at least partially controlling what sensations, perceptions, and observations the other system has. Moreover, by their choices interacting systems can create a social field that is different from and potentially more complex than what either one can separately produce.

The prerequisite for *interaction* between purposeful systems is that they can sense, perceive, observe, and remember the same sorts of things in their shared environment. The minimal level of intersystem *behavior* — that is, where there is an intent to produce a behavior in the other — is *communication.* Before considering the concept of communication we will briefly discuss what is probably the most significant form of interaction — namely, *interpersonal feelings.* For this we need only those concepts that have been introduced in the previous chapters.

Interpersonal feelings

According to *Webster's,* to *blame* is "to find fault with." However, although one may find fault with a book but not blame it, one may blame an author for his book.

1. The radical nature of the change in environment that the presence of other purposeful systems produces has been analyzed by Emery and Trist (1965) in their treatment of the disturbed-reactive environment.

9.1.   *Blame:* One individual (*A*) blames another (*B*) for something (*X*) if *A* believes *B* intentionally produced *X* and *A* is dissatisfied with *X*.

Note that *B* need not be a person but must be an entity to which *A* attributes intentions and hence choice.

The contrary of blame seems to be *gratitude*.

9.2.   *Gratitude:* One individual (*A*) is grateful to another (*B*) for something (*X*) if *A* believes *B* intentionally produced *X* and *A* is satisfied with *X*.

The measures of gratitude and blame are also products of measures of belief and satisfaction or dissatisfaction.

Sympathy, according to *Webster's Collegiate Dictionary*, is "an affinity, association, or relationship between things so that whatever affects one, similarly affects the other or others." If this were taken literally, it would be possible for two persons who did not know each other to be sympathetic with each other if they responded similarly to similar stimuli. This does not seem consistent with common usage in which sympathy seems to connote that the response of one individual produces a similar response in another.

9.3.   *Sympathy:* One individual (*A*) sympathizes with another (*B*) relative to something (*X*) if *B*'s satisfaction (or dissatisfaction) with *X* produces satisfaction (or dissatisfaction) with *X* in *A*.

This definition permits *A* to sympathize with *B* without *B*'s sympathizing with *A*. Sympathy need not be symmetrical. Note that our definition implies that if *A* sympathizes with *B*, *A* is aware of *X* and conscious of *B*. (See definitions of awareness and consciousness in Chapter 4.)

If *B*'s feelings about an *X* fail to produce any feeling in *A*, *A* is unsympathetic with *B*. If *B*'s feelings produce contrary feelings in *A*, *A* may be said to be antipathetic with *B*.

According to *Webster's*, to *appreciate* is "to approve of; to be grateful for," and to be *grateful* is "to be appreciative of benefits received." Gratitude, it seems to us, is directed *to* a responsible person *for* something done. Appreciation is gratitude for the person, not only for what he has done but also for what he can do.

9.4.   *Appreciation:* One individual (*A*) appreciates another (*B*) if *A* believes *B* is capable of producing satisfaction in *A* (that is, fulfilling some of *A*'s objectives.)

Appreciation is passive, but *devotion* is active.

9.5.   *Devotion:* *A* is devoted to *B* if *A* is dissatisfied with *B*'s states of dissatisfaction and satisfied with *B*'s states of satisfaction.

Therefore, if *A* is devoted to *B*, *A* intends to remove *B*'s dissatisfactions and preserve his satisfactions. Note that devotion not only presupposes sympathy but also involves an intention to do something about it.

The contrary to devotion is antagonism, the desire to preserve another's states of dissatisfaction and remove his states of satisfaction. There is no convenient anonym for appreciation; therefore we use disappreciation to represent A's belief that B is capable of producing dissatisfaction in A.

Now let us briefly discuss several feelings on which even angels fear to tread: love, hate, and loyalty. The meanings of these concepts are much too vague and rich for hope of finding any agreement among those who have tried to analyze their meanings. The following definitions were suggested by E. A. Singer, Jr.'s (1923) analysis of these concepts in his essay, "Royce on Love and Loyalty."

9.6. *Love:* A loves B if (1) A appreciates and is devoted to B, and (2) the satisfaction that B produces in A cannot be produced by any other individual.

Thus the lover perceives the loved one as a source of satisfaction, and wants the loved one to be in a state of satisfaction. This produces the willingness of the lover to yield to the will and desires of the loved one. But this much characterizes our relationships with all for whom we care. What distinguishes love from care is the uniqueness bestowed on love's object. It completely individuates its object; there are no substitutes for it. This does not preclude loving more than one person. However, one loved person cannot replace another if the other is still loved.

9.7. *Hate:* A hates B if (1) A disappreciates and is antagonistic to B, (2) the dissatisfaction that B produces in A cannot be produced by any other individual.

So hate is the contrary to love with respect to the first condition, but it shares love's individuating characteristic.

Love and loyalty are often used interchangeably with respect to social groups, especially nations. One is said to love his country or to be loyal to it. The distinction is not usually clear. Following Singer, we believe loyalty is not an individuating feeling.

9.8. *Loyalty:* A is loyal to B if A appreciates and is devoted to B.

Thus loyalty is love without individuation. The object of loyalty is replaceable. Therefore, whether one loves or is merely loyal to one's country depends on the extent to which that country can be replaced by another. The athletic team that one loyally supports is usually replaced easily by another when one moves — not so for a loved object.

The Nature of Communication

In an environment shared by two purposeful individuals or systems, each may be unaware of the presence of the other. However, if one has a feeling about the other it must be aware of their overlapping environments. We now consider those situations in which each of two purposeful individuals or systems is aware that there is another such individual or system in its environment and that the choices of the other can affect what will happen to it. In these situations the *interactions* of the individuals or systems can produce intersystem behavior. One system can affect the behavior of another only by producing a change in one or more of the four components of the other system's choice situation, or in one or more of the other's parameters of choice.

One system may affect the components and parameters of another's choice situation by physically changing the other's environment, as by removing or adding an instrument to it. However, it is possible for one system to affect the other's parameters of choice without changing either its environment or the components of its choice situation. *Communication* is such a way. Furthermore, through communication one system can affect the behavior of another in a completely different environment.

9.9.   *Communication:* One purposeful individual (B) communicates to another (A) when a message[2] produced by B produces a change in one or more of the parameters (P_i, E_{ij}, V_j) of A's purposeful state. B can be referred to as the *sender* and A as the *receiver.*

Several aspects of this definition of communication should be noted. First, A and B may be the same individual; that is, a person may communicate to himself, as in writing a reminder to himself. Second, the sender of the message need not intend or want to communicate to the receiver in order to do so. An interceptor of a message may be communicated to, although unintentionally. Third, the sender and receiver may be widely separated in time and space. Through their writings both Aristotle and Nehru have communicated to, though not with, us.

Finally, note that *both parties in communication must be purposeful. If we push a button to start a machine and the machine has no choice, communication has not taken place.* On the other hand, if we push a button at the front door of a house, though we do not communicate with the bell we do communicate with the occupants of the house; both they and we have alternative ways of pursuing our objectives.

Now we want to concentrate on the communication received and the receiver.

The Value of a Communication

It will be recalled that a purposeful state of an individual (A) is described by the following.

1. The set of available courses of action, C_i.
2. The set of possible outcomes, O_j
3. The environment, S.
4. The state of A.

2. See Chapter 10 for a definition of message.

5. The probabilities of *A* selecting each course of action, P_i.
6. The efficiencies of the courses of action for each objective, E_{ij}.
7. The value of the outcomes to *A*, V_j.

Then, given the available courses of action and possible outcomes, the value of a purposeful state, V^*, must be some function of P_i, E_{ij}, and V_j; that is,

$$V^* = f(P_i, E_{ij}, V_j). \tag{9.1}$$

The nature of the function, f, depends on the definition of the state's value. This value may be defined in several different ways such as in terms of expected return, expected gain, or expected loss. The discussion and measures of state value that follow are independent of the function used. But for illustrative purposes we use expected relative value as the state value; that is,

$$V^* = \sum_{i=1}^{m} \sum_{j=1}^{n} P_i E_{ij} V_j. \tag{9.2}$$

Since $P_i \leq 1.0$ and $E_{ij} \leq 1.0$, then if a measure of relative value is used in which $0 \leq V_j \leq 1$ and $\Sigma V_j = 1.0$, it follows that the minimum and maximum values that the state *value* (V^*) can assume are 0 and 1, respectively.

Receipt of a communication involves a change in the receiver's purposeful state. Let V_1^* represent the value of the initial state (just prior to receipt of the communication) and V_2^* represent the value of the terminal or changed state where the change is the receiver's response to a message. Then the changes must be in one or more of his P_is, E_{ij}s, or V_js, or some combination of these. Therefore, the value of the communication to the receiver is $V_2^* - V_1^*$. Even if only positive absolute values of V_j are used, the value of a communication may be negative: where $V_1^* > V_2^*$. For example, an oral prohibition from a parent may reduce the value of a situation to a child by precluding behavior that is a source of pleasure to him. Incorrect information, as we shall see, can also reduce the value of a purposeful state.

The value of a communication to its sender can be obtained by determining the message-produced change in his expected relative value from his initial to his terminal state. There need be no correlation between the values of a message to the sender and to the receiver. One may benefit, the other may not, or both may benefit or lose (equally or unequally). The parent's communication to his child may increase the value of the parent's state (say, by the elimination of noise) but decrease the value of the child's state.

The value of the communication to third parties can similarly be determined — by finding the message-produced changes in their expected relative value from their initial to their terminal states. One who overhears another's communication may benefit or lose for having heard.

Modes and Measures of Communication

A particular communication may change the receiver's probabilities of choice (P_i), the efficiencies of his choices (E_{ij}), the relative value of the possible outcomes (V_j), or some combination of these. Even where a communication produces a combination of changes in the receiver, each type of change can be studied separately. Each of the three types of change produced by a message can be identified and defined as follows.

9.10.   *Information:* A communication that produces a change in any of the receiver's probabilities of choice informs him, and hence transmits information.

9.11.   *Instruction:* A communication that produces a change in the efficiencies of any of a receiver's courses of action instructs him, and hence transmits instruction.

9.12.   *Motivation:* A communication that produces a change in any of the relative values the receiver places on possible outcomes of his choice motivates him, and hence transmits motivation.

There is apparently one other way in which a purposeful state can be changed: some of the available courses of action that were not potential choices of the receiver before a communication may become potential as a result of the communication. However, such a possibility is covered. Since in a purposeful state the available courses of action are formulated as an exhaustive and exclusive set, every possible choice is included. Therefore, if any choice that was not potential becomes so, this change must be reflected in a change in a probability of selecting one of the alternatives.

Now let us examine each of the three modes of communication in more detail.

INFORMATION (CHANGES IN PROBABILITIES OF CHOICE)

Because of the pervasiveness of the use of information in the restricted (technical) sense of Shannon's information theory (Shannon and Weaver, 1949), it might seem preferable to use another term here. But since the way that we use information here conforms more closely to common usage than does Shannon's, if a change is required it would seem preferable to change Shannon's term. Shannon's usage is based on that of Hartley (1928). Cherry (1957) seems to reflect our opinion.

> In a sense, it is a pity that the mathematical concepts stemming from Hartley have been called "information" at all. The formula for H_n is really a measure of one facet only of the concept of information; it is the statistical rarity of "surprise value" of a source of signs (p. 50).

Despite his terminology, Shannon was concerned with what may better be called the *amount of message* transmitted rather than with the amount of information communicated. He was primarily involved with systems in which each possible message can be coded into a combination of two symbols. For example, if there are four possible messages and two symbols (0 and 1), the messages can be represented as 00, 01, 10, and 11. Then to select one message out of the four, two choices from among the two symbols (that is, binary choices) may be made. One binary choice allows two messages (0 and 1), and three binary choices allow eight messages (000, 001, 010, 100, 110, 101, 011, and 111). In general, x binary choices allow 2^x possible messages.

For Shannon, the amount of information contained in a message is the amount of freedom of choice involved in the selection of the message.[3] A unit of choice is defined as the selection of one out of two equally available symbols. Thus, in selecting one of two equally available symbols, one choice unit is involved and the resulting one-symbol message contains one unit of information.

In general, if there are M equally available messages in a state, the selection of one contains x units of information where $x = \log_2 M$.

Equal availability of the symbols means equal likelihood of choice by the sender. That is, if there are M possible messages and the probability of each being selected is $1/M$, complete freedom of choice exists. If the probability of selecting a particular message (p_i) deviates from $1/M$, the choice is not completely free. In the extreme case if the probability of selecting any one of a set of messages is 1.0, then there is no freedom of choice, and no information can be communicated by the one message that is always selected.

In order to cover cases when choices are not equally likely (as well as when they are), Shannon derived the following general measure of the amount of information (symbolized by H in his system) contained in a state: $H = \Sigma p_i \log p_i$, where p_i is the probability of choice of the ith message. If $\log_2$ is used, then H is expressed in binary units, which are called *bits*. Thus a state that contains two equally likely messages contains one bit of information.

The measure of information[4] to be developed here will also be related to freedom of choice; that is, it will be a function of the probabilities of choice associated with alternative courses of action. It will be a different function, however, because of the difference in selecting between messages and courses of action. The measure developed here is a function of the number of alternative potential courses of action, m.

In Shannon's use of information we cannot speak of how much information a person has, only how much a message has. Clearly, from the behavioral scientists' point of view, the person is much more important.[5]

---

3. An alternative approach to the measurement of syntactic information has been proposed by D. M. MacKay (1950 and 1955). A recent discussion of its application can be found in Payne (1966).

4. Unless we indicate to the contrary, information will henceforth be used as pragmatic information.

5. Attempts to use Shannon's theory of communication in the behavioral sciences has hardly met with success. See Hardy and Kurtz (1963) for an evaluation of these efforts. Also see Schramm (1966), who observed, ". . . we must admit frankly the difficulty of bridging the gap between the [H] formula's concept of information (which is concerned only with the number of binary choices necessary to specify an event in a system) and our concept of information in human communication . . ." (p. 534).

When we talk of the amount of information a person has in a specified situation (purposeful state), we do so in two different but related senses. First, we refer to the number of available courses of action he is aware of — that is, to the number of potential courses of action. For example, a person who is aware of four exits from a particular building has more information than the person who is aware of only two when there are four. The act of informing, then, can consist of converting available but not potential choices into potential choices. A statement such as "There are exits at either end of this hall" may convey information in this sense. The person who has this information (who has these potential choices) may or may not exercise it, depending on his appraisal of the relative efficiencies of the alternative exits. In one sense, then, the amount of information in a state is a monotonically increasing function of the amount of potential choice of courses of action an individual has in that state.

The second sense in which we talk of information involves the *basis* of choice from among the alternative potential courses of action. For example, an individual who knows which exit is nearest to him has a basis for choice and hence has information about the exits. Information in this sense pertains to the efficiencies of the alternatives relative to desired outcomes (a rapid exodus). Suppose, for example, that there are two exits and one is nearer to a person (A) than is the other. If A knows this and his objective (valued outcome) is to leave the building quickly, the choice is *determined* in the sense that A will always select the nearest exit. If he always selects the most distant exit, then he is obviously misinformed (he has information, but it is incorrect). If he selects each exit with equal frequency, then he apparently has no basis for choice (he has no information). In this sense, then, information is the amount of choice that *has been* made. Now let us make this concept more precise.

Consider the case of an individual (A) who is confronted by two potential courses of action, C_1 and C_2. If the probabilities of selecting the courses of action are equal, $P_1 = P_2 = \frac{1}{2}$, the situation may be said to be *indeterminate* for A.

9.13.   *Indeterminate choice situation:* A purposeful state in which a subject's probability of choice of each of the m available courses of action (defined so as to be exclusive and exhaustive) is equal to $1/m$.

A person in an indeterminate state has no basis for choice and hence can be said to have no information about the alternatives. This is clearly the case when one of the alternatives is more efficient that the other. But if the two courses of action are equally efficient, the individual may have information to this effect and select each with equal frequency. Strictly speaking, however, he has no real choice in this situation, since the alternatives are equally efficient. In a situation in which all alternative choices are equally efficient, information has no operational meaning. Such a situation does not constitute a purposeful state. Consequently this discussion has relevance to only those situations in which the alternative courses of action are not equally efficient.

If $P_1 = 1.0$ and $P_2 = 0$, then the situation is *determinate* for the person involved. All the choice that can be made has been made. The maximum possible amount of information is contained in the state. It may not be correct information, but this is another matter that will be considered later.

9.14. *Determinate choice situation:* A purposeful state in which a subject's probability of selecting one of the available courses of action is equal to 1.0.

Now we can define a unit of information as follows.

9.15. *Unit of information:* The amount of information that changes an indeterminate two-choice situation into a determinate choice situation.

Let us consider the general case involving m available courses of action. In order to select one from this set, a minimum of $m-1$ choices from pairs of alternatives (paired comparisons) is required. Table 9.1 illustrates.

Table 9.1

$m = 2$	3	4	5
$\left.\begin{array}{c}C_1\\C_2\end{array}\right\}1$	$\left.\begin{array}{c}\left.\begin{array}{c}C_1\\C_2\end{array}\right\}1\\C_3\end{array}\right\}2$	$\left.\begin{array}{c}\left.\begin{array}{c}\left.\begin{array}{c}C_1\\C_2\end{array}\right\}1\\C_3\end{array}\right\}2\\C_4\end{array}\right\}3$	$\left.\begin{array}{c}\left.\begin{array}{c}\left.\begin{array}{c}\left.\begin{array}{c}C_1\\C_2\end{array}\right\}1\\C_3\end{array}\right\}2\\C_4\end{array}\right\}3\\C_5\end{array}\right\}4$

Implicit in Shannon's bit measure of information is the assumption that an ultimate choice is the result of a series of choices from contracting dichotomous sets. If there are four possible messages, it is assumed these are grouped into two sets of two each — say, $(M_1$ and $M_2)$ and $(M_3$ and $M_4)$. The first choice then consists of selecting one of these sets. The second consists of selecting one of the messages in the selected set. Hence two choices of different type are involved. We assume a procedure of choosing among courses of action that differs from the procedure just described; it involves three paired comparisons, each of the same type. We do not assume choices are necessarily made in this way, although they may be, but we use this concept because it involves the maximum possible number of nonredundant choices.

The maximum amount (number of units) of information that a state can contain, then, is $m-1$ — that is, the amount of information required to choose completely from $m-1$ pairs of alternatives.

We can conceive of the amount of information contained in a purposeful state as a point on a scale bounded at the lower end by no information in a state of indeterminism (no choice has been made) and at the upper end by complete information in a state of determinism (complete choice has been made). Location on this scale will depend on the values of the probabilities of choice, P_i.

Understanding these concepts is facilitated by visualizing a weightless platform scaled from 0 to 1.0 and balanced on a fulcrum located at the value $1/m$. A unit weight represents each course of action. Then two-choice determinate and indeterminate states can be represented, as shown in Figure 9.1. Note that since $\Sigma P_i = 1.0$ these platforms will be in balance for every possible combination of P_is. We shall use this analogy again as new concepts and measures are introduced.

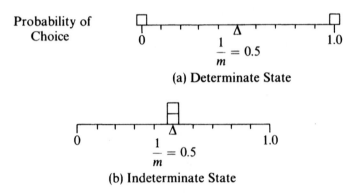

Probability of Choice

(a) Determinate State

(b) Indeterminate State

Figure 9.1.   Physical Analogy of Information in a Purposeful State

In an indeterminate state each $P_i = 1/m$. Therefore, the amount of deviation of a state from indeterminism is

$$\sum_{i=1}^{m} \left| P_i - \frac{1}{m} \right|.$$

For an indeterminate state this sum is equal to zero. In a determinate state one P_i is equal to 1.0, and the remaining $(m-1)$ P_is are equal to zero. Therefore, in such a state

$$\sum_{i=1}^{m} \left| P_i - \frac{1}{m} \right| = \left| 1 - \frac{1}{m} \right| + (m-1)\left| 0 - \frac{1}{m} \right| = 1 - \frac{1}{m} + (m-1)\frac{1}{m} = 1 - \frac{1}{m}$$

$$+ 1 - \frac{1}{m} = 2 - \frac{2}{m}.$$

Given a state with m possible courses of action, the fraction of the maximum possible amount of information it contains is the ratio of (a) its deviation from the corresponding indeterminate state to (b) the deviation of the corresponding determinate state from that indeterminate state:

$$\frac{\sum_{i=1}^{m} \left| P_i - \frac{1}{m} \right|}{2 - \frac{2}{m}}$$

This ratio has a minimum value of zero and a maximum value of one.

The product of this fraction and the maximum amount of information that such a state can contain $(m-1)$ provides a measure of the amount of information (here symbolized by α) in that state.

9.16. *Amount of information in an individual's state* (α):

$$\alpha = (m-1)\frac{\sum\limits_{i=1}^{m}\left|P_i-\dfrac{1}{m}\right|}{2-\dfrac{2}{m}} = \frac{m}{2}\sum\limits_{i=1}^{m}\left|P_i-\frac{1}{m}\right|$$

where m is the number of (exclusively and exhaustively defined) available courses of action and the P_is are the probabilities of the subject's selecting the ith course of action.

The net amount of information communicated is the amount of information contained in the state of the receiver immediately following the communication (the *terminal* state) minus the amount contained in his state immediately preceding the communication.

9.17. *Net amount of information communicated to a receiver* (α_N):

$$\alpha_N = \alpha_2 - \alpha_1 = \left[\frac{m}{2}\sum\limits_{i=1}^{m}\left|P'_i-\frac{1}{m}\right|\right] - \left[\frac{m}{2}\sum\limits_{i=1}^{m}\left|P_i-\frac{1}{m}\right|\right],$$

where α_2 and α_1 are the amounts of information contained in the terminal and initial states, respectively, and P'_i and P_i are the probabilities of choice in the terminal land initial states, respectively.

This measure can take on values from $-(m-1)$ to $(m-1)$. Negative values represent a loss of information (as in going from a determinate to an indeterminate state).

Suppose that in an initial state involving two courses of action, C_1 and C_2, $P_1 = 1.0$ and $P_2 = 0$. This state contains one unit of information. If as a result of communication P_1 is changed to 0 and P_2 to 1.0, the terminal state also contains one unit of information. Hence the *net* amount of information communicated (α_N) is equal to zero. This results, so to speak, because the information in the initial state was removed and replaced by an equal amount of *different* information. Clearly the value of the terminal and initial states to the receiver may differ, and this will be reflected in the measure of the value of information to be developed later. It does seem peculiar, however, to say that no information has been transmitted; one should more properly say that although the *net* amount of information transmitted was zero, there was an *exchange* of information. Therefore if we develop a measure of the *gross* amount of information transmitted, subtraction of the net amount transmitted from this provides a measure of the amount of information exchanged.

In measuring the net amount transmitted we determine the amount by which the initial and terminal states differed from an indeterminate state. Now let us measure the amount by which the terminal state differs from the initial state: $\Sigma \mid P'_i - P_i \mid$. As before, let us take the ratio of this deviation to the maximum distance deviation $(2 - 2/m)$, and multiply it by the maximum amount of information that the state can contain $(m-1)$.

9.18.   *Gross amount of information communicated to receiver* (α_G):

$$\alpha_G = m - 1 \frac{\Sigma \mid P'_i - P_i \mid}{2 - \dfrac{2}{m}} = \frac{m}{2} \Sigma \mid P'_i - P_i \mid.$$

This quantity has a minimum value of zero and (since $\max \Sigma \mid P'_i - P_i \mid$ $= 2.0$) a maximum value of m.

9.19.   *Amount of information exchanged* (α_E):

$$\alpha_E = \alpha_G - \mid \alpha_N \mid.$$

Since $\alpha_G \geq \alpha_N$, this measure has maximum and minimum values of m and 0, respectively.

Again in the example where P_1 changed from 1.0 to 0, and P_2 from 0 to 1.0, since the amount of information in both states was 1.0; α_N, the net amount transmitted was 0. The gross amount of information transmitted in this case is

$$\alpha_G = \frac{2}{2} [(1.0) + (1.0)] = 2.0.$$

Hence the amount of information exchanged is

$$\alpha_E = 2.0 - 0 = 2.0,$$

the maximum amount possible.

In the physical analogy (see Figure 9.2) it is apparent that the sums of the distances from the fulcrum $(1/m)$ in the terminal and initial states are both equal to 1.0. Hence the amounts of information in these states are equal and the net amount of information communicated is equal to zero. However, the total distance traveled by C_1 and C_2 over the P_i-scale is 2.0 (the gross amount of information communicated). The difference between the gross and net

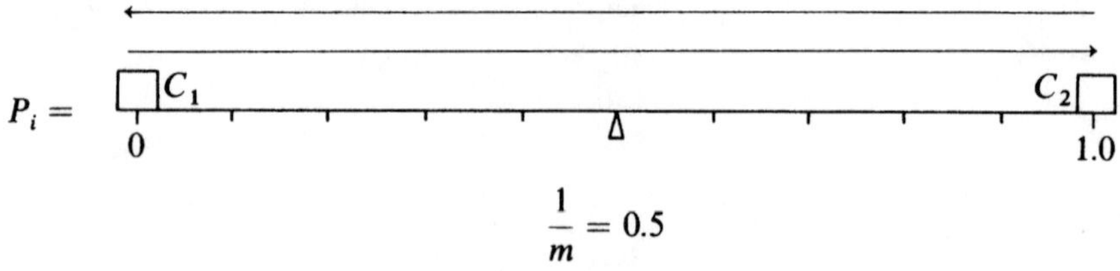

Figure 9.2

amounts of information communicated $(2.0-0 = 2.0)$ is the amount exchanged. The amount exchanged can be interpreted as the amount of movement from the initial state less the minimal amount required to obtain the same amount of information contained in the terminal state.

These measures can be illuminated by considering the slightly more complex examples shown in Table 9.2.

Table 9.2

i	Initial State P_i	Terminal State (a)		Terminal State (b)	
		P_i'	$\lvert P_i' - P_i \rvert$	P_i'	$\lvert P_i' - P_i \rvert$
1	0	0	0	0.6	0.6
2	0.1	0.1	0	0.1	0
3	0.1	0.1	0	0.1	0
4	0.1	0.2	0.1	0.2	0.1
5	0.7	0.6	0.1	0	0.7
$\alpha =$	2.5	2.0		2.0	
$\Sigma \lvert P_i' - P_i \rvert =$			0.2		1.4

The net amount of information communicated in both cases is $2.0-2.5 = -0.5$ units. For the first terminal state (a) the gross amount of information communicated is $5/2(0.2) = 0.5$. Therefore, the amount of information exchanged in this case is $0.5-0.5 = 0$. For the second terminal state (b), however, the gross amount of information communicated is $5/2(1.4) = 3.5$, and hence the amount exchanged is $3.5-0.5 = 3.0$.

Let us return to the physical analogy (see Figure 9.3) note in (a) that the sum of the distances from the fulcrum is decreased and hence a negative net amount of information is transmitted. The gross amount transmitted is proportional to the sum of the distances traveled (0.2). Since this sum is the minimal amount required to reach a terminal state with the distribution of P_is indicated, no information has been exchanged. In the second case (b) of the total movement $(0.1+0.6+0.7 = 1.4)$ it is clear that two moves of distance 0.1 each would have produced the same distribution of P_is. Since $m/2(0.2) = 5/2(0.2) = 0.5$, then $3.5-0.5 = 3.0$ is the amount of information exchanged.

The measure of information that has been developed here depends on how the alternative courses of action are formulated by the investigator. Suppose one investigator formulates two exclusive and exhaustive courses of action

C_1: use of an automobile
C_2: use of any other mode of transportation

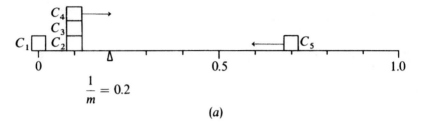

$$\frac{1}{m} = 0.2$$

(a)

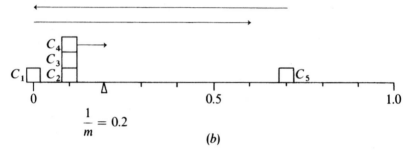

$$\frac{1}{m} = 0.2$$

(b)

Figure 9.3

and another investigator formulates

C_1: use of an automobile
C_2: use of bus
C_3: walking
C_4: use of any other mode of transportation

If the subject always uses an automobile ($P_2 = 1.0$ in both cases), then the first investigator would find one unit of information and the second would find three. Hence the measure depends on the investigator as well as the subject.

Two aspects of this relativity of the measure of information should be noted. First, it is possible to adjust the measures obtained by the two investigators so that they are in agreement. The definitions have been so constructed as to make this possible. Second, the same relativity is present in Shannon's measure of syntactic information. In applying his measure, one can use a letter of the alphabet, a phoneme, a word, or even a message as a unit for which the probabilities of choice are to be determined. The use of different units may yield different (Shannon) amounts of syntactic information in a message.

As long as we can make comparable the results of different investigations of the same thing, that they may yield apparently different results presents no serious methodological problem.

It is also important to observe that the measures of information developed here contain no implication concerning the correctness or incorrectness of the information received. Further, it should be noted that this measure is relative to a specific receiver in a specific state. The same message may convey different amounts of information to different individuals in the same choice environment or to the same individual in different choice environments. Consequently to determine the amount of information transmitted by a message it is necessary to specify the set of individuals and states relative to which the measure is to be made. If more than one individual or state is involved, it is also necessary to specify what statistic (such as an average) is to be used. Generality of information may be defined in terms of the range of individuals and/or states over which it operates.

It should also be noted that messages are not the only possible source of information; one may also obtain information by perception. The measures of information given here are equally applicable to states before and after perception. The measures of instruction and motivation to be developed below are also applicable to perception. This generality is an important property of these measures.

Finally, a message that informs either (1) changes the subject's conception of the choice situation (what choices he believes are possible) and, through such changes, modifies his beliefs in the efficiencies of the alternatives that he perceives; or (2) changes his beliefs in efficiencies without changing his beliefs about available choices.

INSTRUCTION (CHANGES IN EFFICIENCY OF CHOICE)

To inform is to provide a basis for choice — that is, a belief in the greater efficiency of one choice compared to another. Hence information modifies objective probabilities of choice by modifying believed (subjective) probabilities of success. Instruction is concerned with modification of the *objective* probabilities of success — efficiency. The amount of instruction a subject has in a particular state is equivalent to the amount of *control* he can exert over possible outcomes in that state. He has maximum control if he is capable of bringing about any of the possible outcomes by any of the means available to him. To instruct is to impart such a capability where it is lacking.

Consider a course of action C_1 and two (exclusively and exhaustively defined) outcomes, O_1 and O_2. A person has complete control over C_1 if he can use it to make either outcome occur with certainty when he wants that outcome. For example, if he can use an automobile (C_1) to go somewhere (O_1) or not (O_2), he has complete control over the course of action and the outcome. If he cannot change the probability of an outcome's occurring by changing the way he pursues a course of action, then he does not control that course of action and the outcome. Suppose that the efficiency of C_1 for O_1, E_{11}, is equal to 1.0 no matter what the subject wants, and hence the efficiency of C_1 for O_2 must be equal to 0. Then his choice is like pushing a button that releases a mechanically defined course of action over whose outcome he has no control.

A measure of the amount of control a person has in a purposeful state can be developed as follows. Consider one course of action, C_1, and two outcomes, O_1 and O_2. If (*a*) when the relative value of O_1 to the subject is maximum (say, 1.0; that is, $V_1 = 1.0$) and hence $V_2 = 0$, the efficiency of his use of C_1 for O_1 is 1.0 (or $E_{11} = 1.0$), and (*b*) when the relative values are reversed ($V_1 = 0$ and $V_2 = 1.0$), the efficiency of his use of C_1 for O_2 is 1.0 (or $E_{12} = 1.0$), then he has maximum control over C_1. Therefore, the amount of control that a person has over a course of action is reflected in the *range* of its efficiency as a function of the value he places on possible outcomes.

9.20. *Amount of control* (β_{ij}) *an individual has over a particular course of action* (C_i) *relative to a particular outcome* (O_j):

$$\beta_{ij} = (E_{ij} \mid V_j = 1.0) - (E_{ij} \mid V_j = 0).$$

This quantity has a maximum value of 1.0 and a minimum value of -1.0. For example, suppose the course of action is "use of a desk calculator" and the two outcomes are "correct computation" and "incorrect computation." If a subject can always use the calculator correctly when he wants to and always incorrectly when he wants to then he has complete control over use of the desk calculator with respect to the relevant computations.

9.21. *Amount of control* (β_i) *an individual has over a particular course of action* (C_i) *relative to a set of* n *outcomes:*

$$\beta_i = \sum_{j=1}^{n} \beta_{ij}.$$

This measure has maximum and minimum values of n and $-n$, respectively. Now one can generalize over a set of courses of action.

9.22. *Amount of control* (β) *an individual has in a purposeful state relative to a set of* m *courses of action and a set of* n *outcomes;*

$$\beta = \sum_{i=1}^{m} \beta_i = \sum_{i=1}^{m} \sum_{j=1}^{n} \beta_{ij}.$$

This measure has maximum and minimum values of mn and $-mn$, respectively.

The amount of control an individual has in a state is the amount of instruction he has in that state.

9.23. *The net amount of instruction communicated to a receiver* (β_N):

$$\beta_N = \beta_2 - \beta_1,$$

where β_2 and β_1 are the amounts of instruction in the terminal and initial states, respectively.

This measure has maximum and minimum values of $2mn$ and $-2mn$, respectively.

Communication can result in unlearning as well as learning – that is, the loss of control. The gain or the loss of control may be either good or bad for the subject; the amount and value of control must be measured separately. A measure of its value will be developed later.

To obtain a measure of the gross amount of instruction transmitted, we sum over the absolute values of the changes that occur relative to each $C_i - O_j$ combination.

9.24. *The gross amount of instruction communicated to a receiver* (β_G):

$$\beta_G = \sum_{i=1}^{m} \sum_{j=1}^{n} |\beta_{ij}' - \beta_{ij}|,$$

where β_{ij}' refers to the terminal state and β_{ij} refers to the initial state.

Since $|\beta_{ij}' - \beta_{ij}|$ has maximum and minimum values of 2 and 0, respectively, β_G has maximum and minimum values of $2mn$ and 0, respectively.

9.25. *The amount of instruction exchanged* (β_E):

$$\beta_E = \beta_G - |\beta_N|.$$

Since $\beta_G \geq \beta_N$, this measure has maximum and minimum values of $2mn$ and 0, respectively.

Information and instruction are also relative concepts; one can be converted into the other by redefinition of courses of action. Consider the course of action "using a computer" where the outcome of interest is a correct solution to an equation. The subject involved may not be aware of the availability of a packaged program for solving the equation, and hence he does his own programming with, say, a probability of success (efficiency) equal to 0.5. If a message makes him aware of the packaged program, his efficiency in use of the computer may go up to 1.0. Then we can measure the amount of instruction he has received.

On the other hand, we could define two courses of action: C_1, which is "use of the computer with his own program" and C_2, which is "use of the computer with a packaged program." Then before the communication his probability of selecting the first course of action (C_1) may have been 1.0, but after communication the probability of selecting the second course of action (C_2) may change from 0 to 1.0. In this interpretation the message would be said to inform rather than instruct.

Again this relativity of concepts presents no problem as long as we can adjust the two different interpretations of the same objective state of a subject so that they become comparable. The definitions provided here clearly make such adjustment possible.

A single communication may, of course, both inform and instruct. A message that does both can be said to *enlighten* the receiver. The joint effect of information that changes probabilities of choice and instruction that changes efficiencies of choice is a change in probabilities associated with the possible outcomes. Thus whereas information relates to familiarity and instruction to knowledge, *enlightenment relates to understanding.*

If an individual equally values all possible outcomes in a purposeful state, then he has no basis for selecting one from among them to pursue. He can be said to be *unmotivated* in that state. It should be recalled that the outcomes used to define a purposeful state are defined so as to be exclusive and exhaustive. Then since the maximum relative value of an outcome is 1.0, the sum of the relative values over a set of outcomes is also 1.0. Therefore, if relative value is added to one outcome, an equal amount must be subtracted from others.

A state that contains no motivation is described by the condition $V_1 = V_2 = \cdots = V_n = 1/n$. A state that contains complete motivation is one in which one outcome has a relative value of 1.0 and all the others have none. These observations correspond exactly to those made in the discussion of information and probability of choice. Therefore, measures of motivation communicated can be formulated in a way that is completely analogous to the way used to develop measures of information.

9.26.   *Amount of motivation in an individual's state* (γ):

$$\gamma = \frac{n}{2} \sum_{j=1}^{n} \left| V_j - \frac{1}{n} \right|.$$

9.27.   *Net amount of motivation communicated to a receiver* (γ_N):

$$\gamma_N = \gamma_2 - \gamma_1,$$

where γ_2 and γ_1 are the amounts of motivation contained in the terminal and initial states, respectively.

9.28.   *Gross amount of motivation communicated to a receiver* (γ_G):

$$\gamma_G = \frac{n}{2} \Sigma \left| V_j' - V_j \right|,$$

where V_j' and V_j are the relative values of outcomes in the terminal and initial states, respectively.

9.29.   *Amount of motivation exchanged* (γ_E):

$$\gamma_E = \gamma_G - \left| \gamma_N \right|.$$

As was observed in Chapter 2, courses of action and outcomes (means and ends) are relative concepts. By reconceptualizing a subject's purposeful state, an investigator can convert courses of action into outcomes, or outcomes into courses of action. Therefore, by using such transformations it is possible to convert what appears as information in one formulation of another's purposeful state into motivation in another formulation, or, conversely, to convert motivation into information. Finally, since we noted in the last section that instruction and information could be converted into each other, it follows that each of the three measures has a transformation into each of the others.

The Value of the Components of Communication

It will be recalled that the value of a communication to the receiver is given by $V_2{}^* - V_1{}^*$, where these are the values to him of his terminal and initial states, respectively. Using expected relative value for the measure of value of a state, this difference may be rewritten as follows:

$$V_2{}^* - V_1{}^* = \Delta V^* = \sum_{j=1}^{n} \sum_{i=1}^{m} (P_i + \Delta P_i)(E_{ij} + \Delta E_{ij})(V_j + \Delta V_j) - \sum_{j=1}^{n} \sum_{i=1}^{m} P_i E_{ij} V_j.$$

By expansion this equation may be converted into the following.

$$\Delta V^* = \sum_i \sum_j \Delta P_i E_{ij} V_j + \sum_i \sum_j P_i \Delta E_{ij} V_j + \sum_i \sum_j P_i E_{ij} \Delta V_j + \sum_i \sum_j \Delta P_i \Delta E_{ij} V_j + \sum_i \sum_j \Delta P_i E_{ij} \Delta V_j + \sum_i \sum_j P_i \Delta E_{ij} \Delta V_j + \sum_i \sum_j \Delta P_i \Delta E_{ij} \Delta V_j.$$

The first three terms represent the value added to the initial state by the communicated information, instruction, and motivation, respectively.

9.30. *Value of information communicated* $(\Delta V_\alpha{}^*)$:

$$\Delta V_\alpha{}^* = \sum_i \sum_j \Delta P_i E_{ij} V_j.$$

9.31. *Value of instruction communicated* $(\Delta V_\beta{}^*)$:

$$\Delta V_\beta{}^* = \sum_i \sum_j P_i \Delta E_{ij} V_j.$$

9.32. *Value of motivation communicated* $(\Delta V_\gamma{}^*)$:

$$\Delta V_\gamma{}^* = \sum_i \sum_j P_i E_{ij} \Delta V_j.$$

Any of these expressions may be either positive or negative. If $\Delta V_\alpha{}^*$ is negative, the receiver has been *misinformed*; if positive, he has been informed. If $\Delta V_\beta{}^*$ is positive, he has been instructed; if negative, he has been misinstructed. Unfortunately we have no commonly used negative of the verb to instruct. The same remarks apply to $\Delta V_\gamma{}^*$.

The remaining four terms in the equation for ΔV^* represent $\Delta V_{\alpha\beta}{}^*$, $\Delta V_{\alpha\gamma}{}^*$, $\Delta V_{\beta\gamma}{}^*$, and $\Delta V_{\alpha\beta\gamma}{}^*$. For example, $\Delta V_{\alpha\beta}{}^*$ is the joint contribution (*not* the sum of the independent contributions) to value of the information and instruction communicated. The other terms may be similarly interpreted.

It is convenient, then, to think of the value of a communication as the sum of the independent and dependent contributions of information, instruction, and motivation. That is

$$\Delta V^* = \Delta V_\alpha^* + \Delta V_\beta^* + \Delta V_\gamma^* + \Delta V_{\alpha\beta}^* + \Delta V_{\alpha\gamma}^* + \Delta V_{\beta\gamma}^* + \Delta V_{\alpha\beta\gamma}^*.$$

Conclusion

Some attempts to apply the measures developed here are described in Martin (1963). Such applications are not easy. They are time-consuming and costly, and may require a degree of control over subjects that is difficult, if not impossible, to obtain. The situation we are in with respect to these measures is similar to the one a physicist would be in if the only way of measuring the temperature of a body were to determine the mean-squared velocity of its point particles. We have yet to develop thermometers to facilitate measures of human communication; but measures such as have been developed here can take us a giant step toward easy and *relevant* measurement.

Apparently easy measurement may not be measurement at all and may not even be relevant. Good measures have usually evolved through four stages. In the first stage, subjective judgment is used. For example, we estimated the intelligence of people or, at one time in history, the temperature of an object. In the second stage, easier-to-apply *indexes* that correlate highly with expert judgment are sought. The procedure described by Thurstone and Chave (1929) for the construction of attitude tests – a procedure still followed widely – is based on correlation of test scores with expert judgment. Such objective indexes of subjective judgment, however useful they may be, do not yield measures in any strict sense because they involve no unit of measurement and, more important, no idealized operational definition of, and hence standard for, the property being quantified. At the present time, citation counts provide such a subjective index of the value of a scientific article because they are not based on an operational definition and measure of the value of a scientific article.

The third stage of the evolution is the development of idealized operational definitions and measures of the property involved, such as we have tried to develop here, or as in the development of a definition of temperature as mean-squared velocity of point particles. The existence of such measures, even when not practical or easy to apply, as in the above definition of temperature, provides an *objective standard* for which indexes can be sought. Development of such indexes – ones that correlate with, or are structurally related to, the standard (say, use of thermometers) – constitute the fourth stage of the evolution.

Very few of the so-called measures in the behavioral sciences have gone beyond the second stage of this evolution. Even most of the standard psychological tests provide, at best, indexes of human judgment, not of objective measures.

The analysis that yielded the measures defined here show the dangers of indiscriminately applying Shannon's measures to human communication. They do not deal with most of the important characteristics of such communication. The measures proposed here will certainly be modified and replaced in time, but what replaces them should be at least as rich as they are.

We turn now to an analysis of the meaning of message on which our definition of communication is based.

REFERENCES

Cherry, Colin. *On Human Communication.* New York: John Wiley & Sons, 1957.

Emery, F. E., and E. L. Trist. "The Causal Texture of Organizational Environments." *Human Relations* 18 (1965): 21–32.

Hardy, R., and P. Kurtz. "A Current Appraisal of the Behavioral Sciences." *Research Council Bulletin,* Sec. 6 (1963), pp. 99–105.

Hartley, R. V. L. "Transmission of Information." *Bell System Technical Journal* 7 (1928): 535f.

MacKay, D. M. "Quantal Aspects of Scientific Information." *Philosophical Magazine* 4 (1950): 289–311.

Martin, M. W., Jr. "The Measurement of Value of Scientific Information." In *Operations Research in Research and Development,* edited by B. V. Dean, pp. 97–123. New York: John Wiley & Sons, 1963.

Payne, Buryl. "A Descriptive Theory of Information." *Behavioral Science* 11 (1966): 295–305.

Schramm, Wilbur. "Information Theory and Mass Communication." *In Communication and Culture,* edited by A. G. Smith, pp. 521–34. New York: Holt, Rinehart & Winston, 1966.

Shannon, C. E., and W. Weaver. *The Mathematical Theory of Communication.* Urbana: University of Illinois Press, 1949.

Singer, E. A., Jr. *On the Contented Life.* New York: Henry Holt, 1923.

Thurstone, L. L., and E. J. Chave. *The Measurement of Attitudes.* Chicago: University of Chicago Press, 1929.

10

Signs, Messages, and Language

LANGUAGE, *n*. The music with which we charm the serpents guarding another's treasure.

The Devil's Dictionary

Introduction

The definition of *communication* given in Chapter 9 used the concept *message*, which is as yet undefined. Since a message consists of one or more signs, it is first necessary to define *sign*. This chapter includes that definition and also develops a set of measures to characterize sign performance. Using these concepts, *message* and *language* are then defined.

The conceptual development in this chapter is similar in many respects to that provided by Charles Morris (1946 and 1964). The names of the concepts in our treatment are similar to his, but the kinds of definitions given are quite different. Although Morris's work is behaviorally oriented, he does not provide operational definitions of the concepts he treats, and only infrequently do his definitions specify measures of the variables involved. Finally, his treatment of signs is not placed within the general context of purposeful behavior, even though his approach is teleologically oriented. Nevertheless, as will be apparent to those familiar with Morris's work, our debt to him is considerable.

Signs

The task of analyzing the meaning of sign can be divided into two questions: "What can be called signs?" "By virtue of what properties can they be called signs?" The first of these questions is the easier to answer.

It is apparent that objects can be signs — billboards, posters, and, in general, those physical objects we commonly call signs. But behavior patterns can also be signs — such as gestures and speech. Sometimes it is fruitful to consider the properties of objects and behavior as signs rather than objects and behavior themselves. A red light is frequently a sign of danger, but we do not respond to all the properties of the object that throws the light. We may not respond to the material the lamp is made of, but we do respond to its redness and location. This distinction among objects, behavior, and their properties is only a matter of emphasis, since only objects or events (including behavior) have properties; hence a response to a property is also always a response to what has the property. It will be important, however, to identify the properties of an object or event that make it serve as a sign.

At the level of common sense it is apparent that an object, event, or property that is a sign is *a sign of something*. This suggests that something, *X*, is a sign of something else, *Y*, if it can in some sense substitute for *Y*. It is in an analysis of the nature of this substitution that the nature of a sign is to be found.

We have stated (definition 4.1) that a *stimulus* is anything that produces a change in the functional properties of a subject in a purposeful state, and that a *response* is the change in the subject's functional properties produced by a stimulus. Hence a stimulus produces a change in either the subject's probabilities of choice, efficiencies of choice, relative values of outcomes, or some combination of these; that is, it informs, instructs, or motivates him.

A sign is such a stimulus; it produces responses to other stimuli, but we do not restrict these other stimuli to objects or events. These other stimuli may be either concepts or images (both of which we will define later) or signs themselves.

Everything that produces a response produces a response to itself in a trivial sense. Therefore, we do not want to call every stimulus a sign. A closed door produces a turning of its knob, but we do not want to call the door a sign.

According to Morris (1964), a sign produces a *disposition to respond*.

> . . . a disposition to react in a certain way because of the sign (food-seeking behavior or site-probing behavior in the case of bees), has no necessarily "subjective" connotation. Such a disposition can, if one wishes, be interpreted in probabilistic terms, as the probability of reacting in a certain way under certain conditions because of the appearance of the sign (p. 3).

Hence, for Morris, a sign produces a potentiality for response. We prefer, however, to place the potentiality in the sign rather than in the respondent, because, for Morris, an *X* is a sign only if it produces a disposition to respond; when it does not, it is not a sign. It seems to us that *X* should be a sign if it *can* produce the required type of response, even though it may not be doing so in a particular situation.

10.1. *Sign:* anything that is a potential producer of a response to something other than itself

10.2. *Signification of a sign:* something other than the sign that the sign potentially produces a response to.

This definition permits an *X* to be a sign to a potential respondent, even though he is not responding or is not disposed to respond to it at the moment.

We can say a book or a letter contains signs, even though no one is reading it at the moment. Yet we can determine experimentally if the marks in the book have the required potentiality.

Note that there is no requirement that a sign and the thing it produces a response to be in the same environment or even exist at the same time. The name of a person who is in another environment or who has died can produce a response to him. Furthermore, since a purposive state has been so defined that machines (such as computers) can be placed in such states (by appropriate programming), an X may be a sign of something to a machine as well as to a person. We want the definitions of *communication, signs, message,* and *language* to permit communication to and with machines.

The definition of *sign* presented here is very similar to one Morris rejected. He based his rejection on the case of a drug that produces in an individual a sensitivity to something he would not otherwise respond to. Administration of such a drug appears to satisfy the sign requirements, but, Morris argued, this conflicts with common sense. Note, however, that the drug leaves *no choice* to the responder; it *imposes* the increased sensitivity on him. This is critical. If we were to use physical force on a person to make him look at something, the applied force would not be a sign of what he perceives because he would not be free to do otherwise. A stimulus is a producer, not a deterministic cause, of a response. It is a necessary but *not* a sufficient condition of the relevant response. Therefore, something like a drug that is sufficient to produce a response to something else in a given set of circumstances is *not* a stimulus, and hence is not a sign.

It is apparent at the commonsense level that many signs operate in the way we have described. When someone yells *Fire* in a burning building, it may produce a wide variety of purposeful responses to that fire — escape, attempts to subdue the fire or to save contents of the building, and so on. Signs of fire may be spoken or written words, gestures, or objects or events (as a screaming siren or blinking red lights). Note that as a sign of fire smoke differs from the word fire; it is a *natural*, not a man-made or *artifical*, sign. But both operate in the same way: they produce responses to the fire. It is not equally obvious that such signs as "and" or "plus" satisfy these conditions, but we shall consider such less obvious cases later.

The meaning of a sign can be shown schematically, as in Figure 10.1.

The way signs can be studied is conditioned by their essential property's being functional in character. Before turning to a more detailed analysis of how they function, it should first be noted that the structural relationships between different signs may be the subject of study. Such studies form the branch of semiotic called *syntactics*. Morris (1946) defined syntactics as "that branch of semiotic that studies the way in which signs of various classes are combined to form compound signs" (p. 355). Hence the study of grammar is part of syntactics. Much of logic can also be looked at as a part of this branch of semiotic. Since our concern here is with the way signs function little

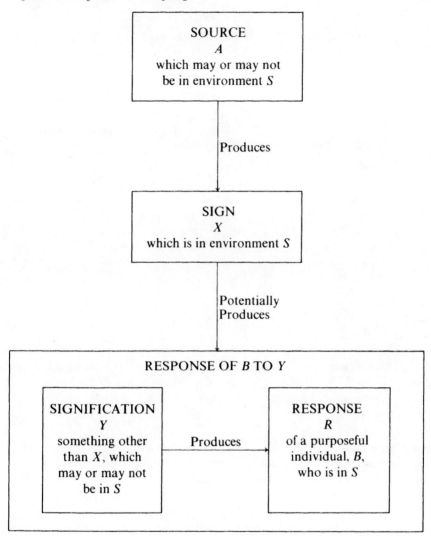

Figure 10.1. Diagram of a Sign's Operation

reference will be made to syntactics. It will come up, however, when we discuss language later in this chapter.

Figure 10.1 provides a basis for analysis of the functioning of signs. We may concentrate our attention on the relationship between the sign, *X*, and what it signifies, *Y*; or we may consider the relationship between the sign and the response, *R*, or respondent, *B*, and/or the source, *A*. Analyses of the first type are called *semantic*; analyses of the second type are called *pragmatic*. Semantics, therefore, is the study of what signs refer to, their signification;

pragmatics is the study of their effects, the characteristics of the responses that they bring about. According to Morris (1964), "Pragmatics is the aspect of semiotic concerned with the origin, uses, and effects of signs" (p. 44). He used *origin* in the same sense that we use *source*.

Semantic Properties of Signs: Denotation and Connotation

The secondary stimulus, Y, to which a sign produces a response (what it signifies) can be considered in two ways — denotatively and connotatively.

10.3   *Denotation of a sign*: the set of objects or events signified by a sign.

Hence the denotation in the shout *Fire* in a building is the fire in that building, but when we speak of fire as in fire prevention we denote a wide range of fires. The denotation of a sign may range from particular to general, may change with circumstances, and vary for different individuals. The statement, "the television program I watched last," may denote different programs to different persons at the same time and to the same person at different times.

10.4.   *Connotation of a sign:* the set of properties (of the objects or events responded to) that produces the response.

Thus the connotation of *matches* may be their ability to light a cigarette or to produce damage to persons and property. Hence the connotation of a sign may also change with circumstances and vary for different individuals. The statement "the last television I watched," may connote different properties (such as humor, drama, news) to different people and to the same person at different times.

Two different signs may have the same denotation but different connotations — as *mate* and *housewife*. Conversely, two different signs may have the same connotation but different denotations — as *matches* and *lighter*.

Denotation and *connotation* are sometimes used synonymously with *meaning*. If *meaning* is so used, it should be borne in mind that this is *semantic*, not pragmatic, meaning. We prefer to use *meaning* in its pragmatic sense, as will be apparent when we discuss this concept.

This discussion of denotation and connotation may seem appropriate for signs that signify *observable* things or properties of such things. But how do these concepts apply to such signs as *centaur, James Bond, snark,* and *angel*? Furthermore, many of the signs we use refer to things that may be or have been observable but that we have never observed, such as names of historic figures or places we have never visited. Both *centaur* and *Abraham Lincoln* fail to produce a response to a relevant observable object. They do, however, produce a response to an *image* or *concept*.[1] Even signs that signify observable

---

1. It will be recalled from the model of choice discussed in Chapter 2 and the discussion of memory in Chapter 4 that images and concepts could be called forth from memory and could be produced or modified by the observations of, or communications received by, the subject.

things may produce responses to images or concepts brought forth from our memory. Sometimes these were produced by the signified things when we observed them in the past. Sometimes they were produced by communication. A description can produce an image of even a nonexistent thing, and an explanation can produce a concept of it.

We might argue that *centaur* denotes the top half of a man joined to the body of a horse, or a drawing of a centaur. In a sense this is so. To one who has never seen a horse or a picture of a horse or a centaur, the word *centaur* is unlikely to denote anything. However, common sense indicates that the respondent to *centaur* is not responding to the parts of a horse and man but to an image or concept. The behaviorist or operationally oriented are disinclined to accept such mentalistic concepts; indeed, it would defeat our purposes here if they were treated as such. But an operational definition of these notions is not impossible.

IMAGES

Note that in common parlance an individual can have the following kinds of image: an image of (1) an object in the same environment (the chair behind me); (2) an object in a different environment (the chair in my bedroom); and (3) a nonexistent object, such as a centaur or James Bond. Hence our definition must be broad enough to cover all these possibilities.

The notion of an image has been a very fruitful one in the development of psychology. It has been used to explain our ability to use past experience in the present or to explain why different people react differently to the same stimulus. It was noted earlier that different observers may describe the same thing differently. This is frequently explained by saying that their images — mental pictures — differed, and it is their images, not the stimulating object, that they describe. In early psychology such images were called *impressions* and *ideas*.

A mental picture was once *assumed* to be one that no one but its possessor could see, hence the earlier prevalence of introspective or subjective psychology. But this assumption is not necessary.

We call the capability of image construction *imagination*, and we feel quite free to say of someone, without asking him, that he has or lacks imagination. On what evidence are such statements based? Somehow we base them on what we have observed. What observations were relevant?

Let us follow a commonsense account of how an image is formed. Suppose you are reading a story to a child and the word horse appears. The child wants to know what a horse is. You may draw one, show a picture of one, or describe it. In so doing, you create an image of a horse in the child. A verbal description of a horse may provide an image of a horse or reveal one, but it is not itself an image of a horse. It is not an image of the horse as a picture is, because the signs used in the verbal description do not themselves have any of the relevant properties of a horse. The picture does. The picture is a sign of a horse that has some of the same (geometric) properties as the thing it signifies. It *looks like* a horse.

10.5. *Iconic sign:* a sign that has some of the same structural properties as the thing(s) it signifies.

Structural properties, as noted earlier, include geometric, kinematic, physical, and morphological properties. Hence iconic signs look, taste, feel, sound, or smell like what they signify; but they need not, and usually do not, function in the same way as the thing they signify. Therefore, iconic signs not only signify but also *represent* what they signify and hence may be a substitute in some circumstances. A photograph, which is a common type of iconic sign, can frequently substitute for the person it represents.

Iconic signs that sounds like what they represent are called *onomatopoeic*; bow-wow, meow, and cock-a-doodle-do are a few.

Iconic signs *individuate*; that is, they represent things or events taken as individuals, differentiated from other things. It is for this reason that we can have an image of *a* horse but not an image of animal. There is no set of structural properties to individuate animals; functional properties are necessary. Or we can have an image of a pistol but not of weapon, because the individuating property of weapon is functional, not structural.

A physical image is an iconic sign. If it is an image of something we have experienced (say, horse), then it facilitates our response to the verbal sign *horse*. The image of a horse increases our probability of responding to the object horse. It is for this reason that books and lectures are so frequently illustrated. Note that we can have a picture of a picture, and hence an image of an image.

Up to this point we have considered only images that can be seen, heard, felt, smelled, or tasted — physical images and images of things that exist. Let us now return to the centaur and images of things that do not exist.

The images of a centaur combines physical properties of man and horse into an individual thing. We have experienced each of the properties involved but not their combination. The image, then, is a combination of properties. If this combination is represented by iconic signs, these signs are a physical image. But the combination of properties is itself an image whether or not it is represented physically.

Images that are not physically represented are called *mental* and, as indicated earlier, are assumed to be inaccessible to all but the person who has it. We can now see why this assumption is false. The combination of properties that form an individual's image (is in his mind) is the same combination that coproduces his responses to noniconic signs. By observation and analysis of his response we can determine what his mental image is. Therefore, a mental image is the collection of structural properties and the relationships between them to which an individual responds. Such images intervene between the sign and what is signified, even when it exists. When it is an image of the real thing, that thing is at least a coproducer of the image. When it does not exist, the image is produced by signs.

10.6.   *Image:* an individuated set of structural properties and the relationships between them to which a subject responds.

CONCEPTS

The difference in common usage between image and concept suggests how to define concept. First we note that concepts are not iconic; they do not look like, sound like, and so on, what they signify. Second, whereas images help us *describe*, concepts help us *explain*. Herein lies the critical difference. *Images connote structural properties, but concepts connote functional properties.*

Explanations are of two sorts. (1) we explain how something comes to be; that is, we identify what produced it. We may explain to a friend the presence of a strange piece of furniture in our home by saying, "It was a gift." (2) We explain a thing by identifying what it can do – what its function is. We may explain a Clipit by "It is used to cut clippings from a newspaper without damaging the sheets below the one being cut."

Hence to say that we cannot conceive of a particular thing is to say that we can't explain it. Either we do not know what could have produced it or we can't determine what it can do, or both.

The definition of a sign developed earlier signifies the authors' conception of a sign: the combination of functional properties of objects or events that explains a particular phenomenon of communication.

10.7.   *Concept:* an individuated set of functional properties and the relationships between them to which a subject responds.

To have an image of *Y* and to have a concept of *Y* are not the same thing. We can have an image of something but not a conception of it. A child may have an image of God but no conception of Him. Conversely, we may have a concept of something for which we have no image. An adult may have a concept of God but no image of Him. Models of reality are either images, conceptions, or some combination of these. A model is a representation of those structural and/or functional properties of reality that the subject believes to exist and to be relevant to his purposes.

SYMBOLS AND SIGNALS

Symbol.   Both symbols and signals are types of signs, but semioticians seem to agree on little more than this with respect to them. Several different meansings are associated with these terms, each of which seems to be justified by common usage. One of these meanings of *symbol* is contained in the following quotation from Suzanne Langer (1948):

> Instead of announcers of things, they [symbols] are reminders. They have been called "substitute signs," for in our present experience they take the place of

things we have perceived in the past, over even things that we can merely imagine by combining memories, things that *might* be in the past and present experience (p. 24).

. . . . it is the conceptions, not the things, that symbols directly mean (p. 49).

Hence, according to Langer, a symbol is a sign that signifies a concept. This is certainly one way that *symbol* is commonly used. For example, it is in this sense that the American flag is a symbol of our concept of our nation, and a skull and crossbones is a symbol of our concept of death. Symbols, in this sense, are frequently, but not necessarily, natural or nonlinguistic signs. Proper names can also be symbols in this sense. *Abraham Lincoln* is a symbol of honesty, but *honesty* itself signifies a concept. It, too, would be a symbol in Langer's sense. This seems to us to be too general a treatment.

Symbol is also commonly used in another sense, particularly in logic and mathematics, but also in more commonplace activities. For example, +, =, and > are commonly called symbols in arithmetic, and $, %, and & are commonplace symbols. In what sense is + different from *plus*? Most would answer that it is just a convenient shorthand for *plus*. It is this sense of symbol that Morris (1946) used when he defined a symbol as a sign "that is produced by its interpreter and that acts as a substitute for some other sign with which it is synonymous" (p. 355). Hence, for Morris, a symbol is a sign of another sign that is produced by the same person who responds to it. "Where an organism provides itself with a sign which is a substitute in the control of its behavior for another sign, signifying what the sign for which it is a substitute signifies, then this sign is a *symbol* . . ." (p. 25).

It does not seem to us that a sign can serve as a symbol only to the one who produced it. Somehow, in a written equation + is as much a symbol to the reader as one the reader writes himself. When the reader sees "Let P_i represent the probability of selecting a course of action C_i," the P_i and C_i become symbols for him as well as for the writer. Nevertheless, it is clear that we use *symbol* in the sense of a substitute for other signs.

Langer used *symbol* as a sign of a concept; Morris used it as a sign of a sign. It seems reasonable to ask whether some have not used *symbol* as a sign of an image. Obviously they have; caricatures are frequently used symbolically.

Symbol, therefore, seems to be used as a sign of an image, concept, or another sign. Now, images, concepts, and signs all have a common property: each represents something other than itself; that is, they can produce responses to something other than themselves. This suggests a definition of *symbol* that synthesizes at least several of its common uses.

10.8.   *Symbol:* a sign that is a potential producer of a response to something, which in turn is a potential producer of a response to something other than itself.

Signal.   Morris (1946) defined a signal as "a sign that is not a symbol" (p. 354). This definition, it seems to us, completely misses the usual sense in which signal is used. In *Webster's Seventh New Collegiate Dictionary,*

(Springfield, Mass.: G. & C. Merriam Co., 1963), *signal* is defined as "an act, event, or watchword that has been agreed upon as the occasion of concerted action" or "a sound or gesture made to give warning or command."

Signals, we believe, are intended to initiate or terminate action. This is certainly true, for example, of a traffic signal, which starts and stops us. But a traffic sign (such as a stop sign) may also stop us. The difference between a traffic sign and a traffic signal, we believe, holds the clue to the essential difference between sign and signal. A signal is always the *behavior* of an object – an act or event; a sign need not be. A constantly red light is a sign of danger, but a traffic light that *changes* its color is called a signal.

Putting these observations together yields the following definition.

10.9. *Signal:* an act of a purposeful individual (or individuals) or of an object whose behavior is produced by such an individual (or individuals), which serves as a sign of that individual's intention that other purposeful individuals or himself (themselves) respond by behaving in a specified way at the time of the act.

Note that an individual can signal himself as in setting an alarm clock or in arranging to be called in a hotel at a certain time in the morning. A traffic signal may be manually operated by a policeman or set by him so that it operates itself in a desired way. Even if it operates itself, its behavior is produced by the one who set it.

Pragmatics

Pragmatics, as we stated, is concerned with the relationship between a sign, its source, and/or its respondent. Our concern here is with the respondent. In Chapter 11 we will consider the interaction of the source and the respondent.

MEANING

Meaning has been used in so many different senses that some, like Morris (1946), exclude the concept from consideration. Cherry (1957) observed, "There is a move today to avoid 'meaning' so far as can possibly be done, in communication studies" (p. 111). He goes on to cite ten different meanings of *meaning* (pp. 112–113). Despite the caution of Morris and Cherry, the analysis of meaning, largely stimulated by the work of Ogden and Richards (1947, originally published in 1923), continues into the present. See, for example, Loundsbury (1966) and Osgood *et al.* (1957). A recent review of the literature on meaning by Marjorie B. Creelman (1966) reaches the following conclusion.

> . . . meaning, the elusive Cinderella, is still at large, evading identification and capture. Perhaps one of the difficulties lies in the various images that her various suitors have of her—images that have led them to seek her different ways. Some see her as a simple-minded creature, some as complex, subtle, and sophisticated. Some

have focused on her intellectual qualities, and some imagine her to be sensitive and emotional. Some, overwhelmed by her mystery, have from the first contented themselves with living with her only in fantasy, concluding that she is essentially unknown and unknowable (p. 207).

We have already pointed out that *meaning* is sometimes applied in the semantic context to refer to what we have called the *denotion* and *connotation*, or the *signification*, of a sign. We see no good reason for using *meaning* in this context where we already have complete and adequate terminology; it would only introduce unnecessary redundancy. This is not so in pragmatics, where there would be a conceptual and terminological gap if meaning were not considered.

Pragmatic philosophers from Peirce to Dewey have pointed out that in practice the meaning of a term does not lie in what it comes from, but in what it leads to; or, as they put it, in the difference it makes in the respondent's behavior. A sign that does not affect behavior has no meaning, no matter what it signifies. Thus the meaning of a sign lies in what it can make one do. When one cries *Fire!* in a crowded theater, the meaning of the cry is not to be found in the flames denoted or the heat connoted but in the effort to escape harm or avoid destruction that it produces. In effect, meaning, though a function of what a sign signifies, is separate from it; it lies not in the signification of a sign but in its *significance*.

Furthermore, meaning is not only applicable to signs but also to any experience or thing that is experienced. All things that act as signs have meaning, but not everything with meaning is a sign. One asks of an event, "What does it mean?" This is equivalent to asking, "What will it lead to?" or "What significance does it have?" In this sense one can, and has, asked about the meaning of life itself. When one is asked what television means to him, he is likely to refer to entertainment, keeping informed about world affairs, and perhaps even education. He does not define television but reveals its significance to him. Meaning is not captured in definitions, signification is.

Cherry (1957) has observed that "the meaning of the utterance to the listener, B," is the selection of the particular response he actually makes, and that, "the meaning of the utterance to the speaker, A," is the selection of a response in B that A intends his utterance to evoke (p. 114). This concept of meaning was also presented by Ogden and Richards (1947), and much earlier by Gardiner (1921–22).

Meaning is a property of a purposeful response to a stimulus. It is quite naturally attributed to the stimulus because the stimulus produces it.

10.10.   *Meaning*: The meaning of a stimulus (sign or otherwise) is the set of functional properties of the response it produces.

Therefore, a sign may have different meanings for different individuals, or different meanings for the same individual at different times. Paul Revere's cry, "The British are coming!" had one meaning for the American Revolutionists and another for the Tories. Or again, "No rain is expected today" may mean one thing to a farmer at work but another when he is vacationing. Its meaning may also change with the seasons. As Cherry (1957) noted, "A 'meaning' is not a label tied around the neck of a spoken word or phrase. It is more like the beauty of a complexion, which lies 'altogether in the eye of its beholder' (but changes with the light!)" (p. 115).

Since the functional properties of different responses to the same sign may differ, the only meaning that *the meaning* of a sign can have lies in a common functional property of these different responses. That is, we may find a more general function that persists among responses that are functionally different at a lower level of generality. For example, in the wide variety of responses to "It will not rain today" we are likely to find a common functional property such as the shedding of protective cover or increased outdoor activity. But even in this sense it may be unlikely that we can find any one meaning for any sign.

For those who prefer to use meaning in a different way that we have, we are willing to qualify our use by referring to it as *pragmatic meaning*.

Morris (1964) discusses three types of signification (semantic properties) of signs and three corresponding "dispositions to react in a certain way" (pragmatic properties). Semantically speaking, a sign, for Morris, is:

1. *Designative,* "insofar as it signifies *observable* properties of the environment or the actor" (as black).
2. *Prescriptive,* "insofar as it signifies how the object or situation is to be reacted to so as to satisfy the governing impulse" (as ought).
3. *Appraisive,* "insofar as it signifies the consummatory properties of some object or situation" (as good) (p. 4).

The corresponding (pragmatic) functions are to produce:

1. "a disposition to react to the designated object as if it had certain observable properties,"
2. "a disposition to act in a certain kind of way to the designated object or situation," and/or
3. "a disposition to act toward a designated object as if it would be satisfying or unsatisfying" (p. 6).

There is a considerable correspondence between these three functions that Morris identified and the three discussed in Chapter 9: (1) *information,* (2) *instruction,* and (3) *motivation.* Furthermore, it is apparent that signs designative in Morris's sense, inform in our sense; those prescriptive, instruct; those that appraise, motivate.

One could pursue considerably further such an analysis of the signification and functions of signs, but since individual signs seldom function independently of other signs it seems more fruitful to discuss the properties of sign combinations — that is, messages. The signification and meaning of a message is never the simple sum of these properties of the component signs; it is a resultant of a considerable interaction between the individual sign properties.

Consider the difficulty of translating a message in an unfamiliar language with the help only of a dictionary.

In sum, the signification and significance of a sign depend on the sign environment and the situation in which it is used. This is why a dictionary must give so many different definitions of most signs.

Sign Measures

Up to this point we have dealt with only qualitative aspects of signs. Now we consider some of their quantitative aspects. Here, too, it is convenient to distinguish between semantic and pragmatic measures.

SEMANTIC EFFICIENCY AND RELATED MEASURES

10.11.   *Semantic efficiency of a sign in an environment* (S): the probability that the sign will produce in an environment a response by the receiver to what the sender intended him to respond.

If the sign represents objects or events, then the semantic efficiency is equivalent to *denotative efficiency*; if the sign represents properties, then its semantic efficiency is equivalent to *connotative efficiency*.

Ambiguous Signs.   Suppose an individual is told to get *the book* off a table on which two books are located. He may get either or both, but he is not likely to pick up a pen rather than a book. In this context the book is *ambiguous* because it has denotative efficiency for more than the item intended. If the instruction had been to get one or the other of the books or the larger book, the ambiguity would be removed. The receiver in the first situation may seek to remove the ambiguity by asking, "Which one?"

The nature of ambiguity, then, lies in the discrepancy between the intended response to a sign and the actual response. The ambiguity exists for the receiver relative to the sender. A receiver may deliberately misinterpret the sender's intention; he may bring a pen in order to annoy the sender. This, however, is not a case of ambiguity. Ambiguity implies that the receiver wants to cooperate with the sender.

10.12.   *Ambiguity:* A sign (X) is denotatively or connotatively ambiguous if (*a*) the sender intends X to denote or connote something (Y), (*b*) X is an efficient denoter or connoter of something other than Y for the receiver, and (*c*) the receiver intends to respond to the denotation or connotation intended by the sender.

That ambiguity is not always undesirable becomes apparent when we realize that it is one of the most important instruments of the verbal artist. The richness of poetry, for example, lies in its having many different denotations and connotations. The ability of ambiguity to stimulate imagination was exploited by James Joyce in *Finnegan's Wake*. In this work, Joyce invented words that deliberately have several denotations and connotations.

Wellingdome Museyroom has many more connotations than Wellington Museum Room. Puns, of course, are a deliberate manipulation of signs to obtain ambiguity, to give signs more than one signification.

The measure of semantic efficiency given above is clearly relative to the intended signification (Y), the environment in which the sign operates (S), and the respondent (A). Now we can determine how the efficiency of a sign depends on these three variables; Y, S, and A. This dependence reflects on the *semantic generality* of a sign. Consideration of its sensitivity to: (1) the signified Y leads to a definition of *signification generality*; (2) the environment, S, leads to a definition of *environmental generality*; and (3) the respondent, A, leads to a definition of *social generality*.

Signification Generality. The word *chair* usually produces a response to only a few objects in a normal room. The word *furniture* usually produces a response to a wider range of objects than does *chair*. Hence *furniture* has a more general denotation than does *chair*. It also has a more general connotation, because the properties of furniture include, but are not exhausted by, the properties of chair.

10.13. *Signification Generality:* If the things signified by one sign, X_1, include all the things signified by a second sign, X_2, X_1 is more general (denotively, connotatively, or both) than is X_2.

We can have a hierarchy of signs relative to the generality of their signification. *Furnishings* is more general than *furniture*, and *furniture* is more general than *chair*.

If there is no overlap of the classes of things denoted by two signs, then the only basis for comparison is the number of things signified. This criterion by itself, however, is not very useful. It serves no useful purpose to assert that *horse* is more general than *buffalo*, because there are more horses than buffalo.

The signification generality and ambiguity of a sign are not to be confused. A general sign may denote a large number of different things, but such is intended. An ambiguous sign denotes more than is intended. Where the intention is that an individual respond to many objects, and he does, the sign is not ambiguous, though general. Therefore, *books* is a more general sign than *novel*, but it may be less ambiguous.

Environmental Generality. As we have already indicated, a sign may have different denotations or connotations in different environments. The denotation of *the man on my right* changes from time to time; it therefore has less denotative *reliability* than does the name of the man. Yet the phrase, "the man on my right" will usually produce responses to the man in the same relative position and hence is connotatively reliable, at least with respect to the property *position*.

10.14. *Environmental Generality* of a sign relative to a particular signification (Y), one or more receivers, and an exclusive and exhaustive classification of environments is the fraction of this set of environments, in which the sign produces responses to Y in the relevant receivers.

Social Generality.   Finally, there is the measure that reflects the number of people for whom a sign signifies the same thing in the same set of conditions.

10.15.   *Social Generality* of a sign relative to a particular signification (Y), a set of receivers, and a specified set of environments is the fraction of the set of receivers in which the sign produces responses to Y in the relevant environments.

Using the concept of the social generality of a sign, two other important sign characteristics can be defined.

10.16.   *Obscure signs:* ones that have a low denotative or connotative efficiency relative to any possible denotation or connotation for most but not all of the members of a social group.

The degree of obscurity is simply the fraction of the group's members for whom the sign is semantically inefficient. Thus archaic words (such as *ere* and *perchance*) are usually called obscure because few people know what they are intended to signify.

10.17   *Esoteric signs:* ones that are obscure to members of one subgroup of a population but efficient when used on members of another when the second subgroup has a common set of objectives not shared by members of the first subgroup.

Thus *homoscedastic*, which is an efficient signifier among mathematical statisticians but not among others in general, is an esoteric sign. The jargon of special interest groups usually consists of esoteric signs.

PRAGMATIC EFFICIENCY AND RELATED MEASURES

10.18.   *Pragmatic Efficiency of a Sign in an Environment* (S) is the probability that the sign produces a response in that environment by the receiver that was intended by its source.

It is apparent that by an extension of the discussion of semantic efficiency we can define three types of pragmatic generality: *response, environmental,* and *social.* Since the extension is straight-forward it is omitted here.

Signs That Affect Other Signs

As noted earlier, signs are normally used in sign-complexes. In such complexes the signs interact. Some signs have a particular role to play in unifying the signs in the complex. These signs have the function of affecting other signs either by *modifying* them, *relating* them, *connecting* them, or *emphasizing* them. It is to these special sign-roles that we now turn. (The discussion which follows relates to that of forms of statements which appears in Appendix II.)

MODIFIERS

10.19. *Qualifier*: a sign that produces a change in the connotation of another sign.

Hence a qualifier attributes a property to what is denoted by another sign and puts what is denoted into a class of things that have the attributed property. For example, in *red book, red* qualifies *book* and directs the response to the book to its redness. Note that in *the book is red, is red* serves the same function. Adjectives, of course, normally qualify nouns. Adverbs similarly qualify verbs.

Qualification may individuate what is modified – that is make the denotation more specific and remove ambiguity. This is so because a sign that changes the connotation of another sign may also change its denotation. *Red book* and *blue book* have different denotations. A qualifier may change the connotation of a sign, however, without affecting its denotation. "The room in which I am working" and "the reading room in which I am working" have the same denotations but may have different connotations.

10.20. *Quantifiers*: signs that affect the number of things denoted by other signs.

Some examples are *all, few, four, many*, and so on. Note that whereas in *four books, four* quantifies, in *fourth book, fourth* qualifies since it signifies a locational property.

RELATORS

10.21. *Relators*: signs that relate the signification of one sign to that of another.

Relators may do this by attributing a property to the signification taken collectively. In "John is the brother of Tom," *is the brother of* relates John and Tom. It attributes a property to the pair, a property that cannot be attributed to either member taken separately. Relators may also signify the similarity or difference between the signification of two signs; for example, "John is younger than Tom." The difference can be quantified, as in "John is five years younger than Tom." Of course, more than two things can be related, as in "John is the brother of Tom and Mary."

CONNECTORS AND DISCONNECTORS

10.22. *Connectors* (*disconnectors*): signs that combine (separate) the signification of two or more other signs.

In "John and Mary are at home" the *and* is used to produce a response to the *joint* presence of John and Mary rather than a response to either taken separately. This expression may have a different connotation than "John is at home. Mary is at home." It is the difference in connotation that *and* signifies.

The role of connectors and disconnectors is most apparent in mathematical expressions. We readily recognize the difference between $4+2$ and $4-2$, and between $(3 \times 2)+2$ and $3 \times (2+2)$. Verbally we get the same results by using *and, or, plus*, and so on. Punctuation marks such as the comma, colon, semicolon, and hyphen serve the same purpose.

Sometimes proximity of signs is sufficient to connect them. For example, we may either say *nice and big toy* or *nice big toy*.

EMPHASIZERS

10.23. *Emphasizers (deemphasizers)*: signs that produce an increase (decrease) in the probability that an individual will respond to a signifier.

In writing, a word or passage may be called to one's attention by italicizing it, or by changing the type face or color of ink in which it is printed. In speaking, changes in intonation or repetition have the same effect. On the other hand, smaller type or a drop in one's voice can be used to deemphasize a sign or a sign complex, as in a footnote or an aside.

It should be noted that things that modify, relate, connect, and emphasize other signs are themselves signs. They either produce responses to other signs or affect their signification. Hence they signify either the change in signification that they produce or the intention of the source that more or less attention be given to other signs.

Messages

10.24. *Message:* a set of one or more signs intended by its producer to produce a response either in another or in himself.

One can, of course, send a message to oneself; such as a reminder entered on a calendar. Furthermore, a message can be sent without the use of words, by gestures. However, messages are normally formed out of *linguistic* signs. It is necessary, therefore, to understand the nature of language if one wants to fully understand the nature of messages.

Language

Not all signs are part of a language. Smoke may be a sign of fire, but it is not an element of a language. The signs that form a language are ones that can be produced by purposeful individuals. Hence the word smoke is an element of our language.

Linguistic signs must satisfy conditions other than that of being produced by purposeful individuals. They must be semantically and pragmatically efficient for a significant portion of the people who use them. Otherwise they could not be used in communication. This efficiency must pertain over a wide range of environments. Hence linguistic signs must be environmentally and socially general in both the semantic and pragmatic sense.

The set of individuals relative to which linguistic signs must have these properties is the set for which they are to serve as a language. Languages are relative in the sense that what constitutes a language for one set of individuals may not for another.

Finally, to form a language there must be more than a set of signs; there must also be a set of rules for combining signs into groups in such a way that the resulting sign complexes have the same properties required of linguistic signs. These rules specify the form that linguistic expressions should take and how the resulting expressions should be interpreted. The rules of our language allow us not only to form "dog bites man" and "man bites dog," but also to interpret these same combinations of words in different ways. *We do not know how to interpret sign complexes that do not satisfy these rules.* If in the last (italicized) sentence we rearrange the words in a randomly selected sequence, we may get "complexes satisfy we do these that no do interpret rules to how sign not know."

Linguistic rules are what Morris would call *prescriptions* and what we call *instructions*; they are messages that increase the efficiency of our communication. Of such rules, Cherry (1957) observed:

> Human languages have an excess of rules, so that some can be broken without serious harm. The rules we call grammar and syntax are not inviolate, but the more we break them, the lower are our chances of successful communication (p. 19).

The rules of a language have two sources — common usage and experts. In *The American Language*, H. L. Mencken described the way Americans actually do use and combine signs. The experts — those who prepare dictionaries, write grammars, and teach the language professionally — prescribe what and how signs ought to be used. The *ought* derives from their beliefs about the communicative efficiency of alternative ways of using linguistic signs. The experts and common usage frequently do not agree. They battle in the classroom and the streets; sometimes one wins, sometimes the other.

Summarizing, then, the following definition can be formulated.

10.25. *Language:* a set of signs as well as instructions for their use such that (1) the signs can be produced by purposeful individuals, (2) the signs are semantically and pragmatically efficient for a significant portion of those who use them, (3) the signs are environmentally and socially general in the semantic and pragmatic sense, and (4) the instructions signify ways of permuting and combining signs in the set to form sign complexes that also satisfy conditions (2) and (4).

It is not possible to specify how efficient and general the signs must be over what portion of the population before a language can be said to exist. By complex social processes, languages grow, evolve, and change in many ways; less efficient and less general signs are dropped (archaic ones) or modified, and new ones are added (such as *turbo jet, transistor*). Languages can be created de novo, as Esperanto was in the last century and as such computer languages as FORTRAN, COBOL, and ALGOL have been only recently. One person can create and use a language for his own purposes. Languages need not be social instruments, but they usually are. Clearly communication between people is greatly facilitated when they share a language, but it is not precluded when they do not share one, as many foreign travelers know.

Conclusion

Up to this point we have considered only the elements of communication — the *material* from which communications are made. In Chapter 11 we take up the process of communication — how signs, messages, and language are used.

REFERENCES

Cherry, Colin. *On Human Communication*. New York: John Wiley & Sons, 1957.
Creelman, M. B. *The Experimental Investigation of Meaning*. New York: Springer Publishing Co., 1966.
Gardiner, A. "The Definition of the Word and the Sentence." *British Journal of Psychology*, 12, Part 4 (1921–1922), pp. 352–61.
Langer, Suzanne. *Philosophy in a New Key*. New York: Penguin Books, 1948
Loundsbury,. F. G. "The Varieties of Meaning." In *Communication and Culture*, edited by A. G. Smith. New York: Holt, Rinehart & Winston, 1966.
Morris, C. W. *Foundations of the Theory of Signs*. Vol. 1, No. 2. International Encyclopedia of Unified Science. Chicago: University of Chicago Press, 1938.
————. *Signs, Language, and Behavior*. New York: Prentice-Hall, 1946.
————. *Signification and Significance*. Cambridge, Mass: The M.I.T. Press, 1964.
Ogden, C. K., and I. A. Richards. *The Meaning of Meaning*. New York: Harcourt, Brace & Co., 1947.
Osgood, C. E., G. J. Suci, and P. H. Tannenbaum. *The Measurement of Meaning*. Urbana: University of Illinois Press, 1957.

11

Models of Communication

NOISE, *n.* A stench in the ear. Undomesticated music. The chief product and authenticating sign of civilization.

The Devil's Dictionary

Introduction

We will consider first the situation in which one purposeful individual chooses a message to go to another purposeful individual about something. Following Heider (1946), we will let *p*, *o*, and *x* represent the person, the other, and the something, all as seen by the individual. Later, when we consider intercommunication between at least two purposeful individuals, we shall use the *A*, *B*, and *X* notation introduced by Newcomb (1966) to distinguish this situation.

Choice of Message: The p-o-x Model

Whether *p* chooses to send a message to *o* about *x*, and the kind of message he chooses to send are matters likely to be affected by the following properties of *p*, some of which will have been produced by the behavior of the other. The other, it should be noted, need not be in the same physical environment; he need not even exist, as when one decides to pass on a message to future generations. Also, the other may simply be some other purposeful state of oneself, as when one writes down a telephone number for later use. Now to the properties:

1. p's *beliefs about* x: pUx.
   What structural and functional properties *p* believes *x* to have; that is, his *image* and *concept* of *x*.
2. p's *attitude toward* x: pLx.
   What *p* feels about *x*: the value he places on it.
3. p's *belief about* o: pUo.
   In particular, how *p* believes *o* will respond to possible messages from *p* about *x*. This, in turn, probably depends on what *p* believes the following properties of *o* to be:

179

    a. o's beliefs about x, oUx: $pU(oUx)$.
    b. o's attitude toward x, oLx: $pU(oLx)$.
    c. o's beliefs about p, oUp: $pU(oUp)$.
    d. o's attitude toward p, oLp: $pU(oLp)$.
4.   p's *attitude toward* o: *pLo.*

Given our definition of communication (9.1) the beliefs that are relevant to p's choice of communicative behavior to o about x are beliefs about the probable choices, efficiencies, and probable outcomes of x for himself, and for o. His feelings and motivations concern the relative value for himself and o. These beliefs are a function of the components of the choice situation, as discussed in Chapter 3. What is significantly different from the purposeful state that we discussed there is:

1.   the components of the state include o, for p, and, at least potentially, p for o.
2. p believes that o is also a purposeful individual capable of knowing and choosing from the courses of action available in the situation.
3. p believes, therefore, that he and o are potential coproducers of change in the parameters of the state of each other and hence of their behaviors.

These are the characteristics of a sociopsychological choice situation as distinct from the psychological choice situation considered in Chapter 3, assuming that the individual system is a person and not a group (Asch, 1950, pp. 161–62).

In this situation one of the most striking changes is that liking, where it refers to another purposeful individual, is operationalized as seeking to *benefit*, and *disliking* as seeking to *harm*. The test of whether p likes o is whether, when the outcomes for p are unaffected, he makes the choices that he believes will help o to better pursue his ends. This is not the same as devotion, love, or loyalty since it implies no notion of sacrifice as they do.

This last step provides us with all the conceptual tools we need to develop measures of the probability of p's choosing a particular course of communicative action. He may elect to inform, instruct, or motivate o with the intention to harm or benefit him. Of course, he may elect to inform, instruct, or motivate o so that o will inform, instruct, or motivate him in such a way that he can benefit or harm the other. He may choose with a more extended course of intercommunication in mind. What he chooses will be a function of the components of the situation, himself, the other, the courses of action (including communicative action), the outcomes, and the environment. The parameters that directly affect his choice will be the usual ones — familiarity, knowledge, understanding, and intention.

We are now theoretically able to solve the problem that Heider (1946) introduced: How do p's beliefs and attitudes about himself, another, and something, coproduce p's choice of behavior with respect to o and x? The only testable hypotheses we can generate about these relations must be ones that specify the familiarity, knowledge, and understanding of *p* and of his model of *o*, and the relative values held by *p* and attributed to *o*. Any or all of these parameters could coproduce the message that *p* sends to *o* about *x*. Knowledge of these parameters and the functions relating them to each other would be sufficient to predict and/or explain *p*'s communicative behavior.

The research program this analysis points up is that of empirically determining the effects of changing one parameter on another, with the others constant. An example of what this entails was given in Chapter 3, where a measure of sensitivity was developed to measure the tendency of a purposeful system to learn more about the things it is most concerned with. Similar measures could be constructed within the framework we have presented to show the sensitivity of familiarity and understanding to intention and vice versa. The relations between the nonintentional parameters would be part of such a research program. It seems, for instance, that understanding is more sensitive to familiarity than to knowledge. Similarly it seems that in some situations familiarity (say, buying a book) lessens the efficiency of that course of action because the person is less likely to read it now that it is in his possession.

Our model spells out the essential requirements for experimentation within the suggested program. If, for instance, experiments were designed to study the effects of familiarity on intention, it would be necessary to control for knowledge and understanding. Failure to do so would make it impossible to interpret the results.

The appeal of Heider's *p-o-x* model was that it suggested certain constellations under which *p* would want to harm or benefit, or like or dislike, or change his beliefs about either. These were constellations that he defined as harmonious or in equilibrium, or disharmonious in disequilibrium. We will discuss these in connection with *A-B-X* situations where both individual purposeful systems are communicating.

Before proceeding to *A-B-X* models we want to make some conceptual distinctions in the general properties of the medium through which *A* can communicate with *B*. Beliefs about these will also enter into *A*'s choice of message.

Noise and the Choice of Message

The message that *A* sends to *B* about *X* may differ from the message *B* receives from *A* about *X*. These may differ structurally or functionally. A vocal message over the telephone may be distorted, cut off, or obscured by *noise*. A printed message may be smeared or torn. A television picture may be obscured by snow. In each of these cases the message received is structurally different from the message sent. Anything that alters the structure of the message produces syntactic noise.

11.1.   *Syntactic noise:* any structural difference between a message sent and the message received.

Even if a message is not changed structurally, it may not be received (that is, interpreted or decoded) as it was sent. What is intended as a compliment by *A* may be interpreted as an insult by *B*: "You look so much younger than you are."

11.2.   *Semantic noise: ambiguity in the denotation or connotation of a message.*

A message may be misinterpreted — that is, *B* responds to the wrong thing — and still produce the type of response intended. *A* may be annoyed by noise he believes is caused by a radio and tell *B*, "Shut that thing off." *B* may turn off the television set, which is actually causing the noise.

11.3.   *Pragmatic noise:* anything that appears in a message or its environment that was not produced by the sender and that decreases the probability of the receiver's responding in the way intended by the sender.

Hence syntactic noise may not produce pragmatic noise; however syntactically noisy a message may be, it may be received correctly and responded to as intended. On the other hand, a syntactically noise-free message may fail to produce the desired response because something diverts the attention of the receiver. Furthermore, as mentioned above, a receiver may respond to a message as intended even if it is ambiguous and hence full of semantic noise. Syntactic and semantic noise *may* produce pragmatic noise, but need not necessarily do so. (For an experimental situation in which it does, see Heise and Miller, 1966.)

11.4.   *The amount of pragmatic noise* in a message received is the difference between the probability that the message sent will produce the sender's intended response by the receiver and the probability that the message received will produce that response.

This measure can vary from $+1$ to -1. A negative measure indicates that the interference has enhanced the sender's chances of success. This may occur when a message sent in a language that is not understood by the receiver is translated into a language that he does understand. Unfortunately we do not have a term to signify negative noise.

THE RECEIVER'S EFFECT ON A MESSAGE

The response to a message that *B* receives from *A* about *X* is a product not only of the message that *A* sent but also of some of *B*'s properties:

1.   *B*'s beliefs about *X*, *BbX*.
2.   *B*'s attitude toward *X*, *BaX*.
3.   *B*'s beliefs about *A*, *BbA*.
4.   *B*'s attitude toward *A*, *BaA*.

Note the similarity to *A*'s relevant beliefs and attitudes.

If *A* combines his relevant beliefs about *B*, the environment, and the medium through which he communicates to *B* into a model that predicts what message *B* will receive and how he will respond to it, given the message *A* has sent, then *A* can use this model to effectively formulate his message. To take a simple case, if *A* knows that *B* will only receive every other word of a message, he can obviously formulate the message so that when received it is what he intends. In more complex cases *A* can use his knowledge of how *B* usually responds to various types of messages to frame a message whose chances of producing the intended response are high — for example, knowing what form of request a person is most likely to respond to. Parents frequently tell children not to do what they want the youngsters to do because they believe a negative response is more likely than a positive one.

REDUNDANCY

If *A* has doubts about either the message *B* will receive or how it will be interpreted, he may repeat the message or send it in several different forms that he indicates are intended to be equivalent. This allows the receiver to select the alternative that is least ambiguous to him. Expressions starting with *that is, i.e., in other words,* and *put another way* have this function. They provide deliberate redundancy in the message.

Like other concepts in communication theory (*noise, information*) *redundancy* can be dealt with at either the syntactic, semantic, or pragmatic level; at each it has a different meaning.

Syntactic redundancy reflects the lack of randomness in the selection of signs, symbols, or messages. For example, most persons can correctly supply the missing letter in Q–ICK: U. The U is therefore redundant because there is relatively little, if any, free choice involved in its selection. Similarly, a message that begins with "A stitch in time" need not be completed for many because they know what follows. Warren Weaver (1966) has put it as follows.

> Having calculated the entropy (or the [syntactic] information or the freedom of choice) of a certain information source, one can compare it to the maximum value this entropy could have, subject only to the condition that the source continue to employ the same symbols. The ratio of the actual to the maximum entropy is called the relative entropy of the source. If the relative entropy of a certain source is, say, eight-tenths, this means roughly that the source is, in its choice of symbols to form a message, about 80 percent as free as it could possibly be with these same symbols. One minus the relative entropy is called *redundancy*. That is to say, this fraction of the message is unnecessary in the sense that if it were missing the message would still be essentially complete, or at least could be completed (p. 21).

Syntactical redundancy can overcome the effects of syntactical noise. A. G. Smith (1966) points this out as follows.

> Redundancy . . . improves the accuracy with which signals are transmitted. . . .
> Redundancy is the repetition of a signal that . . . helps overcome noise.

If the same signal is simply repeated over and over again, the redundancy is 100 per cent. There is no variability or indeterminacy at this high degree of redundancy. The receiver can predict with confidence what the next signal will be. This means . . . that the signal has no surprise and carries no new information. There is too much redundancy for communication. Zero percent redundancy leaves the receiver with sheer unpredictability—the next signal can be anything. At this low degree of redundancy the receiver cannot tell what is noise and what is information. The fact is that communication requires a balance between the predictable and the unpredictable (p. 365).

Semantic noise and redundancy have not been treated as extensively as have their syntactic counterparts. Macy, Christie, and Luce (1966) provide one of the few discussions of these concepts that we have seen. They treat semantic (or coding) noise much as we have—as ambiguity (which, of course, has been discussed extensively, but not as it relates to noise). Semantic redundancy, then, arises from the use of synonyms. The more extra names for the same thing that are used or remembered, the greater the semantic redundancy. The experiment reported by Macy *et al.* (1966) "supports the hypothesis that [semantic] redundancy is used to overcome the errors due to semantic noise" (p. 291).

To the best of our knowledge, pragmatic redundancy has not been dealt with in the literature. It is a difficult concept because it appears to be unrelated to other types of redundancy. Note, first, that a necessary (but not a sufficient) condition for pragmatic redundancy is that it produce no functional response. If it produces such a response, then it is necessary for that response and hence is not redundant. But now we observe that messages completely redundant in the syntactic sense may not be redundant in the pragmatic sense. Seeing or hearing a play that one knows by heart or hearing a memorized musical composition may affect the receiver—produce a response in him. A message, however well it is known, may still do something to the receiver. This is obviously the assumption, if not the fact, behind repetition of commercial messages and pledges of allegiance to the flag.

The same message may produce the same or different responses at different times. "Close the door" when addressed to one of our children, to whom it is a highly redundant message syntactically, is nevertheless effective pragmatically since it produces a behavior that would not otherwise occur. In fact, repeating the message several times in a row often increases the probability that one's child will respond as intended and hence even the repeated messages are not pragmatically redundant. This, too, is a basis for repeated advertising messages.

We noted that failure to elicit a response—a change in the functional properties of the receiver—is only a necessary, not a sufficient, condition for pragmatic redundancy. That it is not a sufficient condition is apparent from a situation in which a person is told something that he either does not believe to be so or does not feel to be right, and he does not respond even though what he is told is completely unfamiliar to him.

Therefore, a message is completely redundant in the pragmatic sense if the response intended by the sender has already occurred and is not reproducible. It is *ineffective* if it fails to produce an intended response when the receiver has *not* so responded previously. If after one has instructed his child to close a door, and he has already done so without its being observed, and the order is repeated, it is pragmatically redundant. The child has already responded and cannot do so again. If, however, his parent tells him to pick up the papers on the floor and he does so but drops some in the process, then a repetition of the message is not pragmatically redundant, even if he is aware of having dropped some papers and knows what his parent will say. Even if he intended to pick up the dropped papers *later*, and his parent's remark produces a response *now*, it produces a change in his behavior and is not pragmatically redundant.

As much as we have said only classifies messages as completely redundant or not; it does not provide a measure of such redundancy.

11.5.   *The amount of pragmatic redundancy* in a message relative to a receiver is the percent of elements of the message (letters, words, sentences, or any message unit appropriate to the inquiry) that can be eliminated without changing the receiver's response to it.

To illustrate how this measure can be applied, we describe an exploratory experiment that several colleagues and one of us conducted to determine the effect of condensation on articles appearing in scientific journals. Since the experiment was conducted for exploratory purposes only, small samples of articles, journals, and subjects were used. This work was not intended to be reported in the literature, but only to indicate whether or not a certain line of inquiry was worth pursuing.

A number of experts in the field of operations research were asked to classify articles that had appeared in recent issues of several journals dealing with operations research. The classes used were above average, average and below average. Eight articles were selected — their quality was agreed on by all the experts — four above and four below average. Letters were sent to the authors of the selected papers, requesting that they prepare an objective examination on the content of their papers — an examination that was to be given to graduate students to whom the papers were to be assigned for reading. They were also asked to provide the answers. All did so.

Other experts who were knowledgeable in the subject matter of the papers were asked to use a red pencil and reduce each paper first to two-thirds and then to one-third of its original length. They did so only by eliminating words, sentences, or paragraphs; not by rewriting. In addition, the abstracts of the articles that had appeared in the journals with them were also used. Therefore, each article was available in four versions: 100, 67, and 33 percent, and abstract.

Each of a group of graduate students who had not previously read the papers were given one version of each paper. Each version of each paper was assigned at random to an equal number of students. After reading the papers, each student took the examinations prepared by the authors of the original articles.

There was no significant difference (at the 0.5 significance level) in the average performance on the examination among those who read the papers in their 100, 67, or 33 percent form. This was true for both the above- and below-average papers. These results indicate, using the measure of pragmatic redundancy constructed here, that each paper was at least 67 percent redundant.

Those who read only the abstracts of the above-average papers obtained an average grade significantly lower than that obtained by those who read the paper in any of its longer forms. The average grade of those who read abstracts of the below-average papers was not significantly lower than the grade of those who had read these papers in one of their longer forms. The redundancy of the poorer papers was therefore significantly greater than that of the better papers, but the amount of redundancy in each of them was surprisingly large. Unfortunately we did not give the examinations to students who. had not read the papers in any form.

If results such as these are reproducible in an experiment large enough and properly designed, they would indicate that a considerable amount of condensation of scientific literature is possible without any significant loss of effectiveness. The amount of condensation justified by study of pragmatic redundancy would probably be much larger than that justified by study of syntactic or semantic redundancy.

The results obtained in this exploratory study help to explain the following observation by Martin and Ackoff (1963).

> The fact that Digests, or Abstracts, are read twice as much [by physicists and chemists] during browsing [as compared with directed reading] might not be expected by some. It is consistent with the findings of the earlier study in which it was found that abstracts are used more as a substitute for articles than as a guide to them (pp. 330–31).

An article that lacks any pragmatic redundancy may also lack readability. The optimal amount of redundancy, however, remains to be determined. It is likely to be dependent on other aspects of the communication situation — for example, the attitudes and beliefs of the participants.

We have already noted that a message that contains syntactically or semantically redundant parts may not be pragmatically redundant. A part of a message, or a message that is pragmatically redundant, however, must be either syntactically or semantically redundant, or both. Hence, a message (or part of one) may be redundant in all three senses.

A message that is pragmatically redundant in the absence of pragmatic noise may not be redundant when such noise is present. For example, a lecturer may repeat important points to be sure he catches some members of the audience during one of their intermittent moments of attention. Furthermore, sheer repetition can often penetrate inattention.

Redundancy is not the only way of overcoming noise; *feedback* is another.

FEEDBACK

If *A* can observe *B* receiving his message while he is sending it, he may obtain information from *B*'s behavior that is usable either in formulating the as yet unsent part of his message or in reformulating the message already sent. Teachers and lecturers, of course, constantly make use of such feedback in formulating their messages to their audience.[1]

11.6. *Feedback:* information received by the sender of a message about the receipt of or response to his message.

Therefore, feedback is a stimulus that produces a response in the sender of a message. More generally, feedback is information obtained by any functional entity about the product of its behavior. The product need not be a message; it may be any type of behavior. The feedback that a message sender receives may itself be a message from the receiver of his message. This observation leads us into consideration of two-way communication.

Two-Party, Two-Way Communication: A-B-X *Model*

Two-way communication between *A* and *B* involves a minimal sequence of messages:

$$[(A \text{ to } B \text{ re } X) \rightarrow (B \text{ from } A \text{ re } X)] \rightarrow [(B \text{ to } A \text{ re } Y) \rightarrow (A \text{ from } B \text{ re } Y)]$$

where → represents *produces* and *X* and *Y* may be either the same or different subjects. The sequence of messages may, of course, be extended to a larger number than two.

The conceptualization of *A*'s communicating to *B* given in the first part of this chapter can also be applied to *B*'s communicating to *A*, and hence the model of a two-way communication emerges from that for one-way communication. The new ingredient is that each message after the first may be (but is not necessarily) a response to any of the preceding messages, the sender's or the receiver's.

In Chapter 9 it was shown that a message may inform, instruct, and/or motivate its receiver, whatever the intention of the sender. The sender, of course, may intend to inform, instruct, or motivate either the receiver or himself.

11.7. *Question:* Any message sent by *A* with the intention of producing a responsive message that will inform, instruct, or motivate *A*, whatever its structure (syntax).

---

1. See chap. viii of Smith (1966) for discussions of the effect of feedback on communication and performance of tasks.

When *A* sends a question to *B*, he *asks* him something. On the other hand, if the intent of *A*'s message to *B* is to inform, instruct, or motivate *B*, *A* *tells* *B* something.

11.8.   *Statement:* any message sent with the intention of informing, instructing, or motivating the receiver.

A *question* and a *request* are related but are not identical.

11.9.   *Request:* If *A* sends to *B* a message that *A* intends to produce a choice of any type of course of action (including, but not necessarily, communication) by *B* that *A* wants, then *A* makes a request of *B*.

Every question is a request for further communication, but not every request is a question; for example, "Please, close the door."

Some other important types of messages related to those just considered require the concept of *reward* and *punishment*.

11.10.   *Reward:* An individual is rewarded for doing (or not doing) something if his action (or lack of action) produces behavior in another (or himself) that increases his probability of obtaining something he wants (benefits him).

11.11.   *Punishment:* An individual is punished for doing (or not doing) something if his action (or lack of action) produces behavior in another (or himself) that decreases his probability of obtaining something he wants (harms him).

11.12.   *Threat:* a message that signifies both an intention by the sender that the receiver does (or does not do) something and an intention by the sender to punish the receiver if he does not do (or does) that something.

11.13.   *Promise:* a message that signifies both the intention of the sender to do something of value to the receiver (commitment), and the intention of the sender to receive punishment if the intended act is not carried out (obligation).

11.14.   *Order:* a request that carries with it a threat of punishment to the receiver if he does not respond as the sender intends he should.

Requests and orders do not require two-way communication, but questions do. Questions require answers.

Minimal two-way communication may consist of (*a*) tell–tell, (*b*) ask–tell, (*c*) ask–ask, (*d*) tell–ask. A communication that terminates with a tell may or may not be complete; one that ends with an ask is necessarily incomplete; it leaves a request unfilled.

An important class of communications between *A* and *B* about an *X* consists of those that can be viewed as attempts to produce agreement or disagreement between *A*'s and *B*'s beliefs and/or attitudes toward *X*. Newcomb (1966) has examined this process and formulated several postulates about such communication. In Appendix III we analyze one of these postulates, and by so doing show how the conceptual system provided here can enrich Newcomb's assertions, make them more precise, and provide the basis for designing effective tests of their validity.

In Appendix III we also attempt a translation of Rapoport's (1960) important hypotheses about debates.

More than Two-Party Communication

Whestley and MacLean (1966) have produced a very provocative conceptual model for research on communications that involve more than two parties. Their concern is *mass* communication, but we believe their concepts can be fused with ours to produce a more general model of what may be called (following Bavelas, 1966) *chain communication* — situations in which *A* communicates to *B* through *C*. We shall refer to *C* as an *intermediary* in this context. The model is extendable to any number of intermediaries and hence to a chain of any length. Furthermore, by reversal of roles (say between *A* and *B*) types of communication networks other than the chain result.

Whestley and MacLean restrict the concept of an intermediary (*C*) to something that acts without purpose (in their sense) and without intention to affect the receiver (in our sense): "*C*s serve as agents of *B*s in selecting and transmitting non-purposively the information *B*s require, especially when the information is beyond the immediate reach of *B*" (p. 87). Why they so restrict the function of the intermediary is not clear. It seems that the intermediary may alter the intended content of the sender's message (by censorship, editorializing, or other) so as to change its effect on the receiver. Then the intermediary's behavior would be intentional in our sense and purposive in theirs. The intermediary obviously may act as a filter and as a condenser of messages, as well as a distorter, collector, or transmitter of messages.

It is possible to formulate a more general conception of social communication than has been developed by Whestley and MacLean. Let us begin with the obvious.

Messages from different sources (*A*s) about the same *X*, even if intended for the same receiver (*B*), may be structurally or functionally dissimilar either: (1) because of the differences in what two or more *A*s observe even when they observe the same *X*; or (2) because of the difference in their relevant beliefs and attitudes involving *X*, *B*s, *C*s, and any other individuals in the system; or (3) because of differences in their abilities to formulate effective messages. Such differences create the need for evaluating alternative sources of information, instruction, and motivation.

When *A*s intentionally send messages about *X*s to *C*s, they may intend the *C*s to be receivers, not intermediaries. The neighborhood gossip may retransmit a message that the sender had not intended to go any further. *C*s may intercept messages not intended or intended not to reach them (as when a newspaper reporter overhears a conversation and reports its content). Indeed, *C*s may conceive of their role as largely that of obtaining from *A*s messages that the *A*s do not intend to make available to *B*s or, for that matter, to Cs. This appears to be so where private investigators, secret agents, or exposé journalists are involved.

We should like to discuss in detail the communication functions that intermediaries (and senders and receivers as well) can perform. First consider the production of a message.

11.15.   *Encoding:* the act of producing a message.

Note that this is encoding in the pragmatic sense. It implies encoding in the syntactical sense, but such encoding does not imply pragmatic encoding. Syntactic encoding can produce a set of signs that are not capable of communicating. In pragmatic encoding, a set of signs is produced to signify something the producer has experienced – perceived, thought, intuited, or felt.

11.16.   *Decoding:* the production of a response by a message to what it signifies.

Decoding in this pragmatic sense similarly implies syntactical decoding, but the converse is not necessarily true.

Although *encoding* is often used synonymously with *translation*, we prefer to use them differently.

11.17.   *Translation:* the act of changing the signs in a message from one language into another.

Thus translation presupposes encoding. The sender, receiver, or intermediary may translate a message.

A message is encoded by the sender and decoded by the receiver. It is *transmitted* from the sender to the receiver.

11.18.   *Transmission:* the behavior by whose means a message produces a response in the receiver.

11.19.   *Channel:* the instruments (objects, events, and their properties) that produce transmission.

In sending a letter the postal service is the channel, in telephonic communication it is the telephone system, and in speech it is the atmosphere.

Intermediaries as well as senders and receivers can affect messages in several ways. It is convenient to consider these in connection with possible roles of intermediaries.

Intermediaries may be passive; that is, they may receive whatever is sent to them and transmit it without intentional modification. As we have already indicated, however, they may actively intervene in the communication between senders and receivers. Such intervention may serve the senders' and receivers' purposes either well or poorly. Rewriting news reports may be useful to the pressured sender and ultimate receiver; but censorship may serve neither's purpose well.

First, consider *passive* intermediaries, ones whose only effect on messages is structural (not functional). In the most extreme case they serve only as a channel: they receive and deliver the message to the receiver. The post office, messengers, and the telephone system act in this way. The intermediary may also transform the signs of a message into structurally different but functionally equivalent signs, as when a secretary takes dictation and types a letter. Frequently such transformations are made to facilitate *storage* of the message until it can be received or is wanted by the receiver. The intermediary may store and subsequently retrieve the message from storage, as in libraries and file systems.

Passive intermediaries, then, are ones that transmit, structurally transform, store, and retrieve messages. They can be classified into one of four types.

1. The *one-to-one* intermediary who receives messages from only one source (*A*) and transmits them to only one receiver (*B*). Such an intermediary can be one- or two-way. If two-way, it also receives messages from *B*, which it transmits to *A*. There seem to be few intermediaries of this sort, except in such contrived situations as are constructed in laboratory experiments involving communication: we have known cases in which two persons who are not on speaking terms will communicate to each other through a third party. Feelers between two nations at war are frequently handled through a third party — often many third parties.

2. The *many–one* intermediary who receives messages from many sources and transmits them to only one receiver. In these cases the intermediary's function can be likened to that of a funnel. A secretary frequently performs this function. Some intelligence officers in the military do so for the senior officer to whom they report. Directors of marketing research often serve in this function for marketing executives.

3. The *one–many* intermediary who receives messages from one source but transmits them to many receivers. Such an intermediary *disperses* messages. A public relations or press officer may serve this function. A book's publisher thus serves its author.

4. The *many–many* intermediary who, of course, receives messages from many sources and transmits them to many sources. Newspapers, journals, and libraries are such intermediaries.

Active intermediaries do more than affect the structure or transmission of messages. As already noted, they may translate messages — transform them from one language into another. In addition they may perform numerous other functions, among the most important of which are *filtration, condensation,* and *editing.*

11.20.   *Filtration:* the selection of a subset for transmission to a receiver, from the set of messages intended for him.

An intermediary may filter messages with the intention of better serving the receiver's purposes, as in transmitting only messages that he believes are of value to the receiver. Or the intermediary may filter for its own or another party's purposes. When it does so, it engages in *censorship.*

11.21. *Censorship:* filtration that is intended to serve the purposes of a party other than the sender or receiver of a message.

The refereeing process used by most professional journals is intended to serve the receivers' purposes and hence is not censorship, but it is filtration. Filtration always involves *evaluation* of messages for their effectiveness. It attempts either to eliminate undesirable responses from the receiver's or someone else's point of view, or to eliminate messages that will produce no response (ones that are completely redundant).

11.22. *Condensation:* the reduction of the number of signs in a message or the transformation of them into a set of signs whose receipt requires less time than did the original message.

The intermediary may either reduce the message while trying to retain its essential content in order to reduce the receiving time required (*digest* the message), or provide a brief description of its content so that the potential receivers can decide whether or not they want to receive the full message (*abstract* the message). A digest is intended to replace the message. An abstract is intended to provide a basis for deciding whether or not to receive the message; thus it serves as an instrument for filtration.

11.23. *Editing:* the act of changing a message with the intention of increasing its effectiveness for the sender and/or the receiver.

Not only editors but also (at least good) secretaries perform this function. The sender himself may perform the editorial function.

When there is an intermediary between A and B, and A intends to communicate to a particular B or class of Bs, his beliefs about and attitudes toward C may also affect his formulation of his message. B's corresponding beliefs and attitudes involving C may also affect what message he receives and how he responds to it. This is particularly so when two different Cs transmit inconsistent messages on the same subject (such as contrary accounts in different newspapers of the same event). Which of conflicting messages on the same subject the receiver believes is largely influenced by his beliefs about and attitudes toward the subject of communication, the senders, and the intermediaries. As Whestley and MacLean have pointed out, a receiver may select that intermediary whom he believes will most efficiently serve his purposes.

THE ARBITRATOR AS INTERMEDIARY

Arbitrators in conflicts between two parties (labor and management or two nations in a dispute) serve as intermediaries operating in both directions. They may meet with each party separately until they have established a basis for direct (nonintermediated) communication between the two parties, or they may meet with both parties together and attempt to direct the communication between them. It is apparent that the attitudes of the conflicting parties toward the intermediator has a considerable effect on his effectiveness in producing agreement. Then A's attitude toward the arbitrator is likely to be strongly influenced by (1) what A believes is C's attitude toward A — $Ab(CaA)$ — and (2) what A believes is C's attitude toward B — $Ab(CaB)$. The same is true for B. A's attitude toward C is likely to be favorable if A believes C's attitude toward A is more favorable (or no less favorable) than is C's attitude toward B.

One function of the arbitrator is to define the issue — the differences between A and B. Hence, he may go through a process much like that advocated by Rapoport (1960) for the parties of a debate. He may formulate A's and B's beliefs and attitudes in a way that is acceptable to them, and he may try to find the conditions in which each believes the other's position is valid. Therefore, he can serve as a facilitator of the type of debating process that Rapoport advocates.

The arbitrator seeks a way of resolving or dissolving the conflict once the problem has been defined. If he does not find a way, then he may try to find an equitable solution, one that removes exploitation and/or reduces the intensity of conflict. (See Chapter 12 for discussion of these concepts).

It should be apparent from this brief discussion that many hypotheses concerning the effectiveness of arbitration can be formulated within the conceptual system constructed here. Examples are hypotheses that relate the arbitrator's effectiveness to the attitudes of the conflicting parties toward him and his attitudes toward them, and hypotheses that relate his effectiveness to the parties' beliefs about familiarity, efficiency, and outcomes.

Communication within Groups

The chain is obviously only one type of network by which multiple parties can be connected. A detailed analysis of different types of communication networks and ways of characterizing them can be found in Bavelas (1966). Experiments dealing with the effects of such networks on communication and task performance can be found in Leavitt (1966), Guetzkow and Simon (1966), Shaw *et al.* (1966), Mulder (1966), and Macy, Jr., *et al.* (1966). Note that a network is a property of a group, not of the separate individuals that compose it.

The most complex network is one in which every party can communicate directly with every other party. For a group of three, four, or five individuals such networks can be represented as is shown in Figure 11.1.

Consider the simplest of these, the three-party network. The attitudes of each party towards the other two are now relevant to the behaviour of each. Even if these attitudes are treated dichotomously (as favorable and unfavorable), there are $2^6 = 64$ possible permutations of attitudes. In general, if there are n persons there are $2^{(n^2 - n)}$ permutations of attitudes. Thus even for five persons there are more than a million permutations of just

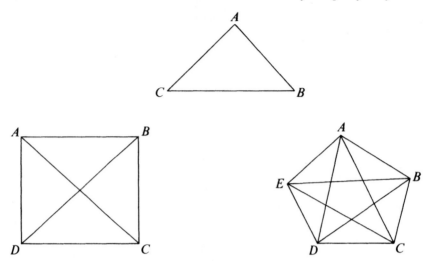

Figure 11.1.   Three-, Four-, and Five-Node Networks

their attitudes. If we ignore the individuality of the participants and treat them as equivalent points in the network, then we can deal only with the combinations (not permutations) of attitudes. For $n = 3$, there are seven such combinations.

Favorable	Unfavorable
6	0
5	1
4	2
3	3
2	4
1	5
0	6

In general, there are $n(n-1)+1$ such combinations. Hence for five persons there are twenty-one combinations of dichotomously treated attitudes. But in order to get down to this number we must give up considering each party uniquely; therefore much of the psychological content of the situation is sacrificed. The reason for making this sacrifice is apparent: a model of an interaction of individuals that treats each person uniquely would be too complex to handle. Remember that we have considered only their attitudes toward each other, and these only dichotomously. We have not considered their attitudes toward X nor any of their beliefs.

It becomes clear why groups are seldom conceptualized as the sum and interactions of their parts. For practical reasons it is necessary either to depersonalize the members of a group or to treat the group itself as an individual, hence the emergence of sociology.

Similar difficulties create physics from mechanics. Even if the behaviour of bodies can be explained in principle when complete knowledge of each of their point particles and their interrelationships is available, it is not feasible to deal with bodies in this atomistic way. Bodies are themselves treated as individuals.

In Chapter 13 we discuss the conceptual transition from purposeful individual to purposeful group as an entity, and indicate how the group can be treated as a teleological system. We also consider how this conceptualization can be made completely compatible with that of the individual we have developed. Chapter 12 is concerned with the concepts of cooperation and conflict introduced here.

REFERENCES

Ackoff, R. L. *et al. Model Study of Escalation: Report of 1964–1965 Studies.* Philadelphia: Management Science Center, University of Pennsylvania, March 1, 1966.
Asch, S. E. *Social Psychology.* New York: Prentice-Hall, 1952.
Bateson, Gregory. "Information, Codification, and Metacommunication." In Smith (1966), pp. 412–26.
Bavelas, Alex. "A Mathematical Model for Group Structure." In Smith (1966), pp. 216–22.
Guetzkow, Harold, and Simon, H. A. "The Impact of Certain Communication Nets Upon Organization and Performance in Task-Oriented Groups." In Smith (1966), pp. 244–53.
Heider, F. "Attitudes and Cognitive Organization." *Journal of Psychology* 21 (1954): 107–12.
———. *The Psychology of Interpersonal Relations.* New York: John Wiley & Sons, 1958.
Heise, G. A., and G. A. Miller. "Problem Solving by Small Groups Using Various Communication Nets." In Smith (1966), pp. 283–85.
Leavitt, H. J. "Some Effects of Certain Communication Patterns on Group Performance." In Smith (1966), pp. 222–43.
Macy, J., Jr., L. S. Christie, and R. D. Luce. "Coding Noise in a Task-Oriented Group." In Smith (1966), pp. 285–94.
Martin, M. W., and R. L. Ackoff. "The Dissemination and Use of Recorded Scientific Information." *Management Science* 9 (January, 1963): 322–36.
Mulder, Mank. "The Power Variable in Communication Experiments." In Smith (1966), pp. 259–74.
Newcomb, T. M. "An Approach to the Study of Communicative Acts." In Smith (1966), pp. 66–79.
Rapoport, Anatol. *Fights, Games, and Debates.* Ann Arbor: The University of Michigan Press, 1960.
Shaw, M. E., G. H. Rothschild, and J. F. Strickland. "Decision Processes in Communication Nets." In Smith (1966), pp. 253–59.
Smith, A. G. *Communication and Culture.* New York: Holt, Rinehart & Winston, 1966.
Weaver, Warren. "The Mathematics of Communication." In Smith (1966), pp. 15–24.
Whestley, B. H., and M. S. MacLean, Jr. "A Conceptual Model for Communications Research." In Smith (1966), pp. 80–87.

12

Conflict, Cooperation, and Competition

DISCUSSION, *n.* A method of confirming others in their errors.
The Devil's Dictionary

Introduction

In the last three chapters we have been concerned with how one purposeful individual can affect another through communication. In this chapter we examine in more detail the kinds of effect one purposeful individual or system can have on another — that is, the nature of their interactions.

Two related concepts are central to this discussion: *conflict* and *co-operation*. From these concepts others will be derived; the most important are *exploitation* and *competition*. We will also consider how the interactions between two individuals can be affected by these individuals or others. Communication, of course, is one of the more important ways of affecting such interactions.

The components and parameters of a choice situation play an important role in this discussion, so let us review them briefly. We continue to use A and B to represent subjects, but we introduce T to represent third parties. S continues to represent the environment of subjects. C_i $(1 \leq i \leq m)$ represents the courses of action available in the environment, and O_j $(1 \leq j \leq n)$ represents the possible outcomes. Both courses of action and outcomes are considered to be so defined as to be exclusive and exhaustive unless otherwise noted. The parameters of the choice situation are: P_i, the probability that C_i will be selected in $S (\Sigma_i P_i = 1.0)$; E_{ij}, the probability that C_i will produce O_j in $S (\Sigma_j E_{ij} = 1.0)$; and V_j, the relative values of O_j to the subject in S. We shall assume that relative values range from zero to one, but this assumption is not critical since appropriate adjustments can be made in what follows to take account of any scale of relative values, including ones with negative values.

The expected relative value (EV) of a choice situation to a particular

196

individual (A) is given by

$$EV_A = \sum_i \sum_j P_i E_{ij} V_j.$$

*EV*s have a maximum value of one and a minimum value of zero.

Cooperation and Conflict

Consider two individuals, A and B. Let $(EV_A \mid B)$ represent the expected relative value to A of his choice situation when B is present in it; and $(EV_A \mid B')$ represent this value when B is *not* present in it. $(EV_B \mid A)$ and $(EV_B \mid A')$ are the corresponding expected relative values for B.

12.1.   *Cooperation, conflict, and independence:* In a particular state (S) if:

  1. $(EV_A \mid B) > (EV_A \mid B')$, then B cooperates with A;
  2. $(EV_A \mid B) < (EV_A \mid B')$, then B conflicts with A;
  3. $(EV_A \mid B) = (EV_A \mid B')$, then A is independent of B.

Therefore, if B's presence increases the expected value of A's state, B cooperates with A; if B's presence reduces this value, he conflicts with A; and if he has no effect on A's expected relative value, A is independent of B.

12.2.   *Degree of cooperation and conflict:* The degree of cooperation of B with A is

$$DC_{BA} = (EV_A \mid B) - (EV_A \mid B').$$

The degree of conflict of B with A is

$$DC'_{BA} = -DC_{BA}.$$

These measures can take on values from -1 to $+1$. Negative values of the degree of cooperation represent conflict and the converse. Note that cooperation and conflict exhaust the ways in which one individual can affect the expected relative values of another.

Nothing in the definitions of cooperation and conflict requires either of the parties to be conscious of, or to intend, his effect on the other. One person may inadvertently affect another whose presence he may not even be aware of, as when one person begins to use a telephone whose extension is being used by another.

12.3.   *Degrees of cooperativeness, hostility, and independence:* If, in an environment occupied by A and B,

  1. B's potential courses of action can be grouped into three exclusive and exhaustive classes

     C_1: courses of action that have efficiency equal to 1.0 for increasing EV_A

     C_2: courses of action that have efficiency equal to 1.0 for decreasing EV_A

     C_3: courses of action that have no effect on EV_A

  2. all the courses of action are equally efficient for all outcomes not affecting A but desired by B, and

3. *B* is aware of these efficiencies, then

P_1 = his degree of cooperativeness toward A,
P_2 = his degree of hostility toward A, and
P_3 = his degree of indifference toward A.

One individual may be cooperative or hostile toward another in a particular situation because of the effect the other has on him. *Ascendancy* is stimulated hostility and reflects a desire to get even with an aggressor. *Aggressiveness* is unstimulated hostility. One can be ascendant without being aggressive; that is, become hostile only if provoked. Although one could be aggressive without being ascendant, this does not seem likely.

Exploitation

The degree to which one individual (B) cooperates or conflicts with another (A) need not equal the degree to which A cooperates or conflicts with B. Thus two individuals may affect each other differently. This difference is a measure of *exploitation*.

12.4. *Degree of exploitation:* The degree to which one individual (B) exploits another (A) is

$$DX_{BA} = DC_{AB} - DC_{BA},$$

and the degree to which A exploits B is

$$DX_{AB} = 1 - DX_{BA} = DC_{BA} - DC_{AB}.$$

This measure can range from -2 to $+2$. By use of this measure we can distinguish between three kinds of exploitation. If DC_{AB} and DC_{BA} are both positive but unequal, then the two individuals cooperate with each other, but unequally. The one who benefits most can be said to be a *benevolent* exploiter of the other. This is the type of exploitation that most colonial powers have claimed for themselves when they have admitted to exploiting their colonies. Many employer–employee relations can also be characterized by this type of relationship.

If DC_{AB} and DC_{BA} are both negative but unequal, then A and B are in conflict with each other, but unequally. The one who suffers least can be said to be the *malevolent* exploiter of the other. Such an exploiter is one who is willing to suffer if he can make another suffer more than he does. This is usually the case when revenge is involved. Many wars are examples of malevolent exploitation.

Finally if one party cooperates with the other but the other is in conflict with him, we have a case of what might facetiously be called *normal* exploitation. This seems to characterize the historic relationship between slave and master.

The degree of exploitation is the difference between the degree of conflict of A with B and B with A, and hence is a measure of the asymmetry of the effects that two individuals have on each other. The sum of these degrees also has significance.

12.5. *Intensity of cooperation (conflict)* between two individuals, both of whom cooperate or conflict with each other, is the sum of the degrees of cooperation (conflict) between them.

This sum has meaning only if A and B are in cooperation or conflict with each other (the signs of DC_{AB} and DC_{BA} are the same). Negative values represent intensity of conflict, and positive values represent intensity of cooperation. Minimum and maximum values are -2 and $+2$, respectively. If $DC_{AB} = DC_{BA} \neq 0$, then even though there is no exploitation there is an intensity of conflict or cooperation. Intensity can increase as exploitation decreases, and exploitation can increase as intensity decreases. On the other hand, they may increase or decrease together.

12.6. *Escalation (de-escalation) of conflict (cooperation):* an increase in the intensity of conflict (cooperation) between two or more parties.

One seldom hears about the escalation (de-escalation) of cooperation but it is clearly as significant as escalation (de-escalation) of conflict.

Competition

In the literature of psychology, social psychology, and sociology there is a good deal of qualitative discussion about the difference between conflict and competition. One of the more commonly cited differences is the presence of physical force in conflict and its absence in competition. This difference does not seem valid to us because, for example, a prizefight is normally thought of as a competition, while a street brawl is thought of as conflict. Although the use of force or physical contact does not seem to be essential to conflict, it can play an important role in it – a role we discuss below.

We make no attempt here to survey the copious literature on the distinction between conflict and cooperation, but we do want to cite the most suggestive definition we have found – that of Katz and Schanck (1937). In essence, they argued that competition is conflict *according to rules* and hence is *constrained* conflict. This does distinguish between a prizefight and a street brawl, but although we can think of no case of competition that does not have rules, we can think of instances of conflict that also have rules. Wars, in contrast to riots, have rules, but we do not believe war is competition. Nations at war are not supposed to use chemical and biological weapons, are supposed to treat prisoners and cililians in certain ways, and so on; *but* these rules are frequently broken, and there is no authority to enforce them and to punish the offender. Therefore, although rules seem necessary for competition they do not seem sufficient. However, we think the essential difference between conflict and competition can be found in the function of those rules that operate where competition occurs.

In a prizefight and other sporting events, rules are imposed by an authority to protect the interests of both the participants and the audience. In economic competition, governments impose rules to protect the public, if not the participants. The rules in economic competition do not prevent the elimination of a participant, but they usually reduce the likelihood of such an occurrence. In a private tennis match or chess game, rules are not imposed by an authority, but they are accepted voluntarily by the players because doing so serves their interests. Therefore although conflict appears in competition, it appears to be constrained by rules that serve either a common purpose of the participants or the purpose of a third party. Let us try to make this more precise.

12.7 *Competition:* Two individuals, A and B, are in competition in an environment (S) if the following conditions are satisfied:

1. A's degree of intention for outcome O_1 in S is greater than his degree of intention for another outcome O_2. The converse holds for B.
2. Of the set of courses of action available to A and B in S $\{C\}$, there is a subset $\{C^*\}$ such that choices by either A or B of any member of this subset that increases (decreases) the probability of O_1 occurring in S, decreases (increases) the probability of O_2 occurring in S. (O_1 and O_2 cannot both occur simultaneously).
3. There is a third outcome (O_3) possible in S, which may occur with O_1 or O_2 and which is intended either by both A and B or by a third party (T).
4. The conflict between A and B relative to O_1 and O_2 in S is efficient relative to O_3 in S.[1]
5. If A (B) selects a course of action not in the subset $\{C^*\}$, the other individual or T can punish him with respect to his pursuit of O_1 (O_2).

It should be apparent that this definition can easily be extended to cover more than two participants.

When the third (or cooperative) outcome (O_3) in competition is a goal or objective of a third party (say, an audience) and *not* of the participants in the conflict, the competition can be said to be *extrinsic*. If O_3 is a common objective of the conflicting parties, the competition can be said to be *intrinsic*. Competition may therefore be both intrinsic and extrinsic, as in a tennis match between friends before an audience.

In intrinsic competition the ratio of the degree of intention of each competitor for the conflicting objective $(O_1$ or $O_2)$ to his degree of intention for the cooperative objective determines whether the competition is dominantly conflict- or cooperation-orientated for him.

---

1. In many cases a stronger condition is satisfied: the probability of O_3 occurring in S increases as the intensity of conflict between A and B relative to O_1 and O_2 increases. For example, the entertainment value of a sporting event generally increases as the intensity of the conflict between participants increases.

The rules of competitive behavior that define the subset of permissible courses of action $\{C^*\}$ are accepted by, and/or imposed on, the participants in order to assure the effectiveness of the conflict for the third (cooperative) objective. In economic competition, conflict between rival companies is supposed to serve the interests of the consumer. Laws and regulations are enforced to make sure it does. In our economic system it is illegal for two competitors to fix prices so as to exploit the consumer. They may, however, exploit each other. Infraction of the rules can result in punishment of the guilty party by the government either by the imposition of fines or by further restrictions on choice. In intrinsic competition an infraction of the rules by one party allows the other to impose some kind of penalty on him.

Ways of affecting conflict

The nature of conflict is such that either the environment in which it takes place or the behavior of one or more of the participants must be changed if the conflict is to be removed or reduced in intensity. To attempt to remove a conflict by changing its environment is to attempt to *dissolve* it; to do so by changing the participants is to *resolve* it. These modes of affecting conflict are available to third parties as well as to the participants.

12.8.   *Dissolution of conflict:* a change in the environment of a conflict so that the participants no longer conflict with each other.

12.9.   *Resolution of conflict:* a change in the behavior or properties of one or both of the participants so that they no longer conflict with each other.

To dissolve or resolve a conflict is to remove it. Curiously, however, when we speak of *solving* a conflict – as we do in the context of the theory of games – we do not necessarily imply removal of the conflict. To solve a conflict is to do as well as possible in the conflict situation. One might go further and suggest that solving a conflict is to rationalize it – to ensure that no more is put at stake and no more harm is intended by either party than is commensurate with such interests as are in conflict.

12.10.   *Solution of conflict:* selection by a participant from among courses of action available to him of the one that maximizes his expected relative value in the conflict situation.

Thus dissolving a conflict involves changing the environment, resolving it involves changing someone other than oneself, and solving it involves changing one's own behavior. Although these modes are exhaustive, they are by no means exclusive. Let us examine them in more detail.

DISSOLVING CONFLICT

Many conflicts that arise from unintended intrusions on the senses can be removed by modifying the environment. Several things can be done to the environment that may change the nature of one party's effect on the other. First, the environment can be modified so that the behavior of one participant no longer has an effect on the other. This is equivalent to separating the opponent from the one affected. If A is flashing a light in a room where B is trying to read and thus comes into conflict with B, a screen can be placed in a position so that it blocks the light. Note that this may allow both A and B to do what they were doing previously, but the conflict is removed. The objective was not to change A's behavior but to change its effect on B. The efficiency of such an effort clearly depends on whether A intends to conflict with B. If he does, such a separation of A and B is not likely to succeed because, for example, A may remove the screen or initiate distracting noises.

Second, conflicts that arise from scarcity can often be dissolved by making available more of whatever is scarce. If two children want the same ball and are in conflict over it, the conflict may be removed by providing a second ball of the same type as the first. If it is impractical or impossible to duplicate what is wanted, then, obviously, so is this mode of dissolving conflict. But where it is practical and possible it is an attractive way of removing conflict, because it does not involve changing the behavior of the opponents. In effect, it separates them.

Separation can also be accomplished by removing one or both of the conflicting parties from the environment. If A can induce B to leave, A has resolved the conflict. If he cannot induce B to leave, he may use physical force to remove B, or, what is equivalent, he may incapacitate B in the original environment. If force is used to remove or incapacitate a participant in a conflict, we have what Rapoport (1961) called a *fight*. A fight may dissolve the conflict from the point of view of the victor, but it does not do so from the point of view of the vanquished. As a result the hostility of the vanquished toward the victor is usually increased so that if an opportunity later presents itself he is likely to initiate another conflict, one that is often more intense than the first. Hence a conflict is not usually dissolved or resolved by a fight; it is usually suppressed temporarily and subsequently escalated.

RESOLUTION OF CONFLICT

Note that in a fight one participant attempts to remove the opponent by changing some of his relevant *structural* properties (such as his location or physical ability to act). This is done in order to affect at least one of his functional properties — his probability of selecting conflicting behavior. One may change this or some other functional property of an opponent without affecting him structurally. For example, one can make the cost of an opponent's selecting a conflict-producing course of action greater than the gain he can expect from it. The imposition of a *threat* on one or both parties of a conflict is to attempt to *deter* the conflict. The threat may be issued either by a participant or by a third party (like the government). The law and police are intended to deter potential criminals.

The threat of punishment or retaliation can be effective only if two conditions are satisfied: (1) the recipient of the threat is aware of the deterrent, and he perceives the expected costs imposed by it as greater than he can expect if he ignores it; and (2) he believes the deterrent will be used only if he selects the undesired course of action. If he does not believe the second – that is, he believes the deterrent will be used against him no matter what he does – then it may very well increase his chances of selecting the course of action it is intended to prevent. Hence the danger in a national policy based on massive deterrence lies in a nation's inability to convince others that this capability will not be used without the specified provocation. Similar remarks can be made about rewards for cooperation.

Note that the use of deterrents may not remove a conflict but only prevent it from escalating. It should also be observed that the use of deterrents is unlikely to reduce hostility even where it reduces the intensity of conflict.

To make an opponent aware of a deterrent or a potential reward may require communication with him, but communication may affect conflict in other ways.

Resolving Conflict by Communication. One party to a conflict may use communication to affect the other's behavior either by *informing* him (changing his probabilities of choice), or by *instructing* him (changing the efficiency of his choice), or by *motivating* him (changing the values that he places on outcomes), or by some combination of these. What Rapoport has called a *debate* is only one way of using communication to resolve a conflict: it is one directed toward changing those beliefs and/or attitudes that produce conflicting behavior.

Suppose one child (*A*) wants the ball that a second child (*B*) is playing with. There may be in the environment a second similar ball that child *A* is not aware of but child *B* is. *B* may inform *A* of the availability of the second ball and thus resolve the conflict. Obviously, this information may also be conveyed by a third party, such as a parent.

In general when one party (*A*) knows how another (*B*) can get what he wants without conflicting with *A*, and *B* does not know this, then *A* may inform *B* of the possible choice that will avoid or remove conflict. A third party may resolve a conflict by informing both parties of appropriate alternatives to what they are doing.

Suppose two persons want to use the one electronic computer available in the environment. If either tries to get exclusive use of the computer because he believes only one at a time can use it efficiently, conflict results. If instruction on how to run both problems simultaneously is supplied one party or an outsider to the one(s) seeking exclusive use, the conflict may be avoided or resolved. In general, instruction may be used to avoid or resolve conflict where two parties can obtain what they want by more efficient use of a course of action already selected by one or both parties.

Finally, if each of two persons in the same environment want something that both cannot have (as two children who want the same ball), conflict may be avoided or resolved by changing the desire of one or both parties through motivational communication. A parent may attempt to distract the child by interesting him in something other than the ball.

When both conflicting parties communicate with each other in an attempt to resolve or prevent escalation of conflict they can be said to be *negotiating*; that is, communication exists between the parties of a conflict, which they intend either to dissolve or resolve their conflict, or to prevent its escalation.

The way a negotiation is organized and the environment in which it is carried out can have considerable effect on its chances for success. Even such things as the arrangement of the room where negotiations take place can influence the outcome. Rapoport's (1960) discussion of ways to make a debate more productive of conflict resolution is relevant to negotiation as well.

Negotiation is often facilitated by a third party — a *mediator* — an individual who is present at negotiation of a conflict that he is not a part of, whose function it is to increase the probability that communication between the conflicting parties produces a resolution of the conflict.

Many conflicts cannot be resolved without outside intervention. It has been pointed out that one of the reasons many conflicts between nations are so difficult to resolve is that there is no third nation whom the conflicting nations respect equally as a neutral. Even in such cases it would still be possible to resolve conflicts if there were a third party strong enough to impose its will on those involved. If there were such a third party — as an effective world government — national conflicts could be *arbitrated* as labor–management disputes are. An *arbitrator* is an individual (or group) who resolves a conflict to which he is not a party, or prevents its escalation, by selecting the courses of action to be followed by the participants in the conflict.

The courts often serve as arbitrators in such areas as civil cases. Even in criminal cases the courts can be looked at as arbitrating a conflict between the accused and the state. Governments or governing bodies of organizations may appoint arbitrators for disputes between their members and impose such arbitration on them, using their power of punishment to make the imposition. In some cases (as in many labor–management disputes) the parties to the conflict themselves agree to the selection of an arbitrator and agree to be bound by his decision.

In many negotiations and arbitrations the objective is not so much to resolve conflict as it is to prevent its escalation. Escalation is likely to occur when one or both parties to a conflict believe they are exploited by the others. Hence most negotiations and arbitrations are directed to removing exploitation, not conflict. The parties involved are primarily motivated by a desire not to be taken advantage of. A conflict in which neither escalation nor de-escalation takes place can be said to have reached *equilibrium* or *stability*.

Inducing and Imposing Cooperation. In a fight at least one participant attempts to impose his will on the other. To impose behavior on someone is to give him no choice. Deterrents, rewards, and communication are used to *induce* (not impose) behavior preferred by the user. To induce behavior is not to remove choice. Rapoport (1961) argued that it is not possible to induce (produce choice of) desired behavior by use of physical force.

> To *induce* an action . . . is most physically impossible. The most you can do is offer a choice between alternatives, for example, "Sign this or die." We call such an offer intimidation by use of force, but in the last analysis, it is the Other who makes the choice. If he chooses not to sign, he cannot be forced to do so, because his nervous system and his muscles cannot be controlled by another in coordinated fashion (p. 215).

It is because of this apparent inability to impose cooperation on conflicting parties that pacifists have to be so passive. They can be passively against conflict and war, but not aggressively for peace. Put another way, one cannot impose cooperation on another without a fight, or at least so it seems.

The ancient Greeks endowed Cupid with the ability to impose love on another without the use of physical force. He was equipped with a unique bow and arrows for this purpose. If such instruments were generally available, it would change the entire logic of war and peace. If one person, *A*, behaved aggressively toward another, *B*, then *B* might shoot him with cooperativeness and thus impose a change of attitude on *A* without denying him choice. Then if *A* wanted to retaliate, he would shoot *B* with cooperativeness toward him.

However, even Cupid's bow and arrows could be used as instruments of conflict. One person could inflict cooperativeness on another in order to make it easier to destroy him. The ideal instrument of peace, therefore, would be one so designed that its user could not impose cooperativeness on another without doing so to himself. Instruments such as the Greeks gave Cupid, or the peace pills or gases that many have dreamed of, could not by themselves provide a permanent removal of conflict. The way they would be used is critical.

Instruments to impose cooperation are becoming a reality. In the May 1966 issue of *Esquire*, in an article, "Mind Control is Good, Bad. (Check One)" (pp. 106–9), A. J. Budrys reviewed recent technological developments that make it possible to impose cooperativeness and other functional properties on men and animals, at least under laboratory conditions. We already have the makings of conflict decontamination chambers. The question of how well we will use the power of Cupid, once we have it, remains open.

SOLUTION OF CONFLICT

When an individual finds his effectiveness reduced by the behavior of another, or his own behavior is reducing the effectiveness of another, he may either remove himself from the conflict environment or change his behavior in that environment. If he restricts himself to looking for a course of action that is intended to minimize the undesirable effect another person can have on him, then he treats the conflict as what is now commonly called a game, and he seeks what is called a solution to it. In such cases a game is used as a representation or model of the conflict situation. Many, if not most, theories of conflict are based on such representation. See, for example, von Neumann and Morgenstern (1953) and Howard (1966).

The methods of disposing of problems that were discussed in Chapter 7 are highly relevant to the search for ways to handle conflicts. We do not repeat them here because the main task of this chapter has been to define and explore the concepts of cooperation and conflict. These concepts are included in Chapter 13 to analyze the properties of social groups and organizations.

Conclusion

In experimental conflict situations when communication between participants is prevented it has been observed that the participants attempt by their actions alone to make their intentions known to, and influence, the others. People tend to cooperate more when they can communicate with each other than when they cannot. An even stronger observation has been made: even when communication is possible but is not used, people tend to cooperate more than when it is prohibited. (These and related findings are reported in Management Science Center, 1967.) This indicates that the mere possibility of communication tends to reduce the hostility between conflicting parties. In the experimental work in this area with which we have been involved, communication has had a greater positive effect on cooperativeness than any of numerous other variables tested.

It is a curious characteristic of our culture that we have expended much more research effort on increasing our effectiveness in conflict than in cooperation. An ability to do the first does not imply an ability to do the second. This imbalance in allocation of research effort and resources is reflected in our ability to wage war more successfully than we wage peace.

Cooperation is not merely the absence of conflict. Furthermore, even if two parties cooperate with each other one may be the benevolent exploiter of the other. Even this kind of asymmetry breeds conflict (as in the outcome of benevolent colonialism). Hence reduction of exploitation among co-operators is as difficult a problem as any involving the control of conflict.

Social groups are normally held together by cooperative interactions among their members. It is not surprising, therefore, that most of the research on cooperation has been done as part of research on group behavior. It is to such behavior that we now turn.

REFERENCES

Howard, Nigel. "The Theory of Meta-Games." "The Mathematics of Meta-Games." *General Systems* 11 (1966): 167–200.

Katz, Daniel, and R. L. Schanck. *Social Psychology.* New York: John Wiley & Sons, 1938.

Management Science Center. *"A Model Study of the Escalation and De-escalation of Conflict."* Mimeographed. Philadelphia: University of Pennsylvania, 1 March, 1967.

Rapoport, Anatol. "Three Modes of Conflict." *Management Science* 7 (1961): 210–18.

von Neumann, J., and O. Morgenstern. *Theory of Games and Economic Behavior.* 3d ed. Princeton, N. J.: Princeton University Press, 1953.

IV

Social Systems and Beyond

Chapter 13 is a consideration of systems whose components are purposeful individuals — social systems — and how they affect and relate to their parts. In Chapter 14 we take the step beyond purpose suggested in Chapter 3, and define and characterize ideal-seeking systems. Finally, Chapter 15 takes us still further, and we come back to the concepts we started with but, we hope, with considerably enriched versions of them.

13

Social Groups as Systems

HUMANITY, *n*. The human race, collectively, exclusive of the anthropoid poets.

The Devil's Dictionary

Introduction

Most sociologists do not observe group behavior but the behavior of individuals in groups. In fact, a great deal of sociology has nothing to do with group behavior. Whereas psychologists are primarily occupied with the uniqueness of each individual's behavior, many sociologists, equally occupied with individual behavior, are preoccupied with similarities of behavior of different members of a group. Therefore, the objects observed are the same in psychology and much of sociology, but the properties of concern are different; one seeks to describe and explain differences, and the other looks for similarities.

The historian, who deals with the behavior of nations, alliances, political parties, revolutionary movements, has been more sociologically oriented than has the sociologist.[1] The economist and management scientist deal with companies, industries, and even nations as entities. To study these entities they do not observe the behavior of their individual members but the behavior of the groups taken as a whole, as an entity. For example, a company's pricing policy, its growth in sales volume, its profits, acquisitions, diversifications — all are group behavior. To be sure, knowledge of them could be obtained by observing individual members of the firm, but this is not the way it is done. A contract between labor and management is the product of negotiation between individuals, but it is also a group product.

Given that we can observe the properties of a social group without observing the properties of its members, it follows that we can also observe its behavior, since behavior is simply a change of properties over time. We can and do speak of a nation's selecting war or negotiation as a means to an end. Since we can talk meaningfully of a group's behavior, we can also discuss the outcomes that it does and does not produce — that is, its function. Hence

---

1. See Stretton (1969) for a detailed exposition of this point.

211

we can also consider the choices of a group and characterize them by use of the same conceptual scheme developed for the study of an individual's choice. A reexamination of the conceptual system developed in this book will reveal that it has no properties that restrict its application to persons (to *psychological* individuals). It is equally applicable to groups (to *social* individuals).

Therefore, it is meaningful to talk of a group's *personality*, but we would prefer to call this its *culture*, for we believe culture is to a group what personality is to an individual: its general choice function. We can also speak of the familiarity, knowledge, understanding, intention, vacillation, traits, as well as the many other properties discussed here. Often we may prefer to call these properties by other names when they refer to groups, but in trying to find other names we discover that the social sciences have hardly dealt with such properties of groups, at least not in a scientific way.

Social Individuals and Groups

13.1. *Social individual:* any collection of psychological individuals that is itself treated as an individual.

Individuation of a social individual requires specification of the rule(s) for inclusion and exclusion of psychological individuals from the collection over a specified period of time. For example, the people whose names appear on a specified page of a telephone directory constitute a social individual, as do residents of the city of New York who own automobiles. In the first group the specification of membership is denoted since the members are identified by name; in the second the specification is connotative since membership properties are given. It is possible in principle, of course, to translate any connotative specification into a denotative list of members.

The populations and the samples drawn from them that are used in social surveys of any kind (censuses or markets surveys) are social individuals. Identification of those who are members of such a collection may be difficult, as those who have conducted social surveys are well aware. Defining a population is the same as identifying a social individual.

What is here called a social individual is sometimes broken into two different types of entities: a *category* and an *aggregation*. According to Cuber (1959):

> A category is any number of persons who are thought of together, whether they are in communication or not. An aggregation is a collectivity of persons who are held together in a physical sense by some factor other than intercommunication (p. 298).

Thus, the people whose names appear on a specified page of a telephone directory would be a category in this sense, whereas those who visit a seaside resort on a specified day would be an aggregation.

A social individual is the most inclusive type of social entity. The principal concern of the social sciences, however, is with a particular type of social individual, the *social group*. This is a less general concept because although all social groups are social individuals, not all social individuals are social groups. The identifying characteristics of social groups have been treated at length but without precision in the literature of sociology. As Mizruchi (1967) points out, "the typical definition of a group includes the assumption that two or more persons are in interaction" (p. 113). To define social group in terms of social interaction or social relationship is to define circularly; hence to leave social interaction and social relationship undefined, as is usually done, is to leave social group undefined. The blatancy of this circularity is reflected in the following statement from Gouldner and Gouldner (1963):

> A group consists of two or more people in interaction: the term *group* refers to repeated and patterned social interaction. We shall use the terms *social interactions* and *group* more or less interchangeably throughout the text . . . (p. 98).

In line with our discussion of the individuality of systems in Chapter 3, we propose a definition that does not suffer from the circularity of asserting that a group is what a group does.

13.2. *Social group:* a purposeful system whose members are purposeful individuals and who are intentionally coproducers of a common objective.

13.3. *Common objective:* an outcome intended by each member of a social individual.

We must be careful to distinguish between *common* and *analogous* objectives. For example, if each member of a collection of people wants a car for himself, the members have analogous objectives. If each member wants every member to have a car for himself, there is a common objective. Analogous objectives are ones that differ only with respect to the individual involved in the outcome. Objectives are not the same unless the individuals involved in them are the same. Analogous objectives are similar but not the same.

All the members of one of two competing teams have a common objective: to beat the other team. The members of the second team also have a common objective: to beat the first team. The common objectives of the two teams are analogous. Members of a group may have more than one common objective. Groups whose members have many common objectives are sometimes referred to as multipurpose.

The intention to coproduce common objectives is what produces the interactions that lead individuals to cohere as a social group. This does not mean that each member must have at least some face-to-face interaction with every other member. It means only that over time each has some contact with some of the others some of the time. The members of a social group can cooperate with one another by some form of communication or through intermediaries. Again this does not imply that means of intracommunication are always available to each member. It does imply that such contact as there is tends to further the common objective.

In groups that are extended over space and time, the complexity of the cooperation required to pursue common objectives imposes formidable secondary tasks on groups. These are largely organizational tasks but by no means entirely so: nor do the organizational tasks simply arise from what is needed for cooperation.

To say the members of a social group share a common objective is not to say that they do not *conflict* (see definitions 12.1 and 12.2) with respect to other objectives or even with respect to the courses of action by which the common objective should be purused. Similarly, we cannot ignore the factors that may lead to relative indifference or *independence* (see definitions 12.1 and 12.2) with respect to achieving the common objective. Such conflicts hinder and disrupt cooperation and communication, and undermine the cohesiveness of groups. Consequently the organization of groups must be adapted to manage conflict and assure adequate communication and cooperation with respect to the group's common objective.

These complexities have long led sociologists toward a systems approach that would identify the parts and their interrelations while still retaining a primary focus on the group as such. There has been an awareness, usually implicit, that even if every part performs as well as possible relative to its subobjective, the total group will often not perform as well as possible relative to the common objective(s). However, even the best of the early empirically oriented systems studies were essentially using closed-systems models and focusing on the cooperative behaviors functional to achieving some common objective. A major landmark in sociological theorizing was Merton's attempt to generalize this approach to encompass dysfunctional effects of conflict (Emery and Trist, 1960). However, Nagel (1956, in Emery, 1969) applied Sommerhoff's theory of systems to show that Merton's systems model was even too primitive to study goal-seeking systems. The main points that Nagel made were the following.

1. The initial parameters of Merton's system are not independent (pp. 312–13).
2. The inability to introduce the individual as anything more than a "role-carrier" renders "vacuous" his distinction between manifest and latent functions (p. 318).
3. The relative value of different functional requirements for a system can be established only by reference to the special material characteristics. A generalized solution cannot be expected (p. 321).
4. There is no recognition of the environment which must be an independent coproducer for any goal-seeking behavior (p. 324).
5. There is no recognition that a real system has only a limited range of states (p. 325).

6. There is no recognition that the functional relations between the parameters of a system may be changing over time (p. 327).

In short, Merton's systems theory is of a class of functioning systems best represented by a working clock. However, the Sommerhoff-Nagel model is still only that of a goal-seeking system. It is not a model of purposeful systems such as we believe social groups to be.

What is required is that social groups be systematically studied at their appropriate system level. This we shall not attempt to do. In Parts I and II we have provided what we think is a systematic treatment of purposeful systems in general and purposeful psychological systems in particular. We believe that the concepts and measures developed for purposeful psychological systems are relevant to the study of social individuals In the earlier chapters of Part III we have dealt with matters of common interest to psychology and sociology. There remain, however, some matters quite central to sociology, and it is these that we now consider.

RELATIONSHIPS BETWEEN SYSTEMS AND THEIR ELEMENTS

Psychologists conceptualize persons as individuals who constitute systems. Social psychologists conceptualize persons as individuals who are elements of systems (social groups), and they are thus primarily concerned with people's interrelationships. Sociologists conceptualize groups as individuals who constitute systems: hence sociologists are preoccupied with collective behavior. These different points of view are not competitive. Each is necessary, each distinct but interrelated.

13.4. *Social system:* a system whose elements are purposeful individuals.

Thus a social group is clearly a social system. Such systems are concrete and dynamic, and are generally, but not necessarily, conceptualized as open.

One of the most important characteristics of a system — one that shows why a system is either more or less than the sum of its parts — is the relationship between its behavior (taking the system as an individual) and that of its elements (taking them as individuals).

The relation between a system and its elements has some of the characteristics of instrumentality discussed at the end of Chapter 2. As we noted there, the instrumentality of a system tends to be of a lower system order than the system. Thus, although a social system is a purposeful system, all of whose elements are purposeful, there is a constant tendency toward *increasing* or *decreasing variety* in the range and level of the behavior of the elements. In that the individual elements are instrumental to the system, the system will be *variety decreasing:* the range of purposeful behavior will be restricted, and increasingly behavior will be at a lower level of multi-goal-seeking or goal-seeking behavior. In that the system is instrumental to its component elements, it will tend to be *variety increasing:* the range of purposeful behavior will be extended, and increasingly behavior will be at the higher level of ideal-seeking (discussed in Chapter 14).

These system tendencies underline some of the basic dilemmas in the design of organizations. For example, in sociotechnical systems concerned with the efficient production of goods and services, it has been difficult to design the system so as to permit the component human elements to behave as purposeful systems, let alone ideal-seeking systems. The apparent success that has arisen from reorganizing work around small, relatively autonomous groups would seem to follow from the shift in instrumentality (Emery and Trist, 1969). When the small social system becomes an instrument for its members there is a tendency for it to become *variety increasing*; they are able to pursue not only production goals but also purposes and even ideals that pertain to themselves.

Similar difficulties have been found in designing sociopsychological systems whose objectives are to change the values, knowledge, and other psychological properties of at least one subset of its members (universities, prisons, hospitals, churches). To the degree that their members are instrumental to these systems' achieving their social purposes there will be a tendency toward *variety reduction*: the very behavior that would manifest the higher values of these systems will tend to be inhibited. Designing for an *increase in variety* in these systems may take us in directions like those of the autonomous work groups (Ackoff, 1968; Emery, 1970).

The relation of instrumentality is inherent in the relation between a purposeful system and its purposeful elements.

A system must be either variety increasing or variety decreasing. A set of elements that collectively neither increase nor decrease variety would have to consist of identical elements; either only one can act at a time, or similar action by multiple units is equivalent to action by only one. In the second case the behavior is nonadditive and hence is redundant. The relationships between the elements would therefore be irrelevant. For example, a set of similar automobiles owned by one person do not constitute a system because he can drive only one at a time and which one he drives makes no difference. On the other hand, a radio with two speakers can provide stereo sound; the speakers each do a different thing, and together they do something that neither can do alone.

Because a system must be either variety increasing or variety decreasing, it must be either more or less than the sum of its parts. This property of systems justifies study of them as individuals and study of the interrelationships of their parts. If systems were variety maintaining, such studies would be unnecessary. We would need to study only their elements as individuals. This shows why psychology is not enough to understand human behavior, why social psychology and sociology are also required.

Not every kind of aggregation of persons constitute a social group. All that do, constitute systems. But social groups are a special kind of system, a purposeful system, all of whose elements are purposeful.

Whether a social group is variety increasing or variety decreasing depends on how it is *organized*. Thus organization or its absence is an important property of social systems. A social group will be variety increasing only if it is so organized that its elements are able to behave in the system as ideal-seeking systems. In the special cases where the social system is degraded to the level of goal-seeking behavior there will be an increase in variety if it is unable to prevent its elements from acting as purposeful systems. Variety reduction will occur if the organization is able to prevent the purposeful behavior of its members. An instructive illustration of this point is Abel's (1951) analysis of the sociology of concentration camps.

An important example of the relation between a system and its elements is that of territorially bound communities that most of mankind lives in. Much of the current interest in the quality of life these provide for their members is bound up in the question of whether the communities are variety increasing or variety reducing, how much so, for whom, and with respect to what aspects of their lives.

We can indicate a set of measures that may throw some light on this relation between communities and their members. Basically we pose the question: Given that the community members are purposeful individuals, how does the functioning of the community affect the parameters of their choices? It is only through these effects that a community can enhance or reduce the variety of choice open to its members.

1. *Probability of Choice.* How likely are the members to choose, as a matter of custom or shared personal preferences, the same courses of action in production of the community's instruments (broadly defined as in definition 2.50)? The greater the likelihood, the greater is the ease of cooperation. It is this measure that is the usual basis of attribution of community spirit.

2. *Efficiency of Choice.* How efficient are the courses of action made possible by the community's instruments, facilities, and services, for how many of the community? Both of these questions are relevant. If the average efficiency of the community's transport is high, because of the high level of car ownership, communality can still suffer if those without cars have access to only very poor public transport.

3. *Probable Outcomes.* How many outcomes are possible and how many are probable for different members of the community? Again both questions are relevant. Havana before Castro probably provided a greater range of possible outcomes to purposeful behavior. Whether for its members there has been a subsequent decline in the quality of the community could be decided only by considering the redistribution of probabilities of outcomes for members.

If we recall that probability of outcome for the individual is a function of both probability of choice and efficiency, we may also ask what is the cor-respondence between the preferred courses of action of the community's members and the efficiency of these courses of action. Sinking resources into a highly efficient parks department may bring pride to the community's elders but adds little to the quality of life for the members who suffer for lack of food.

4. *Relative Value.* What, for the members, are the relative values of the outcomes probable in the community? It may well be that a community that provides wealth and also a high risk of personal violence is one that does less well on the first three measures than does a community that offers less of both.

In setting out these measures of how a community may influence the choice behavior of its members we have not been defining a community but just describing an exhaustive set of categories of the effects that a community can have on its members. A definition follows.

13.5.   *Community:* a social group that provides its members with, or provides them with access to, instruments for the satisfaction of some of their analogous objectives — instruments that some of its members are responsible either for producing and maintaining, or for providing the group with the means for acquiring and maintaining them, and that all its members are responsible for using in a way that does not reduce access to them by any others in the group.

It will be noted that although we selected this example of system–element relation because of the practical importance of territorial communities, the territorial condition occurs neither in the definition nor in the suggestions for measures of the quality of community life. Nevertheless, the conditions we refer to are more likely to pertain in bounded geographic areas. However, what we have said about communities is equally true of social groups whose time span for the pursuit of their purposes is unusually long, compensating for territorial separation (as communities of scholars, in some disciplines), or for groups with a high degree of access to modern forms of communication — those already living in McLuhan's "world village."

Organized and unorganized social systems

Certain types of groups are called *organizations*. We speak of both the organization of activity and the organization of the individuals that act. As we shall see, the activities of organizations are organized, but not all groups whose activities are organized are organizations: their activities may be organized by someone else.

An organization is a social system in which the state of a part can be determined only by reference to the state of the system. The effect of a change in one part or another is mediated by changes in the state of the whole. Given our definition of a social system, it follows that an organized social system has the same properties of self-selection of courses of action in repetitions of the same situation or in varying situations with respect to common objectives.

However, an organized social system presupposes that various choices relevant to system functioning are being made by various parts (division of labor), or that parts are differentially responsible for different parameters of system choice. This potentiality arises because the members of a social system are themselves purposeful individuals, and as such, as noted in Chapter 11, are able to make choices with respect not only to their own purposes but also the purposes of others. Organization is the realization of this potentiality, particularly in regard to the situation where there are four or more others and the complexity of relating to each individual and their potential interrelations starts to rise sharply.

So long as this potentiality is not realized, we are dealing with an *unorganized social group*, one in which the individual elements, although themselves purposeful, cannot make the purposeful choices of the group. The most detailed descriptions of such groups have probably been made by Bion (1961) in his study of small, face-to-face leaderless groups. His observations disclose the same parameters of group choice that we have postulated, but in the apparently paradoxical circumstances of the individual purposeful members behaving at the level of goal-seeking systems. The individuals react more or less adaptively to each new situation. This led Bion to postulate a set of basic group emotions: basic because when the group choice was apparent, the individual seemed only to adapt like a goal-seeking system to the situation; and emotions for the same reason – namely, an absence of conscious individual choice.

The basic emotions that Bion identified were dependency, flight–fight, and pairing. Given our previous discussion of communication between purposeful systems, it seems likely that these phenomena reflect the basic parameters of individual choice that are taken over by group choice at various stages. Thus as intention ceases to be an individual function it is experienced as flight–fight without the usual corresponding feeling that one has chosen to do either. As relative efficiency ceases to be an individual function it is experienced as easy pairing, a miraculous dropping of the barriers of differences between individuals. We have not mentioned the effect of the situation when the unorganized purposeful group determines probability of outcome (the joint variation of efficiency and probability of choice). We feel that this is probably the state of mind of the Bion group when in W (when it is work-oriented).

As Bion points out, he was not the first of even modern social scientists to note these peculiar properties of unorganized social aggregates. Tarde, Le Bon, McDougall, and Freud all gave serious attention to this problem as manifested in various forms of collective or mob behavior.

Our own very cursory analysis supports Bion's observations on one further highly relevant point. Group emotional responses are also properties of organized groups. As we shall see, they may be more attenuated in groups that enhance the variety and level of choice of their members, but may be more accentuated in groups that reduce the variety and lower the level of behavior possible for their members. In organized social systems these are usually referred to as morale problems.

We have not attempted to suggest an explanation of one critical aspect of these phenomena – namely, purposeful members of a system behaving at a subpurposeful level. This we take up after we have considered some of the concepts necessary for the analysis of organizations.

In particular, it seems necessary to spell out the concepts of division of labor, responsibility and authority. Without the first, no part of a system could hope to effectively carry out any of the particular functions of a purposeful system, and without observance of the second and third no part would be likely to survive as a part of a purposeful system. These are weak statements to make about the development of organizational form, but they are the only kinds of scientific statements we can expect. If there is no practiced division of labor, then the probability is low that one part of a system will effectively coproduce with other parts the outcomes the system wants. If there is a practiced division of labor recognized in the agreed allocation of responsibilities and authorities, then the probability that different parts will coproduce the desired outcomes is enhanced.

FUNCTIONAL DIVISION OF LABOR

A functional division of labor occurs in a group when the choices to be made are divided into functionally dissimilar subobjectives, and these subobjectives are assigned to different parts of the group (subgroups). Let us make this more precise.

1. Pursuit of the common objective of a group can be decomposed into a finite set of different choices such that if these choices enable their corresponding subobjectives to be attained, then the common objective will be obtained at least to some degree some of the time. No subset is ever sufficient for obtaining the common objective; hence each choice in the set is necessary. There are always alternative decompositions (and, hence, alternative sets of choices) that are sufficient for obtaining the common objective in some environments. This is the reason that different groups with analogous objectives may and do organize themselves differently, or that one group may reorganize itself without changing its objectives.

To take a very simple case, suppose a car is stalled on a highway, and the common objective of its occupants is to move it to the side of the road. This objective can be decomposed into two necessary and potentially sufficient choices: how to steer the car to the side of the road and how to push it. Hence two people can organize themselves for this purpose, provided they have the capabilities necessary to coproduce the objective. A baseball team divides its objective of beating the opposing team into nine different subgoals: pitching, catching, and so on. A company divides its objective into research and development, purchasing, production, marketing, personnel, finance, legal, and so on. Within marketing, for instance, it may divide its objectives with respect to geographic regions.

2. The members of the social group are divided into subgroups with one or more members in each. An individual may be part of one or more subgroups, but no two subgroups have the same composition. Every member of the social group must be a member of at least one subgroup.

3. Each subobjective is assigned to one subgroup, and each subgroup has at least one subobjective assigned to it. Assignment of a subobjective to a subgroup involves giving the subgroup responsibility for obtaining it. To accept such responsibility is to accept the *right* of the group or its agent to *punish* members of the subgroup if they do not perform satisfactorily.

13.6. *Organizational responsibility:* one psychological or social individual (*A*) is responsible to another individual or social group (*B*) if, when *A*'s behavior does not satisfy *B*, *B* can punish *A* without conflict from *A*.

If a member of a baseball team fails to perform satisfactorily, he may be fired or otherwise penalized. Individual responsibility involves acceptance of the *right* of someone to punish. The person or group to whom responsibility is assigned may not recognize this right. A criminal may not recognize himself as a member of society and hence not accept the right of society to punish him; he feels no responsibility to it (Fingarette, 1967). Society may nevertheless hold the criminal responsible and exercise its authority to impose punishment on him whether or not he accepts society's right to do so. For organizations incapable of complete surveillance of members – and this seems to cover all organizations – the allocation of organizational responsibility assumes that the individual sees himself as a member of the system.

A psychological or social individual can be responsible to himself or itself. This involves punishing oneself for failure to meet an expectation. Such behavior is not uncommon, although it may not be as common as rewarding oneself.

13.7. *Organizational authority:* one psychological or social individual (*A*) has organizational authority over another (*B*), both of whom are members of the same social group, if *A* can redefine the subobjectives that *B* must pursue, or if when *B* fails to satisfy *A* in his pursuit of the objectives of their social group, *A* can punish *B*.

Again we find a potential discrepancy between individual and group definitions. An individual may fail to redefine or to punish, and thus effectively abdicate from his organizational authority. He may redefine another's responsibilities or punish him for his shortcomings when he has no authority to do so; that is, he may arrogate to himself authorities for which he has no corresponding responsibilities.

The concept of division of labor may now be defined.

13.8. *Functional division of labor:* A social group has a functional division of labor if (1) its common objective is divided into a set of different sub-objectives, each necessary and all sufficient for the attainment of the common objective in some environment; (2) each member of the group is a member of some subgroup; (3) no two subgroups have identical membership; (4) each subgroup is responsible to the group for attaining one or more subobjectives; and (5) each subgroup has a unique set of subobjectives.

13.9.   *Organization:* a social group with a functional division of labor relative to its common objective(s).

ORGANIZATIONS AND ORGANISMS

Organisms are frequently used as an analogue of organizations. Herbert Spencer, tried to build a whole sociology in which social groups were treated as organisms. Although his effort failed, the reasons for the failure do not seem to be well known. As a result, efforts like his continue to appear in a wide variety of disguises (Burns and Stalker, 1961). These experiments have failed because there is an essential difference between organisms and organizations, even though many similarities exist. This difference alone would be sufficient to justify the difference between biology and sociology.

Both organisms and organizations are purposeful systems, but *organisms do not contain purposeful elements.* The elements of an organism may be functional, goal-seeking, or multi-goal-seeking, but not purposeful. In an organism only the whole can display will; none of its parts can.

Because an organism is a system that has a functional division of labor it can also be said to be *organized.* Its functionally distinct parts are called *organs.* Their functioning is necessary but not sufficient for accomplishment of the organism's purpose(s).

THE FUNCTIONAL CHARACTERISTICS OF ORGANIZATIONS

The way a task is decomposed and assigned to subgroups of an organization is usually called its *organizational structure.* But this use of structure is different than our use of the term as the contradictory of function. Organizational structure is a functional concept describing the allocation of choice. The simplest aspect involves determination of who is to be responsible for what. The more complex aspects involve determination of which parameters of choice should be influenced by whom (such as staff functions) (Selznick, 1957). In this section we deal with only the simpler aspects.

Any task may be decomposed in a number of different ways; some are more efficient than others. Measurement of the efficiency of an organization's division of labor is not a simple matter. Here we develop such a measure for a very simple organization, and by so doing indicate how a measure can be developed for more complex organizations. (Discussion of a general measure can be found in Sengupta and Ackoff, 1965.)

The objective of any organization can be described in very general terms as one of maximizing its gains (G) minus its losses (L): $\max (G-L)$. Even in the simplest organization there must be at least two controllable variables $(X$ and $Y)$; otherwise there would be no need or advantage to dividing its activity into parts. In pursuit of its objective the group attempts to select values of the controlled variables $(X$ and $Y)$ that maximize $(G-L)$. The group's *objective function*, then, can be represented by

$$\max_{X, Y} (G-L). \tag{1}$$

Suppose the gain (G) is a function (f_1) of only one controlled variable (X):

$$G = f_1(X), \tag{2}$$

and the loss (L) is dependent only on Y:

$$L = f_2(Y). \tag{3}$$

Substituting in equation (1) the values of G and L in equations (2) and (3) yields the following reformulation of the group's objective function:

$$\max_{X, Y} [f_1(X) - f_2(Y)]. \tag{4}$$

Now suppose we want to divide pursuit of this objective into two tasks. One group can be assigned control of X and the other control of Y, and their respective *subobjective functions* could be

$$\max_{X} [f_1(X)] \quad \text{and} \quad \min_{Y} [f_2(Y)].$$

Then, because the gain and loss are independent,

$$\max_{X, Y} [f_1(X) - f_2(Y)] = \max_{X} [f_1(X)] - \min_{Y} [f_2(Y)]. \tag{5}$$

The division of labor (organizational structure) in this situation has no inherent inefficiency; if each subgroup obtains its subobjective, the group as a whole will obtain its objective.

Note that in this case the two subgroups are *independent of each other* because the variable controlled by each has no effect on the performance of the other. Hence these two subgroups *do not form a group* because they are not interrelated.

Now consider that the subgroups are interrelated. The group has the same objective function as in the above situation, but its gain and loss depend on both controllable variables. Hence (3) and (4) become

$$G = f_1(X, Y), \tag{6}$$

and

$$L = f_2(X, Y). \tag{7}$$

It may seem reasonable to assign to one subgroup the subobjective function:

$$\max_X \left[f_1(X, Y) \right],\tag{8}$$

and to the other

$$\min_Y \left[f_2(X, Y) \right].\tag{9}$$

But for most functions (f_1 and f_2), where both relate to the same variables, the following *inequality* holds:

$$\max_{X, Y} \left[f_1(X, Y) - f_2(X, Y) \right] \neq \max_X \left[f_1(X, Y) - \min_Y \left[f_2(X, Y) \right] \right].\tag{10}$$

Therefore,

$$\max_{X, Y} \left[f_1(X, Y) - f_2(X, Y) \right] - \left\{ \max_X \left[f_1(X, Y) \right] - \min_Y \left[f_2(X, Y) \right] \right\} = K > 0.\tag{11}$$

The difference (K) between the best the organization can accomplish given its division of labor and the ideal of joint optimization — $\max_{X, Y} \left[f_1(X, Y) - f_2(X, Y) \right]$ — is a measure of the inefficiency of the organization's division of labor (structure). This measure can be generalized to cover any number of controllable variables, to apply to any subobjective functions, and to take uncontrolled variables into account.

It can be shown that forms of organization that move toward joint optimization increase the range of choices open to those responsible for the functions; that is, they are *variety increasing*. Changes in the other direction are effectively *variety decreasing*.

Using this same approach, we can also derive measures of an organization's inefficiency due to faulty communication and poor decision making. Consider communication first. Subgroup A, which controls X, requires information on what value of Y subgroup B selects, and subgroup B requires information on what value of X subgroup A selects. Suppose they obtain incorrect information: subgroup A believes the value y is used by B where $y \neq Y$, and subgroup B believes the value x is used by A where $x \neq X$. Both use incorrect values. Then their actual performance, assuming they optimize correctly, would be

$$\max_X \left[f_1(X, y) \right] \quad \text{and} \quad \min_Y \left[f_2(x, Y) \right]$$

The difference,

$$\left\{ \max_X \left[f_1(X, Y) \right] - \min_Y \left[f_2(X, Y) \right] \right\} -$$
$$\left\{ \max_X \left[f_1(X, y) \right] - \min_Y \left[f_2(x, Y) \right] \right\},$$

is a measure of inefficiency due to communication. (As we shall see below, if the organizational structure is inefficient, communication inefficiency can be negative.) The magnitude of this inefficiency due to communication depends on the functions f_1 and f_2, and hence on the organization's structure. This is consistent with the widely held belief that some organizations are more sensitive to poor communication than others because of differences in their structures. In this simple case the joint contribution of structure and communication to the organization's inefficiency can be measured by

$$\max_{X, Y} \left[f_1 (X, Y) - f_2 (X, Y) \right] -$$
$$\left\{ \max_{X} \left[f_1 (X, y) \right] - \min_{Y} \left[f_2 (x, Y) \right] \right\}$$

Finally, suppose that the subgroups do not correctly maximize and minimize their subobjective functions. Let max* and min* represent such faulty optimization. Then

$$\left\{ \max_{X} \left[f_1 (X, Y) \right] - \min_{Y} \left[f_2 (X, Y) \right] \right\} -$$
$$\left\{ \max^* _{X} \left[f_1 (X, Y) \right] - \min^* _{Y} \left[f_2 (X, Y) \right] \right\}$$

represents decision-making inefficiency. Note that here, too, the effect of decision making on the system's efficiency depends on the mathematical properties of the functions f_1 and f_2 and, hence, on the system's structure. In fact, where structural inefficiency exists, faulty decision making and communication may be desirable. This is illustrated by the following simplified version of a real business situation.

Consider a retailing organization that has two subgroups: a purchasing and a sales department. The purchasing department buys a product at the beginning of each month in a quantity X, which it determines. The purchased items are placed in stock until sold. The sales department sets the price (Y) at which the item is to be sold; the lower the price, the more can be sold, on the average. The amount that will be sold in any period can only be predicted subject to a known distribution of errors. This yields a Price Demand curve such as is shown in Figure 13.1. In this case both departments know this curve. Only items in stock can be sold. Back orders are not permitted; that is, customers will not wait for the item.

Suppose the purchasing department is assigned the subobjective of minimizing the cost of inventory while at the same time providing sufficient stock to meet its own estimate of demand. The sales department is assigned the subobjective of maximizing gross profits where this profit is equal to [number of items sold (sales price − cost of purchase)]. Now if the sales department sets a price Y_1 for the next period, it forecasts that an optimistic quantity, X_1, will be sold. (See Figure 13.1.) It tends to overestimate sales and order too much, because its performance suffers if it cannot meet demand but not if items are left in stock. The purchasing department, on the other

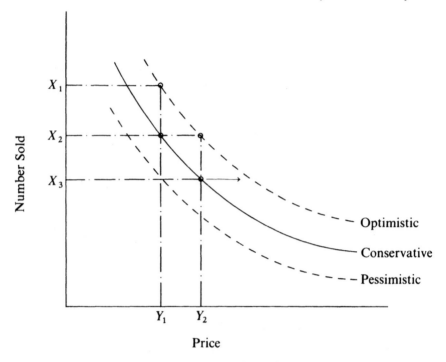

Figure 13.1.   Price–Demand Curve

hand, makes a conservative estimate of sales (X_2) and buys only an amount sufficient to meet this forecast because, if it overbuys, the inventory-carrying costs increase, and the purchasing department suffers. The sales department, of course, wants the purchasing department to use an optimistic forecast of sales, because its own performance suffers if orders are not fulfilled but not if anything is left over in inventory. When the purchasing department selects an order quantity X_2 to meet a conservative forecast of sales based on the price Y_1, the sales department is informed of the fact and responds by raising its price to Y_2 for which X_2 is an optimistic forecast of demand. When it does so, the purchasing department revises X_2 to a lower value, say X_3, which corresponds to a conservative estimate of sales for price Y_2, and so on. The limit of this process is reached when the purchasing department buys nothing, and hence nothing can be sold.

In the real situation, the limit was not reached because both departments wanted to keep the company in business, and they did so by variety reduction — by restricting communication between them. The sales department did not tell the purchasing department what price it was going to set, and the purchasing department did not tell the sales department how many items it was going to buy. Each had to predict what the other would do. Stability was obtained by regressing to a lower level of system functioning.

It is also apparent in this simplified example that less than optimization of the subobjective functions was better than optimization because the organization's structure was deficient.

In this case a slight change in the subobjective functions could remove the problem and the need for deliberately withholding information. If the sales department's responsibilities were extended to include responsibility for inventories produced by optimistic sales forecasts, and the purchasing department's were extended to include lost sales, the organization's structural deficiency would be removed.

Structural inefficiency can be reduced or removed by *reorganizing* the group. But this is not the only way. It is possible to control subgroups without changing their subobjectives so that they make decisions that minimize such inefficiency. For a discussion of methods see Sengupta and Ackoff (1965).

Types of Organized Social Groups

There are many ways of classifying social groups. Two are particularly important. They involve *nodality* and *geneity*.

A *uninodal* organization is one that is hierarchically structured. It has a pyramid of authority topped by an ultimate decision maker who can resolve differences between decision makers at any lower level. A *multinodal* organization has no such ultimate authority and thus requires *agreement* between two or more autonomous decision makers.

A *homogeneous* organization is one that has greater control over its members than its members have over it, and hence tends to be variety decreasing. A *heterogeneous* organization is one whose members have greater control over it than it has over them, and hence tends to be variety increasing.

Each type represents a range on a scale. Therefore, in every organization, except a few at the extremes, there are both homogeneous and heterogeneous, and uninodal and multinodal characteristics, but one type usually dominates the other. Corporations, for example, tend to be dominantly uninodal and homogeneous, while cities and universities tend to be multinodal and heterogeneous. There are also uninodal heterogeneous and multinodal homogeneous organizations.

Within these categories there are large numbers of types of social aggregations and groups, such as crowds, mobs, teams, audiences, and publics. We only consider two extreme types here, types that will illustrate the relevance of the dimensions we have introduced. More than this could easily take us into another book.

PRISONS: UNINODAL AND HOMOGENEOUS

Are there special characteristics that tend to emerge in systems at this extreme of uninodality and homogeneity? Two significant tendencies can be observed in prisons (Emery, 1970).

1. At this extreme of homogeneity there is a marked reduction in the variety of purposeful behavior that can be pursued by inmates or staff. Rigid scheduling of the daily round of activities and a proliferation of regulations mean that most behaviors of the inmates and staff will be simply goal-directed. In each situation they will tend to do only one thing, more or less adaptively.

2. At this extreme of uninodality the chief decision maker (the governor or warden) approximates to the mathematical function we defined in Chapter 3 as π. To maintain this function he will tend to restrict the advice he takes from subordinates to advice that affects only one or two of the parameters of the choices he has to make. It is his business to make decisions on the basis of the whole set of parameters. In line with this he tends to assume that it will be his responsibility to make the decision to meet the inevitable important contingencies; hence he must retain as great a reserve of power as possible, delegating responsibility only for specified courses of action to meet predicted situations.

The nonadaptive aspects of the system tendencies described above (which occur because the elements are themselves purposeful) give rise to derivative tendencies. The most obvious is the persistent struggle of the inmates to create an informal underground system. Less obvious is the tendency of the staff to create a mushroom culture around the chief decision maker. They keep him in the dark and feed him informational manure. If he is interested in the stability of the system rather than in its other purposes, he accepts it.

AGRICULTURAL EXTENSION SERVICES: MULTINODAL AND HETEROGENEOUS

Those who provide these services, taken together with the farmers they serve, provide an extreme case of multinodality and heterogeneity. The farmers make their own decisions and have more control over the extension system than do those who provide the services. Again we can ask the same question: What special characteristics emerge in systems at this extreme? Two parallel but opposite tendencies can be discerned (Emery and Oeser, and Tully, 1958).

1. The farmers resist advice and advisers that do not extend their variety of purposeful behavior.

2. The heterogeneity of the system is manifested by the farmer's reluctance to relinquish control over his goal-directed behavior (say, crop-spraying practices) even in densely settled irrigation areas, as well as by his reluctance to relinquish control over his purposeful behavior unless convinced that control is going to be exercised by some cooperative that effectively embodies ideals he holds (a body that would not be tempted to make a shift in its purposes that he would not make).

Between such systems as prisons and agricultural extension services lie a great variety of naturalistic groups — crowds, mobs, associations, teams, audiences, publics, communities, societies. These various social groupings have been studied from antiquity and more particularly since the emergence of sociology as a discipline. We are suggesting that more rigor may be achieved by studying (1) their nodality and geneity, and (2) the effects the various components of the choice situation have on the parameters of choice for such groups.

The Culture of Social Systems — a Note

As we stated in the introduction to this chapter, culture is to the social group what personality is to the psychological individual. Culture likewise is a function of such parameters as familiarity, knowledge, understanding, and intention.

If a social group is distinctive for the ways in which its members communicate with one another and influence one another's behavior, then that distinctiveness — its culture — must manifest itself with respect to some or all of the parameters of choice. Any group that has functioned over a long period must be expected to have developed characteristic ways of behaving.

A very similar conclusion has been arrived at by Hall and Trager (Hall, 1959).

> . . . what I would like to propose here: a theory which suggests that culture has three levels. I have termed these the formal, informal, and technical, familiar terms but with new and expanded meanings.
>
> Trager and I arrived at this tripartite theory as a result of some rather detailed and lengthy observations as to the way in which Americans talk about and handle time (p. 66).

The special meanings they indicate for formal, informal, and technical closely approximate our definitions of familiarity, understanding, and knowledge. Thus the formal level of culture is what is traditional and communicated by information; the technical level is what is knowledge and communicated by instruction; the informal culture is what somehow or another has to be comprehended or understood (as, "when you grow up you will understand" or "when you get the hang of it"). Hall and Trager do not handle the fourth parameter, relative value, at the same level of generality we have proposed. They handle it in terms of their ten Primary Message Systems (such as subsistence, territorially).

Not surprisingly, their ostensive definitions are sometimes hard to grasp in the context of their discussions. They are often blurred and occasionally, we believe, inconsistent. Nevertheless, the fruitfulness of their work suggests how much more fruitful it would be to work over the same ground with a rigorous set of concepts, those involving not only the basic parameters of choice but also awareness, learning, belief, memory, and so on. However, this is a task we are not prepared to take on here.

A Methodology for Social Research

In attempting to develop understanding through research of social phenomena, particularly ones involving large social groups, the investigator is confronted with what initially appears to be an almost hopeless task. For example, each instance of large-scale social conflict — a war, a strike, or a riot — appears to be infinitely complex, unique, and characterizable only by intangibles. Dealing with such problems, however, is not new to science, whose progress can be measured largely by the extent to which it has converted what initially appeared to be hopelessly complex into what eventually appeared to be relatively simple. Simplicity comes at the end, not at the beginning, of research. At one time heat and electricity seemed to be as difficult to understand as large-scale social conflicts seem to be today.

At the beginning of scientific inquiry into a new area, every theory proposed, no matter how complex, seems too simple. Once science has achieved some measure of success in an area, however, every theory, no matter how simple, seems too complex. As understanding of a class of phenomena increases, the number of variables required to explain it decreases, and the explanation of their interactions and effects becomes increasingly obvious.

The principle method by which science has explored the unknown is experimentation. It is not possible, however, to conduct experiments on large-scale social systems. We cannot bring international conflicts into the laboratory, nor experiment on them in their natural environment, nor do we have the right or capability of intervening in them; we cannot run the risk of intensifying them by experimental manipulation. Furthermore, we cannot perform quantitative analyses on past conflicts, because histories and descriptions of these conflicts have not been recorded reliably or in a quantitative form. Records of past conflicts do not provide us with sufficient facts to allow us to find in them dynamic regularities or consistent causal principles.

In a sense the researcher into the operations of many social systems is in a situation similar to that of the early atronomers; the system they studied also seemed to be infinitely complex and yet incapable of being subjected to experimentation. However, astronomers eventually developed mathematical representations (models) of the systems, and analyzed or conducted experiments on these models. Today such experiments are called "simulations."

In order to proceed as the astronomer has it is necessary to have ordered, accurate, quantitative descriptions of the behavior of the system under study. Newton's work depended on Kepler's, and Kepler's on Brahe's. Without Brahe's detailed and fastidious accumulation of relevant facts, Keplerian laws and the Newtonian theory could not have been developed. The corresponding type of quantitative descriptions of large-scale social phenomena required before theoretical work can be begun is not available. There are few impersonal and objective descriptions of past or current international conflicts because different observers seldom record the same so-called facts, and analysts seldom draw the same conclusions from even the same set of facts. Therefore, one might attempt to understand the dynamics of large-scale social conflict by first seeking accurate descriptions of real conflicts. But even today this is very difficult, if not impossible. However, there is an alternative method for just such situations in which the problem of preparing quantitative descriptions of real large-scale social phenomena has a secondary role. When this method succeeds, it provides the criteria of relevance and techniques of data evaluation required before accurate and reliable descriptions of complex social phenomena are possible. We continue to use the example of large-scale social conflict in developing the characteristics of this method.

Conflict, like many other social phenomena, has been studied extensively. In previous research three approaches to the problem have been taken. The first (exemplified by Anatol Rapoport's simple [Prisoner's Dilemma] conflict games [1965]) involved two-person groups in laboratory situations. Rapoport developed a mathematical model that explains this particular conflict game. He recognizes that inferences cannot legitimately be drawn from highly controlled but simple conflict situations to the very complex but uncontrolled ones found in reality. His work simply provides what he calls "insights" into real large-scale social conflicts (Rapoport, 1960 and 1965). This is not a meager accomplishment, but until we can learn how to infer to real situations from conflict situations that can be studied in the laboratory, it is not likely that we will develop a scientific theory that applies directly to the dynamics of real large-scale social conflicts.

The second approach to the study of large-scale social conflicts involves the use of relatively complex experimental situations, such as international poltical games. Examples of this approach are in the work of Harold Guetzkow (1963) and Bloomfield (1965).

Although the gap between these games and reality appears to be, and may be, smaller than in simple two-person games, the inferential problem remains for two reasons. First, these games resemble reality because they reproduce many of its properties, but there is no assurance that these properties are related to each other in the games as they are in reality. Therefore, inferences cannot legitimately be drawn from games whose structure is not known to a reality whose structure is not known. Second, because of the complexity of these games precise quantitative description of what happens in most of them has not been possible. Again, such comments do not minimize the value of the insights these games have provided.

The third type of approach involves analysis of real conflict situations by either (1) traditional historical analysis, (2) new techniques of analyzing communications between conflicting parties, or (3) statistical analysis of political, social, and economic variables. Examples of rigorous efforts using this approach include the work done at the Foreign Policy Research Institute of the University of Pennsylvania and the work of Yale's *Dimensionality of Nations* project.

The low degree of relevance and reliability of available data can make difficult the analysis of real situations. At best the types of statistical analyses involved in this third approach yield descriptions, not explanations, of what has taken place. Hence, even if completely successful they can yield only accurate predictions, not control, of what will take place. Most of the conclusions reached by any analysis of reality have not been reproducible in any objective way. In brief, such analyses have not yet produced a body of knowledge that can be called scientific. The results obtained are often vague and frequently inconsistent, and seldom justify a status higher than that of a conjecture.

In the method described here an effort is made to incorporate the strengths of each of these three approaches and to avoid or minimize their difficulties. This method tries to retain the value of both controlled experimentation and rigorous quantitative analysis contained in the first type of approach, as well as the realism of the second and third approaches. If anything other than real social phenomena is to be studied, however, the principal methodological problem that must be overcome is inference from a situation that substitutes for reality to reality itself.

The method is shown schematically in Figure 13.2, again illustratively using research into large-scale social conflict.[2]

First, the literature relevant to the real situation under study is reviewed, and all hypotheses and conjectures concerning the phenomenon in question are extracted from it. Since some of these statements will overlap, the resulting list is edited and condensed. (In large-scale social conflict, well over 100 such statements were yielded by this process.)

Next the variables involved in each of these hypotheses and conjectures are extracted and listed. This list is also edited. The variables in the final list are then ordered in terms of the frequency with which they appear in the hypotheses and conjectures. (For example, in the conflict case communication was the most frequently cited variable.) This ordering provides an initial priority that can be used in the experimental work described below.

As will become apparent in a moment, these variables must eventually be given operational definitions so that they can be used experimentally. The conceptual system constructed here may provide some of the required definitions, and others can be derived from those that are provided here.

Now a relatively complex experimental situation is constructed, one that we call an artificial reality (or rich game). It should be as simple a situation as possible and yet satisfy the following conditions.

   1. It is rich enough to test a large number of hypotheses that have been formulated about whatever type of phenomenon is relevant (as the dynamics

---

2. A complete account of the conflict research that makes use of this method can be found in Management Science Center (1969). See also Emshoff (1971) and Emshoff and Ackoff (1968).

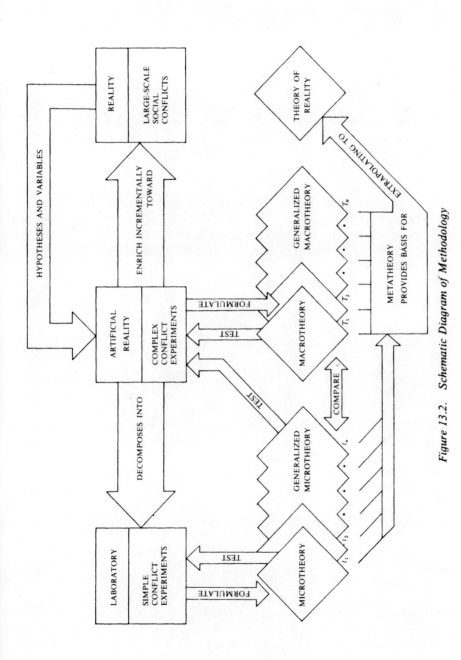

Figure 13.2.   Schematic Diagram of Methodology

of large-scale social conflict). (Clearly such tests cannot confirm any hypotheses about reality, but they can limit the generality of hypotheses or show how they can or should be generalized.) The purpose behind this condition is to assure use of an experimental situation that is realistic enough so that most assertions made about the real situation are applicable to it.

2. There must be explicit operational definitions of the variables manipulated in the situation, including the scales used in measuring them and of the variables by which simplification of reality has taken place (as by holding a variable constant). Identification of these factors makes it possible to design successively enriched experimental situations by the addition of complexities, one at a time or in controlled combination.

3. The relevant behavior in the experimental situation must be describable in quantitative terms.

4. The situation must be decomposable into a set of simpler experimental situations, and where possible these simpler situations should be ones that have already been experimented on or closely resemble situations that have been researched. This enables one to relate the results obtained here to previous work.

The experimental situation that satisfies these conditions is not used as a model of reality but rather as a reality to be modeled; hence its name artificial reality. It is used to generate a history, which is to be explained by the first macrotheory to be constructed. The history is generated by experimentation (like playing the rich game in laboratory conditions), which is designed to test hypotheses about real conflict that have been translated into operational and quantitative terms and adapted to this artificial world.

Experiments are also conducted using decomposed parts of the artificial reality—that is, using simpler conflict situations. These laboratory experiments are used to construct a microtheory to explain their results. A generalized microtheory that explains a variety of simple conflict situations is then sought; the essential differentiating characteristics of a variety of simple situations enter the theory as variables. Finally, generalization of the microtheory to the artificial reality is attempted. Such a generalization in this context is called macrotheory.[3]

A simultaneous effort is made to formulate a macrotheory of the artificial reality by direct analysis of the history it generates. These two theoretical efforts interact until a satisfactory macrotheory (T_1) of the artificial reality is developed.

Once a satisfactory macrotheory (T_1) is developed, the initial artificial reality (R_1) can be modified to provide a more realistic conflict situation (R_2), such as by converting something that was held constant in R_1 into a variable. Efforts can then be made to generalize the earlier theory (T_1) so that it applies to R_2. The output is a more general macrotheory T_2 of which T_1 is a special

3. Efforts to develop such a theory are described in Emshoff (1968), Emshoff and Ackoff (1968), and Emshoff (1971).

case. T_2 is tested against history generated by experimentation with R_2. This procedure is continued, and hopefully produces a sequence of successively more general macrotheories: $T_1, T_2, \ldots, T_n$.

As this set of theories expands, it can be analyzed to find principles that explain how the theories must be generalized in order to apply to more realistic artificial realities. That is, a *metatheory* is sought, one that yields a procedure for generating either t_{n+1}, given $t_1, t_2, \ldots, t_m$, or T_{n+1}, given $T_1, T_2, \ldots, T_n$. These can then be tested in a new artificial reality' R_{n+1} which is a modification of R_n. The development of such a metatheory makes possible larger jumps toward theories of real conflicts, hopefully to a theory that applies to reality in all its complexity.

The plan encompassed in this methodology cannot be carried out in a short period of time. Its complete realization for even one type of phenomenon takes considerable time. The time required depends on the amount of research effort devoted to its realization. This time can be reduced by cooperative efforts because the methodology provides a framework for organizing and integrating the efforts of a large number of research units.

Conclusion

Up to Chapter 9 this book is occupied with purposeful individuals and their behavior. In Chapters 9–12 we dealt with the interactions of purposeful individuals. In this chapter we have been concerned with *systems* of such individuals and their behavior, and thus have made the transition from the domain of psychology, through social psychology, to that of sociology.

Clearly this chapter has presented only a sketch of a conceptual system for the social sciences. We hope, however, that the earlier treatment of purposeful individuals makes clear how the elaboration of the material presented in this chapter can be carried out.

We have moved from mechanical individuals to purposeful systems. Two final steps of generalization remain. First, in Chapter 14, we look at what lies beyond purpose, *ideals*; then in Chapter 15 we try to close the conceptual cycle by using teleological concepts to define those structural notions with which this effort began.

REFERENCES

Ackoff, R. L. "Toward an Idealized University." *Management Science* 15 (1968): B121–31

Abel, T. "The Sociology of Concentration Camps." *Social Forces* 30 (1951): 150–54.

Bion, W. R. *Experiences in Groups*. London: Tavistock Publications, 1961.

Bloomfield, L. P. "The Political-Military Exercise: A Progress Report." *ORBIS* 8 (1965): 854–70.

Buckley, Walter. *Sociology and Modern Systems Theory*. Englewood Cliffs, N.J.: Prentice-Hall, 1967.

Burns, T., and G. M. Stalker. *The Management of Innovation.* London: Tavistock Press, 1961.

———. *Analysis of Behavioral Systems.* New York: Macmillan, 1971.

Churchman, C. W. *The Systems Approach.* New York: Delacorte Press, 1968.

Cuber, J. F. *Sociology: A Synopsis of Principles.* 4th ed. New York: Appleton-Century-Crofts, 1959.

Emery, F. E. *Systems Thinking.* Harmondsworth, England: Penguin Books, 1969.

———. *Freedom and Justice within Prison Walls.* London: Tavistock Publications, 1970.

Emery, F. E., Oeser, O. A., and J. Tully. *Information, Decision and Action.* Melbourne, Australia: Melbourne University Press, 1958.

Emery, F. E., and E. L. Trist. "Socio-technical Systems." In F. E. Emery (1969), pp. 281–96.

Emshoff, J. R. *Analysis of Behavioral Systems.* New York: The Macmillan Co., 1971.

Emshoff, J. R., and R. L. Ackoff. "Prediction, Explanation, and Control of Conflict." *Peace Research Society. Papers XII.* Cambridge Conference (1968), pp. 109–15.

Fingarette, H. *On Responsibility.* New York: Basic Books, 1967.

Gouldner, A. W., and H. P. Gouldner. *Modern Sociology.* New York: Harcourt, Brace & World, 1963.

Guetzkow, Harold, *et al. Simulation in Inter-Nation Relations.* Englewood Cliffs, N.J.: Prentice-Hall, 1963.

Hall, E. T. *The Silent Language.* New York: Doubleday, 1959.

Management Science Center. *Conflicts and Their Escalation: Metagame Analysis.* Report ACDA/ST-149. Philadelphia: University of Pennsylvania, 29 May 1969.

Merton, R. K. *Social Theory and Social Structure.* Glencoe, Ill.: The Free Press, 1949.

Mizruchi, E. H. *The Substance of Sociology.* New York: Appleton-Century-Crofts, 1967.

Nagel, E. "A Formalization of Functionalism." In F. E. Emery (1969), pp. 297–329.

Rapoport, Anatol. *Fights, Games, and Debates.* Ann Arbor: The University of Michigan Press, 1960.

———. *The Prisoner's Dilemma.* Ann Arbor: The University of Michigan Press, 1965.

Selznick, P. *Leadership in Administration.* New York: Harper & Row, 1957.

Sengupta, S. S., and R. L. Ackoff. "Systems Theory from an Operations Research Point of View." *IEEE Transactions on Systems Science and Cybernetics* 1 (November 1965): 9–13.

Sommerhoff, G. "The Abstract Characteristics of Living Systems." In F. E. Emery (1969), pp. 147–202.

Stretton, H. *The Political Sciences.* New York: Basic Books, 1969.

14

Ideal-Seeking Systems

PERFECTION, *n.* An imaginary state or quality distinguished from the actual by an element known as excellence; an attribute of the critic.

The Devil's Dictionary

Introduction

It is a peculiarity of man and some of the social systems of which he is a part that they can pursue outcomes and states they know cannot be obtained. Yet they draw satisfaction from approaching states that cannot be reached. The approach is called *progress* and the end-state is called an *ideal*.

Many wise men have observed that there is more satisfaction in pursuing an end than in attaining it; to play a game well yields more satisfaction than does winning it. Also, some have observed that the researcher's and manager's objective is not so much to solve problems as it is to create more challenging and important problems to work on by solving the one at hand. This is to say that the continuous pursuit of more desirable ends is an end in itself, and hence attainment of a specific end can be conceptualized as a means to such pursuit.

Such observations suggest that a pervasive objective of man and the social systems of which he is a part is the successful pursuit of increasingly desirable objectives. If this is so, then it is reasonable for man and the social systems of which he is part to formulate objectives that can be pursued without end but can be continually approached. Man seeks objectives that enable him to convert the attainment of every goal into a means for the attainment of a new and more desirable goal. The ultimate objective in such a sequence cannot be obtainable; otherwise its attainment would put an end to the process. An end that satisfies these conditions is an *ideal*.

Ideal pursuit can provide cohesiveness and continuity to extended and unpredictable processes, to life and history. Thus the formulation and pursuit of ideals is a means by which man puts meaning and significance into his life and into the history of which he is a part. It also provides the possibility of deriving satisfaction from a life that must end but that can contribute to a history that may not.

Speculation about ideals and their pursuit has been engaged in almost

237

exclusively by philosophers, particularly those concerned with the field of *ethics.* Ideals have received almost no attention from scientist. This is partially due to the widespread belief among scientists that a science of ethics is not possible or that justification for identifying any ideal with the Ultimate Good is not a scientific matter.[1] Suppose, however, that as scientists we could specify an ideal whose attainment logically entails the ability to attain any other ideal and without whose attainment no other ideal could be attained; then we would have identified a necessary and sufficient condition for ideal pursuit. Consequently, an analysis of the functions required for pursuit of this ideal — one we may call a *metaideal* — could provide insight into the general nature of ideal-seeking systems.

We believe there is such an ideal and that such an analysis is possible. This belief is based on the following analysis of the history of ethics.

Ethics has been largely concerned with a search for the Ultimate Good — that is, a criterion that can be used for ethical evaluation of each act by any entity (individual or system) that can display choice. Many different criteria have been proposed throughout history, but these offerings can be gathered into two classes: the *purposeful* and *nonpurposeful.*

Nonpurposeful (ateleological) ethical criteria are supposed to be independent of what anyone's or any group's purposes are and hence independent of what they want.

Such criteria take the form of maxims or rules of conduct. The *Ten Commandments* are a case in point; the *Golden Rule* is another. Historically two kinds of difficulty have arisen with such rules.

First, alternative and at least partially incompatible sets of rules are available. Which of these is the best? This raises to another and higher level the problem of selecting an ultimate ethical criterion. Since nonpurposeful ethics cannot be justified in terms of its consequences to purposeful individuals and systems (its *products*); it must be justified in terms of its *producer*, where it comes from. Thus defense of a nonpurposeful ethics rests on the authority of its source. For this reason such rules have usually been attributed to an ultimate authority, God. This does not solve the problem because there is a set of competing gods available and the ethics they are alleged to have issued differ significantly. Furthermore, for each god multiple agents have reported the source as issuing different ethics. Hence a still higher level criterion is required for selecting among competing authorities, even those claimed to be ultimate. No rational criterion for so doing has ever been provided. Therefore, the ultimate justification for acceptance of a nonpurposeful ethics is an act of faith. This clearly denies science a role in justifying an ethics. More important, however, is that acceptance of such an ethics leaves society with no rational way of dissolving conflicts within it or between societies. Unless one nonpurposeful ethics is universally accepted,

---

1. C. W. Churchman (1961) has made the strongest case to the contrary of which we are aware.

conflict is a natural consequence. And man has found no practical way of promoting such acceptance.

Second, nonpurposeful rules that come from a single authority are always internally inconsistent. E. A. Singer, Jr. (1923) asked:

> ... are these maxims at least consistent with one another? Does one bid us to be truthful?—then another bids us be kind! But how in this vale of perplexities is one always to be truthful yet never unkind?
>
> For these reasons, most have abandoned the attempt to define the moral good in terms of maxims, which they take rather to be hypothetical goods in disguise. They are rules indeed, but only rules of thumb holding "for the most part." If they vary with time and place, if within the most circumscribed communities they contradict one another, this is because they cannot pretend to be good in themselves, but are only the means by which the community accepting them has found by experience to be best fitted for attaining a certain end. It is indeed the end that justifies the means . . . (pp 73–4).

Thus, curiously enough, the efforts to establish an ateleological ethics drives one to a consideration of what somebody — an individual, a god, or a community—*wants*, with their purposes, or to the consequences of accepting such an ethics. Again, the only alternative is an act of faith that bears with it the preclusion of ethical progress and the acceptance of a permanent state of conflict within and between communities.

Purposeful ethics attempts to define the Ultimate Good in terms of wants and consequences. The earliest form of such an ethics argues (as Protagoras did) that whatever a person wants is *good for him*: "Man is the measure of all things." Although such an ethics does not justify everything a person does, it does justify whatever he does that serves his purposes *well*. Thus inefficiency becomes evil, and evil is relative: it varies from person to person and from situation to situation.

Such an ethics provides no more assistance in resolving conflicts within and between persons than does one that is nonpurposeful. But since science can reduce inefficiency, this point of view does make a science of ethics possible, but it does so by reducing ethics to technology.

One attempt to overcome such an ethics' tolerance for conflict within and between individuals consists of defining the Ultimate Good in terms of what a community (or a majority of its members) wants. However, this does not eliminate the problem; it just raises it to another level. It provides no way of dissolving conflicts between communities. Furthermore, it leaves us with the considerable difficulty of defining the greatest good for the greatest number.[2]

The next and ultimate step in this process is apparent: to seek something that everybody and every community at any time (past, present, or future) has, does, or will want, and that they must want at least as much as,

2. See Churchman (1961, Chap. 2).

if not more than, anything else. Thus the search for a universal and dominating objective was launched.

In the eighteenth century David Hume made an effort to find such an objective, but without success. Numerous subsequent efforts also met with failure. These failures were used as an argument for nonpurposeful ethics. Early in this century, however, E. A. Singer, Jr., observed that such searches were directed at the wrong thing: they were looking at what people desire rather than at the nature of desire itself.

> Now suppose there was something you would have to have whether you wanted to bisect a line, or break a safe, or do anything else in the world; then, whatever you happened to desire, you would have to desire that something. . . . The condition of attaining any end in the world is such control of the world's machinery as shall give you power to get what you want (p. 109).

Ironically, this wisdom was common among children but was completely overlooked by mature philosophers. When children are confronted with the familiar fable that involves the granting of three wishes, many are bright enough to observe that they would require only one; then they would wish that all their wishes come true. One cannot wish for anything, even for the absence of desire, without wishing for the ability to realize that wish. Thus the ability or *power* to satisfy desire is universally desired and must be desired at least as much as anything else is. This is the desire for *omnipotence*. Little wonder that in every conception of God — man's formulation of an ideal being — omnipotence is one of His essential attributes.

Without omnipotence no ideal could be attained; with it, all could be. The notion of omnipotence, however, leaves us with the problem of what an ideal is. Our purpose here is not to discuss this problem philosophically, but much of what is said is relevant to philosophy. Rather, our objective is to lay a conceptual foundation on which scientific study of ideals and their pursuit can be based. What we have to say should be equally applicable to psychological or social systems.

The Nature of Ideals and Their Pursuit

It will be recalled that the *goal* of a system in a particular situation was defined as a preferred outcome that can be obtained within a specified period of time. Further, an *objective* of a system was defined as a preferred outcome that cannot be obtained within a specified time period but can be obtained over a longer time period.

A purposeful system is of a qualitatively higher order than is a goal-seeking system: it can pursue objectives. A goal-seeking system selects its course of action only with respect to a goal — the outcome that can occur in the situation with which it is confronted. A purposeful system can choose courses of action with respect to a criterion, an objective, which is not necessarily a possible outcome in the period considered, but is a possible outcome of future situations of which the current situation's outcomes are potential coproducers. If a purposeful system fails to achieve its goal in one situation, it may change its goal in order to better pursue the same objective. If a system consistently sacrifices its goals for the sake of its objectives, we can be sure it is a purposeful system.

However, *only those purposeful systems can be ideal-seeking that can choose between objectives*. They are able to (1) maintain progress toward an ideal by choosing another objective when one is achieved, or the effort to achieve it has failed, and (2) consistently sacrifice objectives for the sake of ideals.

An ideal (definition 2.33) is to an objective what an objective is to a goal. It is an objective that cannot be obtained in any time period but can be approached without limit.

Objectives can be ordered with respect to ideals just as goals can be ordered with respect to objectives. But an ideal is an outcome that cannot be obtained in principle. However, what appears impossible to attain at one moment of time is often accomplished at a later time. About two centuries ago Bishop Berkeley argued that it was impossible to measure distances less than 1/1,000 of an inch. Today we measure distances of 1/10,000,000 of an inch. Hence what we formulate as an ideal at one time may become an objective at another. Today we see errorless observation as an ideal, a state we believe to be impossible to obtain in principle. Movement with the speed of light appears to be an ideal of some.

A purposeful system or individual is ideal-seeking if, on attainment of any of its objectives, it chooses another objective that more closely approximates its ideal.

An ideal-seeking system or individual is necessarily one that is purposeful, but not all purposeful entities seek ideals. The capability of seeking ideals may well be a characteristic that distinguishes man from anything he can make, including computers.

It has been repeatedly observed that without ideals man's life is purposeless. This can be taken to mean that where there are no citeria for choosing between purposes, the choice of purpose is itself purposeless. If we are to distinguish between those purposeful systems that are ideal-seeking and those that are not, we must distinguish the criteria that enable the ideal-seeking ones to choose between their purposes. Our consideration of the historical treatment of ideals suggested that omnipotence was the one ideal that, if achieved, would make it possible to achieve all other conceivable ideals. However, omnipotence is to ideal-seeking systems what the personality function π is to purposeful systems. Just as we felt that this function could not be studied directly, so we feel that it is not possible to directly study omnipotence or the Ultimate Good. We do think it possible to approach the subject through study of those ideals that have evolved to affect the parameters of choice when the object of the choice is choice of purpose.

Ideals Influencing Choice of Purposes

Some insight into the nature of ideal pursuit can be provided by attempting to determine what is required in order to choose between purposes. The answer to this should determine the basic properties of ideal-seeking systems. We would expect that the different parameters of choice would be reflected in different ideals, and they are. Although choice of purposes will have outcomes different than choice of courses of action, the parameters of choice cannot be different. By exploring the criteria for choice of purposes that each parameter presents, we should identify the central and enduring ideals of ideal-seeking systems. This should bring us nearer to understanding the overriding ideal of omnipotence, or the Ultimate Good.

First we will identify the necessary functions of a system that is ideal-seeking. Then we will analyze each in more detail. Four general functions are required, each corresponding to one of the parameters of a choice situation. Furthermore, each is directed at what will turn out to be a familiar subideal.

Progress toward the ideal of omnipotence requires progress toward the maximization of (1) the availability of efficient choices, (2) the efficiency of choices made, (3) the compatibility of outcomes obtained, and (4) the relative values of these outcomes.

1. An ideal-seeking system requires *resources* that would make it possible for it to select perfectly efficient means for any of its objectives. By a resource we mean anything other than the system itself which can be a coproducer of the outcome it wants. Thus resources are part of the individual's environment. Then an environmental state we can refer to as the ideal *politico-economic state of* PLENTY is necessary for attainment of the ideal of omnipotence.

2. Necessary resources must be discovered or developed, and the system must have the ability to select the right resources at the right time, and have the ability to use them with perfect self-knowledge and knowledge of the environment. Such a state of knowledge can be referred to as the ideal *scientific state of* TRUTH.

3. An ideal-seeking system could obtain *all* its objectives only if there were no conflict between the outcomes it produced nor between any of these outcomes and those produced by others. Thus, *peace of mind* and *peace on earth* (good will toward men) are necessary conditions for omnipotence. A conflict-free internal and external state can be referred to as the ideal *ethico-moral state of the* GOOD.

4. Finally, and least obvious, is that the ideal of omnipotence becomes vacuous if all desire, all relative value and intention, is eliminated; that is, if a state of Nirvana is attained. Therefore, omnipotence presupposes its exercise, and this in turn requires that more desirable goals and objectives replace old ones once these have been obtained. Thus in an ideal state systems would enlarge their desires, and the succeeding objectives they sought would be more desirable. In an ideal state all purposeful individuals and systems would

be ideal-seeking. Such a state can be referred to as the ideal *aesthetic state of* BEAUTY. Below we try to justify attributing this desire-enlargement function to beauty.

Thus the pursuit of the ancient triad of ideals – the TRUE, the GOOD, and the BEAUTIFUL – are necessary for the pursuit of omnipotence; and the modern ideal, PLENTY, completes the requirements. We shall now try to show that familiar social institutions have the function of facilitating pursuit of one or more of these subideals.

Institutional Functions and Ideal Pursuit

Pursuit of the environmental state we have referred to as a state of PLENTY involves what would normally be called the politico-economic institutions of society. We begin by examining these in more detail.

THE QUEST FOR PLENTY: POLITICO-ECONOMIC FUNCTIONS

1. The community must make available in some environments the resources (goods and services) required for pursuit of objectives, and it must do so in sufficient quantities to permit to all who so desire the simultaneous pursuit of similar objectives. This is the function of *production*, which is embodied in the institutions of business and industry and in departments of public works.

2. These resources must either be placed in environments to which individuals have access, or persons must be provided with access to environments where resources are located. This is the function of *distribution*, which is embodied in the marketing (wholesaling and retailing) and transportation systems.

3. Individuals must be able to acquire the right to use whatever available resources they require. Therefore persons must either be given or given use of these resources, or they must be able to rent or buy them. This requires instruments of *exchange* (like the monetary system). They must be able to acquire these instruments of exchange.

3.1. Some individuals can acquire instruments of exchange by exchanging their labor (employment), or by investing, renting, or selling their accumulation of these instruments or other resources. This is accomplished through *financial* institutions.

3.2. Those who cannot provide for themselves must be provided for. These include the young, old, and incapacitated. To provide for them is a *welfare* function that is accomplished either privately, primarily through the family, or publicly through public welfare or charitable institutions.

4. An individual who uses a resource must be assured of continued availability of that resource (*property rights*), and he must be assured of non-interference with his self-capabilities. Such assurances must be maintained against various types of enemies:

4.1. Others in the community. This is the *legal* and *police* function.

4.2. Other communities. This is the *military* function.

4.3. Accidental or natural damage. This *accident prevention* function involves fire departments, police departments, flood control agencies, health departments, and others. Where accidents do occur, retribution is required. This is the function of *insurance.*

4.4. Natural deterioration with use or over time. This is the *maintenance* function, which is carried out by many private and public service agencies, including medical institutions.

THE QUEST FOR TRUTH: SCIENTIFIC FUNCTIONS

1. The community must produce the knowledge necessary for the development of new and more efficient instruments. This is the *basic research* function, which is carried out by a variety of institutions, including those of higher education.

2. Available knowledge must be used to develop more efficient instruments for more objectives. This is the *applied research* (or technological or developmental) function. It is carried out by many of the same institutions as is basic research.

3. It is necessary to disseminate knowledge on how to develop knowledge, and how to use it and its products. This is an *educational* function. It is carried out not only by educational institutions in the narrow sense, but also by the family, the press, and so on.

THE QUEST FOR THE GOOD: ETHICO-MORAL FUNCTIONS

1. As indicated above, it is necessary to remove conflict of objectives within individuals, to produce peace of mind. This has traditionally been a function of ethics, particularly as set forth by religious institutions. More recently this function has been increasingly taken over by scientifically based mental-health institutions, hence the conflict between some organized religions and the practice of psychiatry.

2. It is also necessary to remove conflicts between individuals. Educational, religious, diplomatic, legal, and other types of institution try to perform such functions, but as yet no very efficient means for so doing have been developed.

THE QUEST FOR BEAUTY: AESTHETIC FUNCTIONS

The aesthetic function is the least understood of the four. A complete justification for the treatment given to it here would require much more space than is appropriate in this book. Therefore we provide only a brief, but we hope suggestive, sketch.

1. An ideal-seeking community must continually renew its members so that they are capable and desirous of striving for something better. But con-

tinuous striving for the unattainable exhausts men both mentally and physically. When mentally or physically fatigued, man can neither create new instruments nor conceive of new means or ends. It is necessary, therefore, to provide him with a change of pace that he may be renewed, that the creator may be recreated. This is a *cathartic* function embodied in recreational institutions – sports, cinema, television, and so on. In art the comic is the cathartic form.

2. It is also necessary to inspire men to create and fashion new conceptions of the possible, and to implement them. Through beauty, art creates what may be called the *creative mood*, a disposition to create, and the *heroic mood*, a disposition to sacrifice present values for those of the future. This *inspirational* function is embodied in artistic, religious, and philosophical activities. In art the tragic is the inspirational form.

Art leads men to find new meanings and commitments in life, and the man that leads other men moves them with visions of the possible and desire for the unattainable. Thus leadership can be considered to be an art form.

The Generality of Ideal-Seeking Functions

The generality of these functions – politico-economic, scientific, ethico-moral, and aesthetic – derives from their necessity in the pursuit of any ideal. Perhaps the best way to grasp this generality is to turn the functions in on themselves.

Consider the scientific ideal in isolation, the ideal of perfect and complete knowledge.[3] There is clearly a politico-economic aspect of scientific progress. The resources required by science will have to be produced, distributed, and made acquirable, protected, maintained, and so on. There is also a scientific function involved in the pursuit of the scientific ideal: to provide science with the most efficient instruments possible in the development and use of knowledge. This science of science is precisely what *methodology* is all about.

There is also an ethico-moral aspect to scientific progress. It involves the elimination of conflicts between sciences and between scientific and non-scientific activities. One need only mention inter- and intradisciplinary conflicts or the conflict between science and religion to appreciate the need for this function. Finally the need for recreation and inspiration within science, the aesthetic function, is also apparent. It is not accidental that a scientific work that inspires others is so often called beautiful. Nor is it accidental that there are so many scientific games (such as puzzles) to provide recreation to scientists.

One could apply all four ideal-seeking functions to any of the four functions, not only to science as we have done above. Thus there is not only an ethical function in science, but there is a scientific function in ethics. If ethics has the function we have attributed to it and if the ULTIMATE GOOD is

---

3. A detailed analysis of pursuit of the scientific ideal can be found in Ackoff (1962, Chap. 15).

omnipotence for all, then science can clearly contribute to progress toward it and to measurement of that progress. *This does not reduce ethics to science* any more than science is reduced to ethics when we consider the dissolution of conflict relevant to its practice.

It appears that an ideal-seeking system must be capable of successfully pursuing each of the four ideals that we have identified. A system can be purposeful without having this capability. It can be restricted only to purposes that can be attained with what is available in the kinds of environment it now experiences.

But note that unlimited progress on any of the four fronts seems to require cooperation of other ideal-seeking individuals. Therefore, a very important characteristic of ideal-seeking individuals seems to be that they must belong to an ideal-seeking system if they are to make significant progress toward their ideal.

Furthermore, it is apparent that a system cannot continuously pursue or make progress toward an ideal if it must engage in conflict with other purposeful systems. Hence an ideal-seeking system must seek autonomy. This can be attained either by isolating itself or by expanding to include all its potential or actual enemies. Isolation is no longer technically possible. Therefore the historic evolution toward a single autonomous world state — an evolution from the family as an autonomous unit to the clan, then the tribe, to the city, now the nation — can be interpreted as an important aspect of ideal pursuit.

Other properties of ideal-pursuing entities also become apparent. It is clear that such a system must be able to derive at least as much satisfaction from progress toward an ideal as it does from attaining a short-run goal. Only if this is so would it be willing to *sacrifice* a short-run and immediate source of satisfaction for a longer range one. An ideal-seeking system must be willing to sacrifice the present for the future, because progress toward an ideal cannot take place along a straight line. This ability to see the long-range consequences of current activity, the ability to do the right thing for the right long-run reason, is the essence of *wisdom*.

The distinction between knowledge and wisdom is important. Knowledge is a means-oriented concept. Wisdom is end- as well as means-oriented. Knowledge is more common than wisdom.

We suspect that the property connoted by *civilized* as applied to societies is analogous to the property attributed to individuals by the adjective wise. A fully developed *culture*, as we use this term, may be uncivilized. Wisdom and civilization refer to the *character*, not merely to the personality, of an individual or the culture of a society.

Conclusion

Identification and analysis of ideal-seeking systems is in its infancy. The category is still generally unfamiliar. If we consider the twenty years it has taken to get from goal-seeking to purposeful systems, we can hardly expect the next step to be much quicker. The Understanding of this aspect of system behavior, however, seems to be essential if we are to solve the problems of adapting to the increasingly turbulent environments we are producing for ourselves.

REFERENCES

Ackoff, R. L. *Scientific Method: Optimizing Applied Research Decisions*. New York: John Wiley & Sons, 1962.

Churchman, C. W. *Prediction and Optimal Decision*. Englewood Cliffs, N.J.: Prentice Hall, 1961.

Singer, E. A., Jr. *On the Contented Life*. New York: Henry Holt, 1923 and 1936.

15

Epilogue: Rounding the Conceptual Circle

LOGIC, *n.* The art of thinking and reasoning in strict accordance with the limitations and incapacities of the human misunderstanding.

The Devil's Dictionary

Introduction

We began construction of a conceptual system in Chapter 2 by assuming the meanings of a few logical, temporal, and spatial concepts, and we used them to define concepts of mechanics and physics. Thus, starting with concepts taken from the formal sciences, we developed a few central concepts of the physical sciences and, using them, then proceeded to the behavioral sciences. The order of this development reflects the commonly held belief that the concepts of science, and hence the sciences themselves, are hierarchical in nature. The concepts of the formal and physical sciences are believed to be fundamental in some sense, and the concepts of the behavioral sciences are believed to be derived from them. This hierarchical conception of science is not one we share for reasons that are discussed in detail in Churchman and Ackoff (1950, Chap. 13) and Ackoff (1962, p. 170f).

We believe that all the concepts of science are interdependent, and therefore illumination of the meaning of any member of the system of scientific concepts can illuminate to varying degrees, each of the other concepts in the system. As we have noted earlier, historical ordering is often confused with logical or epistemological ordering. We do not take the concepts we began with to be basic in any way, but rather we maintain that they are definable in terms of the concepts derived from them. To show that this is the case is not to close a vicious circle, but to complete a cycle in which the initial concepts are enriched. It opens the way for another such cycle in which the meanings of all the concepts can be further enhanced.

In this the last lap on our circle we begin with a treatment of *logic* in behavioral terms and end with the extraction of the basic concepts of space and time with which construction of our conceptual system began. Logic, geometry, and kinematics are instruments of social beings. They were created

248

to serve a social purpose and hence can be better understood in terms of these purposes. In this epilogue we try to make these purposes clear.

We shall close the conceptual circle in outline only. To do more would require another work at least as long as this one.

Logic

15.1. *Propositions:* messages that potentially or actually produce changes in familiarity, knowledge, or understanding of their receivers.

Thus propositions are instruments by means of which one person can increase or decrease another's or his own probabilities or efficiencies of choice.

Grammarians and logicians normally define *proposition* in structural rather than functional terms, as, "a sentence or part of a sentence consisting of a subject and a predicate united by a copula." An instance would be, "Paper is white." Paper is the subject, white the predicate, and is the copula. The problem with such a rule is that exceptions are easy to find. "John is running" is a proposition by this rule, but "John runs" is not. Of course we can create another rule that converts "John runs" into "John is running," but if we start on this track we never reach an end to construction of *ad hoc* structural rules. Furthermore, "Beauty is frozen" may have the necessary form, but it conveys no meaning in most contexts and hence does not *function* as a proposition.

On the other hand, an expression such as "sit down" may change a person's probability of sitting down in a particular environment, but it would not usually affect his familiarity with, or knowledge, or understanding of this course of action. Therefore, it is not a proposition. Orders or prescriptions may change behavior without changing any psychological property of the one who obeys them.

Messages that affect only a person's intentions do not act as propositions. They are nevertheless statements. A proposition may affect intentions, but if so, this is an accidental rather than an essential property of it.

ANALYTIC AND SYNTHETIC PROPOSITIONS

Classification of propositions into *analytic* and *synthetic* is essential for the development of the logic of propositions. This distinction was first introduced by Immanuel Kant (1724–1804). In Kant's terms an analytic proposition is one the connotation of whose predicate is contained in that of its subject. According to this criterion, the proposition "A triangle is a three-sided figure," would be considered to be analytic. But "The radio is not working" would be synthetic.

Kant did not make clear how one can determine whether the connotation of the predicate is contained in that of the subject; that is, he did not define contained in.

It is often said that analytic statements tell us nothing about the world; they have no denotation. This seems to imply that the denotation of an analytic statement is not some real event; thus "The radio is not working" denotes some possible event we can respond to, but "Triangles are three-sided figures" does not. We know from our previous discussion, however, that all signs must have a denotation (Chap. 10). Then what is the denotation of an analytic proposition?

Analytic propositions seems to be concerned with *the way signs are used.* For example, "A triangle is a three-sided figure" tells us we can interchange the terms *triangle* and *three-sided figure* whenever they appear. Or again, "Green apples are green" tells us that we have a right to call green apples green. This may be obvious to those familiar with the language, but nevertheless it deals with linguistic usage. Analytic propositions are, in effect, linguistic rules established by a society. Hence we may say that the connotation of such a proposition is an *intention* of the society to have the terms used in a particular way, and its denotation is the use of the terms in the intended way. Because intention is a property of a purposeful individual, it is connoted and behavior is denoted. Thus the proposition "Green apples are green" is normally analytic; it actually connotes the intention of English-speaking people to employ the terms in the following way: when an individual responds to things denoted by *green apples*, he should also respond to the property green of these things.

Generalizing on this illustration, we can formulate the following definition.

15.2 *Analytic proposition:* a proposition that connotes the following kind of intention of the society in whose language it is expressed: if one or a set of signs has a certain denotation, connotation, or meaning, then another specific sign or set of signs should have a certain denotation, connotation, or meaning.

The proposition "If some *As* are *Bs*, then some *Bs* are *As*" is analytic. It connotes the intention that the meaning of "some *As* are *Bs*" and the meaning of "some *Bs* are *As*" be the same.

Analytic propositions must be studied with respect to some particular language and society. Hence the study of such statements is a social study; to determine whether or not any particular proposition is analytic we must determine whether it signifies the relevant society's intentions with respect to the use of linguistic signs. The determination of analyticity is not purely a formal problem; it requires significant psychological and social research.

It should be noted that many expressions that appear to be analytic in form are not analytic in certain contexts. For example, when it is said that in the West "Men are men," the expression is not usually analytic. Rather than inform us about the use of the sign *men*, it evaluates Western men. It is equivalent to saying that "Men of the West do not have any of the physical and personality traits that characterize women." For a proposition to be analytic it must perform a certain function, not merely have a specified form.

Now, by using the concepts developed thus far, we can begin to define the discipline of logic, since logic is a study of the analytic signs of a language.

All analytic propositions of a language belong to the logic of the language, but in view of the modern meaning of *formal* logic we cannot say the reverse: logic consists only of these analytic propositions. In order to find the complete criteria for the logic of a language we must deal with the notion of a *variable*.

VARIABLES

The concept *variable* is of great importance in all scientific work. In algebra, for example, we express important rules such as $a + b = b + a$ by use of variables — as and bs that refer to any number whatsoever. More specifically, the as and bs are directives that tell us they can be replaced by any numbers, as long as replacement is consistent.

Variables are signs of other signs and hence are symbols. Furthermore, a variable signifies a certain property of the signs signified: these signs, along with a certain manipulation, are coproducers of a transformation of the expression in which the variable appears into another that has some particular property, as into a particular type of signifier, or a proposition, or others. In general the manipulations signified consist of replacing the symbols by signs. In other words, the criterion for a variable can be stated as follows.

15.3. *Variable:* a symbol in a sign complex that (1) potentially or actually increases familiarity with substitution of any one of a specific set of signs for the symbol, and (2) signifies that the resulting sign complex should have some specified property.

15.4. *Sign function:* a sign complex containing one or more variables.

For example, Mr. X is a sign function. It is intended to lead us to substitute any name that designates a male member of the human species, and the resulting sign complex is supposed to designate some one person. In the sign function $x > 4$ we are to substitute any number that is greater than 4, and the resulting sign complex will be a true proposition.

15.5. *Value of a sign function:* the value of a sign complex that results from substituting an appropriate sign for a symbol in a sign function.

Thus a value of Mr. X is Mr. Jones, and another is Mr. Smith. A value of $x > 4$ is $5 > 4$, and this is a proposition. Hence $x > 4$ is called a *propositional function*.

Social intentions with respect to the use of signs can be expressed by propositional functions. For example, if in "If $x > y$ and $y > z$, then $x > z$" numbers are substituted for x, y, and z so that $x > y$ and $y > z$ are true, then it is the society's intention that $x > z$ be true.

An important rule in logic is that of *substitution*. This rule states that in an expression containing variables of a certain kind we may make a specified type of sign substitution for the variables, and the resulting expression will be valid. In general, the rule of substitution signifies a social intention that in certain expressions containing variables it is proper to regard the sign complex that results from the variable's replacement by one of a set of specified signs as a sign that has a certain property (such as denotation or connotation).

Now consider a sign function whose values are analytic propositions. "All *A* is *A*" is such a proposition. Another is "Whatever is both *A* and *B* is *A*." Thus "Whatever is both green and a table is a table" is an analytic proposition.

15.6. *Basic logic:* the set of sign functions whose values are analytic propositions.

Formal logic contains more than what we have called basic logic. Other rules are required.

LINGUISTIC RULES

English grammar consists of many types of rules concerning the way society intends messages to be constructed. But there is one type of rule that is of special importance to logic; for example, "If all *A*s are *B*s and all *B*s are *C*s, then all *A*s are *C*s." This expression connotes society's intention to have "all *A*s are *C*s" be true if "All *A*s are *B*s and all *B*s are *C*s" is true. This rule is an analytic proposition that is concerned with the process of *deduction*.

15.7. *Rule of deduction:* a proposition that connotes society's intention that if one sign complex is true or false, then another sign complex ought to be true or false.

Rules of deduction are analytic and hence belong to the basic logic of the language. Further, the rules of deduction apply to analytic propositions. Therefore, by their use we can derive additional propositions that are as true as those from which they are derived.

The definition of *rules of deduction* employed the concepts *true* and *false*. These, of course, are very important and deserve much more space than we can give them here.

15.8. *True (false):* a proposition is true (false) for a subject in a choice environment relative to an end of that individual if it is a potential or actual producer of a response that is for that end in that environment more (less) efficient than the behavior of that subject would have been in the absence of that proposition.

This definition makes precise the pragmatic concept of truth as that which works. It translates *works* into *efficiency*. The truth of a proposition so defined is not absolute, but is relative to the subject, his (its) environment, and his (its) end. If any one or more of these change, the truth of the proposition may also change. Truths may be more or less general, depending on the range of individuals, environments, and ends they apply to. An absolute truth would be one that would apply to every individual in every environment, whatever his ends. Now back to logic.

15.9. *Formal logic:* the set of all sign functions whose values are analytic, plus all sign functions that can be derived from them by deductive rules.

Thus formal logic is an aspect of a society's language, and the determination of its properties depends on what we take the society to be. Sometimes the society is taken to be all the users of a language; sometimes it is restricted to the experts in a field. The formal logic of professional logicians may be quite different from that of most English-speaking people.

Before we can move conceptually from logic to kinematics we must first reconsider the nature of an *individual* (see definition 2.11), but this time in functional terms.

Individuation and Identification

In the beginning of this effort we assumed the meanings of *property*, *individual*, and *class*, which are important components of formal logic and science in general.

We usually think of a property as something that belongs to an object or event independently of the observer of that object or event. But when we reflect on the way an observer determines whether or not an object or event has a certain property, it becomes clear that what we mean by a property is what it can do to him in certain circumstances. We say a body is heavy if lifting it requires a great deal of effort, or if when it is placed on a scale a certain reading can be made (responded to).

15.10. *Property:* a potentiality for producing a specified type of response in a subject in a specified choice environment.

When we say something is an individual for a person we mean it acts as a unit for him, that its properties cohere and act on him as a whole. We do not separate the weight of a table from the table, since we think it is an essential property of the table. We can separate from it the package lying on top of the table, but not its legs. That is, we recognize that the function the table has for us requires its having legs and weight, but not a package lying on it. The table is for us, then, a collection of properties essential to perform a certain function; the table is an instrument we incorporate into a specific type of our purposeful behavior.

15.11. *Individual:* A set of properties to which a subject A responds in a choice environment S is an individual to A if (1) that set of properties is virtually certain to produce a response R by A in S, (2) the removal of any one of the set of properties reduces the probability of R by A in S to virtually zero, and (3) no other set of properties satisfies conditions (1) and (2).

In effect, a set of properties is said to be an individual if we can find an environment and a response such that the collection of properties has a unique characteristic: it is virtually necessary and sufficient (practically certain) to produce a specified response in that environment.

15.12. *Essential properties of an individual:* the properties that are individually necessary and collectively sufficient to produce the response *R*, which defines the individual.

Not all properties of an individual are essential. It usually has nonessential properties as well. Visibility is an essential property of paper, but whiteness or yellowness is not. The defining response (say, writing) may change with a change in color of the paper, but not functionally. That is, different colored inks may be used by the person, but writing may still occur. Then whiteness and yellowness produce structural not functional changes in the defining response, and thus are nonessential properties of paper.

A property of an individual that produces a functional change in the defining response, but does not do so invariably, is also a nonessential property of that individual. For example, city sidewalks are ordinarily lightly colored. That the lightness of their color is nonessential is clear, for we would not expect its absence (a darker color) to assure nonuse of the sidewalk. Nor would we expect its presence to add to the probability of the occurrence of walking.

What constitutes an individual for a subject may change in different environments, and different things may constitute individuals for different subjects in the same environment. When packing books for shipment each book is an individual. For the student reading an assignment, each page or paragraph may be an individual. For a typesetter, each letter is an individual. There is nothing absolute about individuality. It is a functional not a structural property that lies in the observer as much as in the observed.

Collections of individuals may themselves be individuals. An individual may conceive of his library, as well as each book in it, as an individual. Consider a collection of individuals that is an entity to an observer, each element of which is essential; that is, if any element is removed, the response to the collection changes functionally. Such a collection constitutes a *set*. Thus a pair of shoes, a matched pen and pencil, and the volumes of an encyclopedia constitute sets.

15.13. *Set of individuals:* a collection of individuals that is itself an individual; the inclusion of each member is essential.

15.14. *Class of individuals:* a collection of individuals, each of which may be replaced by any other of the collection in an environment without affecting the subject's response to the one substituted for.

The members of a class have the same relevant properties for a subject. Thus a collection of objects may constitute a class to a subject in one state but not in another. For one purpose, any volume of a set of books may be as good as another (as a paperweight); for another purpose, the content of each volume may be relevant (for reference).

What a person treats as an individual has the property of oneness; it is *one* thing. Two things may be the same (members of the same class) or different, but two things that are the same in every respect are not two but one thing. Let us consider in more detail the processes by which a person treats two things as two or one.

When a person treats a set of properties as an individual, he *individualizes*. The process of individualization is basic to all purposeful activity. Mental growth is closely related to the development of our ability to individualize and classify. The infant is said at first to experience undifferentiated masses of properties; only gradually does it gain the ability to individualize even itself. When individualization begins, consciousness dawns and the learning process starts.

But mere individualization is not enough if we are to learn most efficiently from our experience; we must be able to *relate* our experiences.

15.15. *Relation between objects and/or events:* a property or properties of a set of objects and/or events that they do not have taken separately.

If John and Mary are married, then married is a property of the pair. Marriage is not usually taken as an essential property of the individuals involved, but it is usually so considered for the pair.

We learn through experience, and learning involves the ability to apply what is learned at one time and place to another time and place. In order to do so we must be able to recognize likenesses and differences. Such recognition takes place through *identification* and *individuation*. Roughly put, identification is the process of treating individuals as the same; individuation is the process of treating them as different. The two processes may take place simultaneously, as we shall see.

Of the many available ways of individuating and identifying objects and events, the most general that man has devised involves the use of space-time coordinates. In order to understand spatial and temporal concepts we must understand their function — how they facilitate individuation and identification.

Let us first consider identification in a single environment. This environment, of course, is not necessarily defined at a moment of time but may extend over a period of time. Suppose a person who is alone in his office and wants to communicate to another person can use either a pencil or a typewriter to prepare a message. Then he may identify the pencil and typewriter by the function of communication. If he wants to keep papers from blowing away, he may use either a book or an ashtray to serve as a weight. Here he identifies the book and the ashtray by their structural property (weight) as well as their function.

Therefore, when a person who is pursuing a particular goal in a particular environment exhibits responses to two things, and those responses have a common property (p_2), then he identifies the two things by a property p_1 that produces the common property of his responses, p_2. To identify two or more things by one property is, of course, not equivalent to considering the two things to be identical. A person normally considers a pen and a typewriter to be different in some structural properties as well as in properties that are functional (such as mobility, legibility, time to produce a message).

If a person's responses to two things are alike in all respects, then the person makes a complete identification of these things. They are exactly the same thing for him. Hence they are one, not two, things for him. If at the other extreme the responses to two things are completely different, then the things are completely different for the person, and a complete individuation has taken place.

Now consider identification and individuation in different environments. What does it mean to say, for example, that a person takes this house to be the same one he was in yesterday? The most obvious answer is that he takes them to be the same house if he responds to them in the same way. This is not an adequate answer. When we meet a friend casually and when we see him about to be run down by a truck, our responses may be entirely different because our ends are different. To take care of such cases we can use a technique already employed; we said that a person may have a high intention for some end even though he does not pursue it in this environment. The test for intention is based on making an adjustment of observed behavior to what would occur if a certain type of intention environment prevailed. Analogously here we say that an individual identifies two things if we can assure ourselves that he would respond in the same manner to them were the environmental conditions the same.

15.16. *Identification and individuation:* a subject *identifies* two things perceived at different times if, were he in the same choice environment at these times, he would respond to the things in the same way. If not, he *individuates* the two things.

To facilitate the process of identification, *identification signs* are frequently used. This is the type of sign designed to evoke a similar response to an object or event in various environments. The name of a person, a label on a box, or a number on a house may all serve as identification signs. Such signs may be unreliable, as when two persons have the same name. Only space-time properties are sufficient to guarantee reliable identification.

Time

To determine what time means to a subject it is necessary to make clear the meaning of change in an individual. If an essential property of an individual changes, that individual changes to another individual or ceases to exist. An individual changes and remains the same individual when its nonessential properties change. When a subject responds to a change in such a property, he responds to a change *in* (not of) the individual. Thus we respond to a change in a friend's clothes, but he is the same friend. Even though two different friends wear the same clothing, we respond to them differently.

A change of an individual's nonessential property is an event. People develop ways of individuating events that occur to the same individual, even to themselves. A person may differentiate between breakfasts by their content, location, or by those with whom he had the meal. Some of these individuating properties may be adequate only in special circumstances. He may have the same breakfast with the same people at the same place on different days. Two events that occur to the same individual may be the same with respect to every property save one, time. Two events that occur to the same individual at the same time cannot be otherwise identical; they must differ in some respect, otherwise they would not be two events.

15.17. *Time:* a property of events that is sufficient to enable one individual to individuate any two changes in the same property of the same individual.

Note that this is a functional, not a structural, definition of time. Time is defined by what it does, not what it is in some metaphysical or physical sense. It can be defined structurally in particular environments. If the positions of hands of a clock in the environment of two events is sufficient to distinguish between them, then this positional difference defines time structurally in that environment. It is apparent that different types of structural differences do the same thing in different types of environment (such as position of the sun, length of shadows, and amount of sand in the bottom of an hourglass). But no single type of structural difference in events occurring to the same individual is sufficient for individuating them in all circumstances. This is why time is a functional concept. Difficulties in defining it have derived from the effort to do so in structural terms.

We tend to identify the meaning of time with the way we measure it, and we usually measure it in a way that relates to the rotation of the earth around the sun (structurally). Hence we erroneously conclude that time is a structural concept. The error becomes apparent in situations when astronomical measures do not serve our purposes well. In measuring the rate of growth of plants, C. W. Thornthwaite (1953) found the use of astronomically measured time inadequate. He therefore sought a biological clock, and found one in the pea plant. He used time between appearances of successive nodes on the pea plant as units of time. These units were of different duration when measured astronomically, but they made possible more useful prediction and control of harvests than did hours and days. We measure time by use of events that are identical in all respects save time, and in principle these can be any type of event, not only ones that are astronomical. Which we use should be determined by our purposes.

This is of particular importance for the study of psychological and social systems. The momentary present of these systems has no correspondence with any particular structural definition of momentary present — for example, a split second in the flow of consciousness (Mead, 1932; Emery, 1967). The properties and events that functionally define the momentary present must be determined by our purposes. Therefore, let us take a functional look at the concept of a moment.

A moment of time is a period so short that an event cannot occur within it. Hence there is no basis for differentiating between parts of this period; it has no parts. Put another way, suppose a person has no way of differentiating between two times, t_1 and t_2. Then t_1 and t_2 are the same time for him and the period t_1-t_2 is a moment of time. Thus a moment of time is a period of time whose beginning and end cannot be individuated by a person.

15.18.   *Momentariness:* a property of an individual that is sufficient to preclude a response to change of that individual.

15.19.   *Moment of time:* an individual whose only essential property is momentariness.

Thus a moment is an individual that precludes any response to change in itself.

In this book we have often referred to the properties of an individual at a moment of time. In considering changes in an individual we compared an individual at different moments of time. We referred to these static cross sections of an individual as a *state* of that individual. Remember that we defined the *state of an individual* as the set of its properties at a moment of time.

We are now in a position to deal with the concept of a *time-slice* in functional terms. But first let us make clear that when we say two individuals have the same momentary property we mean that a person identifies the two individuals with respect to their time property.

15.20.   A *time-slice* relative to a subject A is a collection of individuals; one of the essential properties of the collection is its momentariness; all the members of the collection have the same essential momentary property; and the collection includes all objects and events that A responds to and that have this momentary property.

The members of the collection that define a time-slice can be said to exist *simultaneously* for the subject. A room constitutes a time-slice for a person if he reacts to this room and the objects in it as a collection in such a way that the entire room and each thing in it have the same momentary property for him, and if these constitute all the objects relevant to him and have this same momentary property.

The next task is to put some *order* into a set of moments or time-slices — to see what gives time its direction. The idea of before and after seems to be one of the most difficult of all concepts to define. Indeed, we find the typical reaction to this difficulty expressed by even our most eminent philosophers and scientists. Einstein (1923) wrote:

> The experiences of an individual appear to us arranged in a series of events; in
> this series the single events which we remember appear to be ordered according

to the criterion of "earlier" and "later," which cannot be analyzed further. There exists, therefore, for the individual, an I-time, or subjective time. This in itself is not measurable (p. 1).

Analyses of the unanalyzable and conceptions of the inconceivable (such as Einstein himself made in other areas) have provided the milestones along the road of scientific progress. When concepts are widely regarded as indefinable, it indicates that they require some kind of very basic reformulation and reorientation. Such a reorientation is provided here by our dealing with time in functional not structural terms.

An important attempt to define time in terms of purposive behavior was made by the American pragmatic philosopher Charles Peirce. For Peirce (1940), "future conduct is the only conduct that is subject to self-control" (p. 261). This suggested to him a functional criterion for distinguishing the past from the future.

> One of the most marked features about the law of mind is that it makes time have a definite direction of flow from past to future. The relation of past to future is, in reference to the law of mind, different from the relation of future to past. This makes one of the great contrasts between the law of mind and the law of physical force, there is no more distinction between the two opposite directions in time than between moving northward and moving southward.
>
> In order, therefore, to analyze the law of mind, we must begin by asking what the flow of time consists in. Now, we find that in reference to any individual state of feeling, all others are of two classes, those which affect this one (or have a tendency to affect it . . .), and those which do not. The present is affectable by the past but not by the future . . .
>
> If, of two states, each is absolutely unaffectable by the other, they are to be regarded as parts of the same state. They are contemporaneous (p. 343).

Roughly, then, Peirce thought that one state or time-slice preceded another for a person if he treated one as potentially affecting the other, but not vice versa. This is an insight we want to employ in defining the direction of time, though there are several details we shall want to refine to avoid a vicious circle. Peirce's insight was that purposeful individuals distinguish the past from the future on the basis of what they believe they can control. With respect to the future, there are always things their present behavior can accomplish, but they do not regard their present behavior as having any potential influence on the past. Even a man in a prison cell, or a paralytic, thinks of himself as capable of changing the future in some respect, even though it is only a change in his own behavior, as from sitting to walking or a change of a recollected image.

Instead of saying that for a purposeful individual the future is always potentially changeable, we change the terminology and say tentatively that the future (as opposed to the past) is what a purposeful individual takes to be potentially producible by his behavior. But the notion *produce* already contains the notion of the future; the producer was defined as preceding the product.

To avoid this difficulty we define a relationship like producer–product in all respects save that of precedence. This can be done by eliminating reference to time in the definitions of *necessity* and *sufficiency*, and calling the resulting concepts *necessity** and *sufficiency**. Then we can define *essentiality* as follows.

15.20.   *Essentiality:* A thing x of class X in an environment $\bar{x}$ of class $\bar{X}$ is essential for another object y of class Y in an environment $\bar{y}$ of class $\bar{Y}$ at another time if x in $\bar{x}$ is necessary* and insufficient* for y in $\bar{y}$.

There is nothing in this definition that orders x and y temporally. It may seem paradoxical, however, to say that an x that comes after a y can be essential for it, but such an assertion can be meaningful. For example, we not only say that an explosion yesterday was necessary for the damaged building we see today, but we may also say that the presence of an undamaged building today is essential for there not having been an explosion in it yesterday. Or it is necessary* though insufficient* that we do not receive a letter from someone today to prove that it was not sent to us earlier.

If one event or state (x_1) is essential for another (x_2), then the nonoccurrence of the second (x_2') is essential for the nonoccurrence of the first (x_1'). But x_2 is neither necessary* nor sufficient* for x_1. When a person believes that one event or state (x_1) is essential for another (x_2), then he also believes that x_2' is essential for x_1', and that x_2 is not essential for x_1.

15.22.   *Precedence:* a property of two events or states that occur at different times that is sufficient to preclude a belief that one of these events or states is essential for the other.

If one event or state (x_2) is precluded from being believed to be essential for another (x_1), but x_1 is not precluded from being believed to be essential for x_2, then x_1 precedes x_2.

If one moment of time (t_1) precedes another (t_2), and the second precedes a third (t_3), then t_2 lies between t_1 and t_3. A period of time (a duration) can be defined by two moments of time and all the moments that come between them.

15.23.   *Duration of time* $(t_1–t_n)$: a collection of moments of time for a subject, of which t_1 and t_n are members, every moment lying between t_1 and t_n are members, and no moment not lying between t_1 and t_n is a member.

We have now defined in functional terms all the temporal concepts that have been used throughout this effort. Only spatial concepts remain to be similarly treated.

Space

15.24.   *Location* for a subject is a property of a time-slice that is sufficient to enable him (it) to individuate any two individuals in that time-slice.

Location is the one property with respect to which any two individuals in the same time-slice cannot be the same for a person. Location, however, is not always necessary for individuation, as we have already seen. Objects may be individuated by use of other properties.

Points in space are analogous to moments of time.

15.25. *Point in space:* an individual whose only essential property is location and that cannot be responded to as more than one individual.

What characterizes a point is its indivisibility and the fact that it has location as its only essential property.

In order to define a line it is convenient to be able to speak of a point's changing its location. Then we could define a line as a path of a point that changes its location. But a point has been defined as having location as its only essential property; therefore, if its location changes it is no longer the same point. We can avoid this difficulty by considering the method by which a point is located.

Location is usually specified with respect to some coordinate system.

15.26. *Spatial coordinate system:* a set of signs which denote locations.

Such a system is usually, but not always, composed of a reference point, called a *point of origin,* and a set of distances from that point (as in an ordinary line graph). Now a single point may be located relative to any number of different coordinate systems. A point on a piece of paper lying on a desk may be signified by reference to either the paper itself, or the top of the desk, or the room, or others. Now if the paper is moved, the location of the point relative to the paper remains unchanged, but it changes relative to the top of the desk or room. Relative to the piece of paper the point has not changed, but relative to the desk and room it is no longer the same point.

Thus a point whose location has not changed relative to one coordinate system but has changed relative to another can be said to have moved or changed its location. Now we can define the path of a point, or a *line.*

15.27. *Line* (p_1-p_n): if a point p is located at p_1 relative to a coordinate system CS_1 at time t_1, and is located at p_n relative to CS_1 at time t_n, but has not changed its location relative to another coordinate system CS_2, then the path of p (or line p_1-p_n) is a collection of points relative to CS_1 of which (1) p_1 and p_n are members, (2) every location of p in the time interval t_1-t_n is a member, and (3) only locations of p in this time interval are members.

The similarity of the definition of a line and a temporal duration is apparent, since duration is really the temporal path of a temporal point. But whereas a temporal duration is one-directional, a spatial path is not. There are many possible paths between two points in space and many different ways that a path between two points may be traveled. For example, one may move back and forth along a path, retracing previously used path segments. A point can return to a previous location, but a moment cannot. Put another way, there is only one path and one distance between two points in time, but not so in space. Generalizing on the definition of a line, we can define a *surface* as a path of a line over time, and a *volume* as the path of a surface over time.

In principle a line may contain an infinite number of points, but in practice an individual can individuate only a finite number of these. How many he can individuate depends on his measurement capabilities. Using this fact, we can define a *straight line* as follows.

15.28.   *Straight line:* the path of a point relative to a surface between two locations on that surface, which contains the minimum number of locations that an subject can individuate.

Since two points may be on different surfaces, a straight line between them on one surface may not be a straight line or even a line on another. Thus straight lines on a surface of a sphere lie on great circles. But a straight line connecting two points on the surface of a sphere relative to a plane on which both lie would be different.

15.29.   *Length of a line:* the number of points a line contains that a subject can individuate.

The use of units of length is a convenient transformation of this number. To say that one line is two inches long and another is four, is to say that the second line contains twice as many individuateable points.

Consider the case in which two straight lines of equal length have only one point in common. These are called *intersecting lines*. If a person responds differently to these lines, he responds to a difference in their *direction*.

15.30.   *Directions of lines:* a property of lines of equal length with only one point in common, which is sufficient to enable a subject to individuate them.

Direction and distance are two essential properties of lines. We may also speak of the location of a line. If an individual responds differently to two lines of equal length and the same direction, he responds to a difference in their locations.

With the concepts that have been defined here, all the remaining concepts needed for geometry (and kinematics and mechanics) can be derived.

Conclusion

We could continue to define concepts in geometry and kinematics, but we have gone far enough for our purposes. We have tried to show that functional concepts of behavior can be used to illuminate the meaning of concepts of formal science, which are often taken as indefinable. Our position throughout has been that the concepts of science form a system, and that the wide range of concepts used in science, functional as well as structural, are compatible.

REFERENCES

Ackoff, R. L. *Scientific Method: Optimizing Applied Research Decisions.* New York: John Wiley & Sons, 1962.

Churchman C. W. *Prediction and Optimal Decision.* Englewood Cliffs, N.J.: Prentice-Hall, 1961.

Churchman, C. W., and R. L. Ackoff. *Methods of Inquiry.* St. Louis: Educational Publishers, 1950.

Einstein, Albert. *The Meaning of Relativity.* Princeton, N.J.: Princeton University Press, 1923.

Emery, F. E. "The Next Thirty Years: Concepts, Methods and Anticipations." *Human Relations* 20 (1967): 199–235.

Mead, G. H. *The Philosophy of the Present.* LaSalle, Ill.: Open Court, 1932 and 1959.

Peirce, C. S. *The Philosophy of Peirce, Selected Writings.* Edited by Justus Buchler. New York: Harcourt, Brace, 1940.

Thornthwaite, C. W. "Operations Research in Agriculture." *Journal of the Operations Research Society of America* 1 (1953): 33–38.

Appendix I

Errors of Observation

There are four possible sources of error in observation: (1) the observer himself, (2) the observed, (3) the instruments used in making observations, and (4) the environment in which the observations are made. Furthermore three possible types of error can be produced by these sources: (*a*) observing inaccurately (as miscounting or mismeasuring), (b) not seeing something that is there, and (*c*) seeing something that is not there. Because of these errors we consider some people to be better observers than others, and several tests have been developed for evaluation of observers.

Kirk and Talbot (1966) have named these three types of observational error as (*a*) *systematic* or *stretch* distortion, (*b*) *fog* distortion, and (*c*) *mirage.* Each of these types of error can be produced by any of the four sources of error. (See table I.1.)

SYSTEMATIC DISTORTION

In SD [systematic distortion] no information is lost. Rather, it is changed or recorded in an orderly or systematic way. Distortions of this kind are like the distortions a rubber sheet might undergo, so long as it is not torn. Thus, SD can be eliminated or "corrected for" by the application of a rule specifying the appropriate "topological transformation" (p. 310).

Kirk and Talbot cite the following example of systematic distortion produced by an observer.

Astronomer Maskelyne fired his assistant, Kinnebrooke, because the latter was clearly incompetent. Charged with clocking upper transits of certain reference stars, Kinnebrooke consistently clocked them "late" (p. 308).

They illustrate instrument-produced systematic distortion as follows.

Some auto rear-view mirrors are cylindrically convex so that a driver may scan

265

at a glance far more than a "flat-mirror glimpse" of the territory behind him. Again, he sees images which are tall and thin, and they require "getting used to."

A bathroom scale that is improperly set will also produce a systematic bias in readings of persons' weights.

An example of observed-produced systematic distortion is found in a subject who, on being interviewed, always, or almost always lies. If he always lied we could easily correct for this distortion by attaching a "not" to his main verbs.

Environment-produced systematic distortion is introduced, say, by a non-white light when we are trying to determine the color of objects. Changing temperatures will also change the length of metal bars and hence may produce distorted observations. These could be corrected if we know the temperature and the coefficients of linear expansion of the metals under observation.

Table I.1.   Sources and types of errors of observation

Sources of Error	Types of Error		
	Systematic	Fog	Mirage
1. Observer			
2. Observed			
3. Instruments			
4. Environment			

FOG

Fog occurs when an observer does not see what is there. In such distortion ". . . information is lost, mashed out, 'fogged' over . . ." (p. 313). An observer may not be able to hear sounds above an abnormally low frequency or volume if he is partially deaf. If he is color blind, then, of course, he fails to observe color.

Recording equipment may also fail to pick up low-volume sounds or high frequencies. Film may fail to capture color. (If it distorts color, the result is systematic distortion, not fog).

Noise in an environment may result in our failure to hear certain sounds. Glare may prevent our seeing objects that would otherwise be clearly visible.

A subject in an interview who lapses into a language or use of words that we do not understand introduces fog into the exchange. Ambiguity is a type of fog. For example, some feel that James Joyce produced an inpenetrable verbal fog in *Finnegan's Wake.*

MIRAGE

"In mirage distortion (MD) we see something that 'isn't there.' Far from withholding information from us, MD gives us extra, unwanted information" (p. 316).

Most of us have seen or heard things that were not there or tasted ingredients in food that were not there. A subject in an interview can deliberately (or not) produce in us a belief of the occurrence of an event that never took place. A burglar alarm system may go off because of an internal defect when no intruder is present. A false alarm is a mirage. In a very noisy environment we may hear things that were not said.

Hence there are four sources and three types of observational error. Implicitly or explicitly each observer has relevant beliefs with respect to each, and these determine whether or not use will be made of the data obtained. When the observer believes that error is present, he may be able to correct for it if he knows its source and nature. For example, he can correct for the bias of the bathroom scale or the late response of another observer. By interpolation he can fill in missing data, and by a wide variety of tests he can eliminate inconsistent data. The theory of data adjustment is frequently used in science for just this purpose (Deming, 1943).

References

Deming, W. E. *Statistical Adjustment of Data.* New York: John Wiley & Son, 1943.
Kirk, J. R., and G. D. Talbot. "The Distortion of Information." In *Communication and Culture,* edited by A. G. Smith, pp. 308–21. New York: Holt, Rinehart & Winston, 1966.

Appendix II

The Form of Perceptions and Observations

The form of observations is reflected in the form of messages about them. Such messages contain statements, and these in turn contain expressions. Therefore, we examine the form of both statements and expressions that deal with observations. The scheme we will use is the following.

1. Form of statements:
   a. Predication — classification
   b. Comparative
   c. Functional
2. Form of expressions
   a. Qualitative
   b. Quantitative

FORM OF STATEMENTS

A statement may be represented abstractly as $(F(x_1, x_2, ..., x_n)$, where $x_1, x_2, ..., x_n$ represents the things observed, and F represents a relationship among them. The things observed are referred to as arguments, F is referred to as the predicate, and n is the degree of the predicate.

For $n = 1$ (a predicate of degree 1), we have a predicational type of statement. The statement *Charles is a male* has the form $F(x)$, where x denotes the subject, *Charles*, and F denotes the (monadic) predicate, *is a male*.

For $n > 1$, we have a relational statement. *New York is east of Chicago* has the form $F(x_1, x_2)$, where x_1 and x_2 denote *New York* and *Chicago*, and F denotes the predicate, *is east of.*

A statement that contains a triadic predicate (a predicate of degree 3) is *Chicago lies between New York and Denver*, which has the form $F(x_1, x_2, x_3)$. It should be noted that the statement *Charles and Tom are males* may be

268

intended as an abbreviation of *Charles is a male and Tom is a male*, which has the form $F(x_1)$ and $F(x_2)$ rather than $F(x_1, x_2)$.

Predication and Classification. As indicated above, a simple predicational type of statement is one that has the form $F(x)$, as in *Charles is a male*. Such a statement attributes a property to an object, event, or some combination of these.

A compound predicational statement combines two or more simple ones. *Charles is a male* $[F_1(x)]$ and *Charles is an adult* $[F_2(x)]$ can be combined into *Charles is an adult male*. This statement can be represented by $F_1(x)$ and $F_2(x)$. Similarly, the statement *Charles and Tom are adult males* combines two compound predicational statements, and can be represented by $F_1(x_1)$, $F_1(x_2)$, $F_2(x_1)$, and $F_2)x_2$. This symbolism makes explicit that confirmation of the statement requires four attributions.

In order to confirm simple predicational statements, it is necessary to (a) identify the subject and (b) define the attributed property. Identification, as we have already seen, involves specifying a set of properties sufficient to differentiate the subject from any other possible subjects. Hence identification involves a compound predicational statement, $[F_1(x), F_2(x), ..., F_m(x)]$, where $F_1, F_2, ..., F_m$ are sufficient to identify x.

It will be noted that the statement *Charles is a male* is equivalent to *Charles is a member of the set of males*. That is, every predicational statement *classifies* its subject. Therefore, corresponding to each (monadic) predicate (F) defined over a set (X) there is a subset of X consisting of all those members of X that have the predicate F. A simple predicate applied to a set, then, creates two classes. If there are m predicates, 2^m classes can be constructed.

Relations and Comparisons. A statement with a predicate of degree greater than 1 is called a relational statement. In $F(x_1, x_2)$ a property is attributed to x_1 and x_2 taken collectively. In the statement *Charles is the brother of Horace*, the predicate, *is a brother of*, cannot be attributed to either subject taken separately, as can the predicate, *are male*. It will be noted that in this statement we can revise the order of the subjects, *Charles* (x_1) and *Horace* (x_2); that is, $F(x_1, x_2)$ implies $F(x_2, x_1)$.

Where the predicate holds for every pair of subjects in a set, the relation is said to be symmetric over the set. Such a relation *does not order* the subjects, but a relation that is not symmetric may. An example is *Charles is younger than Horace*. Here $F(x_1, x_2)$ does not imply $F(x_2, x_1)$. *Charles* and *Horace* are said to be an ordered pair.

To order more than two subjects a relation must be transitive in addition to not being symmetric. A (dyadic) predicate is said to be transitive if and only if, for any triplet of arguments, x, y, and z, $F(x, y)$ and $F(y, z)$ together imply $F(x, z)$. A comparative statement is any statement whose principal predicate is an ordering relation. For example, the predicate *is less than* defined over the set of real numbers provides an ordering of the real numbers.

Ordering relations are of two types, quasi and strict, depending on whether the relation is reflexive or irreflexive. A (dyadic) relation F defined over a set X is said to be reflexive if and only if $F(x, x)$ is true for every x in X. It is said to be irreflexive if and only if $F(x, x)$ is false for every x in X.

Examples of quasi-ordering relations are *less than or equal to* over the set of real numbers, *is at least as tall as* over the set of human beings, and *implies* over the set of statements. Examples of strict ordering relations are *is less than* over the set of real numbers, *is the ancestor of* over the set of human beings, and *is a proper subset of* over the set of sets. There are many different types of ordering relations; some are discussed in detail by Ackoff (1962, Chap. 6).

Functions. A particularly important class of relational statements consists of ones involving a functional relation. In a statement of the form $F(x_1, x_2 ..., x_n)$, where $n > 1$, if when F and all but one of the x's are specified, the value of the remaining x is completely determined, then F is a *strong* functional relation. Consider the (dyadic) statement *Gloria is the spouse of Charles*, which can be represented as $F(x_1, x_2)$. Once F is specified as "is the spouse of" and either x_1 or x_2 is specified (Gloria or Charles), then the value of the other is completely determined. This statement may be rewritten as either $x_1 = f_1(x_2)$ or $x_2 = f_2(x_1)$.

Consider the triadic predicate F defined over the real numbers such that $F(x_1, x_2, x_3)$ means x_1 is the sum of x_2 and x_3. Such a predicate yields a function for all its arguments, and we may write

$$x_1 = f_1(x_2, x_3),$$
$$x_2 = f_2(x_1, x_3),$$
$$x_3 = f_3(x_2, x_3).$$

In this case,

$$f_1(x_2, x_3) = x_2 + x_3,$$
$$f_2(x_1, x_3) = x_3 - x_1,$$
$$f_3(x_1, x_2) = x_2 - x_1.$$

Note the important property of statements involving strong functional relations: if the value of any (independent) argument inside the functional bracket is changed, the value of the (dependent) argument on the left side of the equation must be changed.

Now let us consider a *weak* functional relation: the dyadic predicate *is the father of* in the domain of human beings. $F(x_1, x_2)$ means x_1 is the father of x_2. For any given value of x_2 there is only one value of x_1 such that $F(x_1, x_2)$ is true. In this case, however, specifying x_1 does not determine x_2, since x_1 may be the father of several persons. In general, a predicate is a weak functional relation for its kth argument if and only if (1) when the values of all arguments except the kth are fixed, precisely one value for the kth argument is determined, and (2) a change in an x other than x_k may not necessitate a change in x_k.

In the statement F.D.R. *was the father of James Roosevelt*, if *F.D.R.* is changed, *James Roosevelt* must be also; but if *James Roosevelt* is changed, *F.D.R.* need not be (if one of his other offspring is substituted for James). In the earlier example when F denotes *is the spouse of*, both x_1 and x_2 were sufficient to completely determine the other. Here, x_2 is sufficient (relative to the predicate *was the father of*) to determine x_1, but x_1 is not sufficient to determine x_2. However, x_1 is sufficient to specify a class of subjects, any one of which when substituted for x_2 makes the statement true; therefore, x_1 bounds the values of x_2.

When we examine the type of statements that take the form $x_1 = f(x_2, x_3, ...)$, we observe three different types that are characterized by the property of the function. Consider first the familiar law of freely falling bodies.

$$s = \tfrac{1}{2} g t^2,$$

in which s is the distance traveled, g is the gravitational constant, and t is the time from release. We note that (for nonnegative s, g, and t)

$$s = f_1(g, t),$$

where

$$f_1(g, t) = \tfrac{1}{2} g t^2$$
$$g = f_2(s, t),$$

where

$$f_2(s, t) = 2s/t^2$$
$$t = f_3(s, g),$$

where

$$f_3(s, g) = \sqrt{2s/g}.$$

Clearly the functional relation involved in this law is strong, since the value of each argument is completely determined by the other two.

Now consider a statement of the form $x_1 = f(x_2, x_3, ..., x_k)$, where x_2, x_3 ..., x_k is a subset of a set of arguments sufficient to completely determine the value of x_1. The subset, then, only partially determines (bounds) the value of x_1. Suppose that, in fact, (1) $x_1 = x_2 + x_3$, (2) x_2 and x_3 are independent, and (3) x_3 can assume three different values: -1, 0, and 1. Suppose further that we do not know about x_3, but we do know that the value of x_1 depends on the value of x_2 and something else. Then from observation we could determine that either (a) $x_1 = x_2 - 1$, or (b) $x_1 = x_2$, or (c) $x_1 = x_2 + 1$.

Suppose also that the probabilities of observing each were $p(a) = 0.25$, $p(b) = 0.25$, and $p(c) = 0.50$. We could now compute $E(x_1)$, the expected value of x_1:

$$E(x_1) = 0.25 (x_2 - 1) + 0.25 (x_2) + 0.50 (x_2 + 1)$$
$$= 0.25x_2 - 0.25 + 0.25x_2 + 0.50x_2 + 0.50$$
$$= x_2 + 0.25$$

Now, although the expected value of x_1, $E(x_1)$, is completely determined, the value of x_1 is not. We know that a change in x_2 is *not* sufficient to result in a change in x_1, since a change in x_3 may compensate for it. But we do know that knowledge of the value of x_2 is necessary for determining the value of x_1. Then x_2 is not a deterministic cause of x_1, but (as we have already considered in Chapter 2) it is a probabilistic cause or producer of x_1.

Suppose that we do not know whether the value of x_1 depends on the value of x_2; that is, we know of no necessary connection between x_1 and x_2, but we have observed that x_1 tends to increase as does x_2. Once again we may express x_1 as a function of x_2, but this is a pseudo function since x_2 is not sufficient for, and we do not know that it is necessary for, determining the value of x_1. We cannot say that x_2 is either the cause or the producer of x_1, but we may be able to say that they are correlated.

Consider a person who usually brushes his teeth once a day, just before going to sleep at night. Brushing his teeth is neither necessary nor sufficient for his going to sleep, and hence is neither the cause nor the producer of his retiring for the night. And yet the two events usually occur together. Again, in a large city it was discovered that people who live in neighborhoods where there is a heavy sootfall are more likely to get tuberculosis than are people who live in neighborhoods with less sootfall. Yet medical research has shown that sootfall is neither necessary nor sufficient for the occurrence of tuberculosis. Hence the values of two variables may tend to change together, and yet the variables may not be causally connected. Such variables are said to be correlated.

The knowledge that two things tend or do not tend to change together can, nevertheless, be very useful. When we see a person brush his teeth at night, we can predict with some assurance that he is about to retire. That is, we can use our knowledge of the value of one variable to predict the value of another.

FORM OF EXPRESSIONS IN STATEMENTS: QUALITY AND QUANTITY

Compare the following two statements: *John is heavy* and *John weighs 150 pounds*. Both appear to be simple predicational statements of the form $F(x_1)$, where x_1 denotes *is heavy* in the first and *weighs 150 pounds* in the second. The obvious difference between these two statements is that the second contains a number. What is not so obvious is that because the second statement contains a number in what appears to be its predicate, it should be represented as a functional statement of the form $F(x_1, x_2)$, where F denotes *is equal to*, x_1 denotes *John's weight*, and x_2 denotes *150 pounds*. This is a weak function, since specification of F and x_1 completely determines x_2, but F and x_2 do not determine x_1.

A transformation similar to changing *John weighs 150 pounds* into *John's weight is equal to 150 pounds* cannot be performed on *John is heavy*. We can transform this statement into *John's weight is greater than W pounds or John's weight is greater than* W_1 *pounds and less than* W_2 *pounds.* There is, however, no reasonable transformation of *John is heavy* into a statement containing the relationship of strict equality.

Not all statements that contain numbers are quantitative statements. Numbers may be used in statements for a variety of purposes:

1. To identify (or name) the subject, as *This is a prisoner number 59241.*
2. To identify the class in which the subject is placed, as *He was in the graduating class of 1951.*
3. To identify the number of subjects in a class, as *Twenty-three universities offer courses in this subject.*
4. To identify the rank order of a subject in a class, as *General Motors is the number one manufacturer of automobiles.*
5. To identify the number of units on a scale that corresponds to the subject's property, as *John is six feet and one inch tall.*

Only the last three of these represent what is called measurement.

Measurement. As we saw (in Chapter 7), to think about something is to manipulate a representation of that thing. As we also saw later (in Chapter 10), such representations are called *signs.* If a sign that represents what is thought about has some of the same relevant properties as what it represents — say, it looks like what it represents — the thought process usually is facilitated. It is possible to go even further to facilitate thought. Man has created systems of signs (as letters and numbers) between whose elements he has established certain relationships (as, an order). When such signs are used to represent things related to each other in some of the same ways the signs are taken to be, measurement has taken place.

Measurement is the use of man-made signs (see definition 10.1.) to represent things believed to be related to each other in some of the same ways that the user believes the signs to be related.

This definition has made use of the concept *belief,* which is considered in Chapter 5.

REFERENCE

Ackoff, R. L. *Scientific Method: Optimizing Applied Research Decisions.* New York: John Wiley & Sons, 1962.

Appendix III

On Newcomb's and Rapoport's Hypotheses

NEWCOMB'S HYPOTHESIS ON TWO-WAY COMMUNICATION

If, in this analysis, we do injustice to Newcomb's intentions, it is not intentional. We try to get at what *he* means, but if we fail it is not because the type of operational translation into an objective teleology that we attempt is of no value, but because we do not understand him. To some, what we are about to do may appear like nitpicking. However, it is intended to support, by example, several fundamental criticisms of much of contemporary behavioral science: (1) the psychology and social psychology of communication is rife with imprecise definitions and inconsistent use of concepts, (2) a systematic way of assigning numbers to a phenomenon is not sufficient to produce measurements, and (3) the use of quantitative relationships in assertions about communication does not necessarily produce a quantitative theory of communication.

Newcomb's first postulate is as follows.

> The stronger the forces toward A's co-orientation in respect to B and X, (a) the greater A's strain toward symmetry with B in respect to X; and (b) the greater the likelihood of increased symmetry as a consequence of one or more communicative acts (p. 69).

He defined the key terms in this postulate as follows.

> "Co-orientation" . . . represents an assumption; namely, that A's orientation toward B and toward X are interdependent (pp. 66–7).
> A's orientation toward X, including both attitude toward X as an object to be approached or avoided (characterized by sign and intensity) and cognitive attributes (beliefs and cognitive structuring).
> A's orientation toward B, in exactly the same sense. For purposes of avoiding confusing terms, we shall speak of positive and negative *attraction* toward A and

B as persons, and as favorable and unfavorable *attitudes* toward B. We shall refer to lateral similarities of A's and B's orientation to X as *symmetrical* relationships (p. 67).

This last definition is illuminated by the discussion preceding it.

In order to examine the possible relationships of similarity and difference between A and B, we shall make use of simple dichotomies in regard to these four relationships [A's orientation toward X and B, and B's orientation toward X and A]. That is, with respect to a given X at a given time, A and B will be regarded as cathectically [i.e., with respect to feeling] alike ($+ +$ or $- -$) or different ($+ -$ or $- +$) in attitude and in attraction; and as cognitively alike or different. We shall also make use of simple dichotomies of degree—i.e., more alike, less alike (p. 67).

First consider Newcomb's condition: "the stronger the forces toward A's co-orientation in respect to B and X." *A*'s co-orientation according to Newcomb is characterized by four variables:

1. *A*'s attitude toward *X*.
2. *A*'s cognitive attributes (beliefs and cognitive structuring) of *X*.
3. *A*'s attraction toward *B*.
4. *A*'s cognitive attributes of *B*.

Although we can see how *A*'s attraction toward *B* and attitude toward *X* can each be represented on a single scale and hence treated dichotomously (alike or different), Newcomb is not clear on how to so represent "beliefs and cognitive structuring." The number of relevant beliefs that *A* can have about either *X* or *B* may be very large. In what conditions are *sets* of measures of beliefs to be taken to be alike or different?

What of "the stronger the forces toward . . ."? We would translate this to refer to the strength of the interdependence of the variables listed above. Let us assume we needed only one measure to represent beliefs.

First, what interdependencies are to be measured: between *A*'s and *B*'s attitudes, and between *A*'s and *B*'s beliefs; or between *A*'s beliefs and attitudes, and *B*'s beliefs and attitudes? If the first, then there will be *two* measures of interdependency. How are these to be aggregated? If the second, it is even more difficult to see how interdependency is to be represented, because *four* relationships are involved: (1) *A*'s attitude and *B*'s belief, (2) *A*'s attitude and *B*'s attitude, (3) *A*'s belief and *B*'s attitude, and (4) *A*'s belief and *B*'s belief. This assumes, of course, that only one belief is involved.

Further, what does interdependency mean? Is a correlation implied? Positive, or negative, or both? Or is interdependency the probability that a change is one of the related measures will produce a change in the other? Of the same magnitude? In the same direction?

Unless interdependency is defined operationally in measurable terms, and unless the variables involved are identified and similarly defined, the postulate itself has no operational significance.

Continuing with the first consequence of the premise we have been examining—"the greater *A*'s strain toward symmetry with B in respect to X"—we must clarify *strain* and *symmetry*. It seems to us that by strain Newcomb intended to connote something very much like what we have called intention. A measure of symmetry involves the same difficulties discussed above with respect to interdependencies. Newcomb refers to "lateral similarities;" therefore, several comparisons are involved. If each produces a judgement of like or different how are these to be aggregated? Are we to take the ratio of likes to the total number of comparisons? If we do, we would be assuming that each comparison is equally important. Is this what Newcomb meant to imply?

The second conclusion—"the greater the likelihood of increased symmetry as a consequence of one or more communicative acts"—appears to be translatable into "the greater the probability that a specified number of communicative acts will produce an increase in symmetry." But this translation and the original both require a definition of a communicative act. Is the voicing of one word one act? Or is it the production of one continuous uninterrupted message? Is it independent of the length of the message or its duration?

Now let us try to use what we have done here to formulate a less general hypothesis than Newcomb's, but one of the same type, and to make it less ambiguous than his. First, we shall restrict attention to attitudes and again use *AaB* to represent *A*'s attitude toward *B*. Following the discussion in Chapter 6, by *A*'s attitude toward *B* we mean *A*'s intention to retain *B* in his environment (hence satisfaction with *B*'s presence). The degree of this intention can range between 0 and 1. If this measure is greater than 0.5, *A* can be said to have a favorable attitude toward *B*; if it is less than 0.5, his attitude is unfavorable; and if equal to 0.5, *A* is indifferent to *B*.

Now we want to make precise the following statement: *A*'s attitude toward *X* depends on both his attitude toward *B* and *B*'s attitude toward *X*; that is, *AaX* depends on *AaB* and *BaX*.

With Newcomb let us treat attitudes dichotomously and let $(AaB)^+$ represent a favorable attitude, and $(AaB)^-$ an unfavorable one. Then we can say that *AaX* depends on *AaB* and *BaX* if the probability that *AaX* is favorable (or unfavorable) is greater if *AaB* and *BaX* are favorable. Now an interesting point arises: the probability that *AaX* is favorable (or unfavorable) may be greater when both *AaB* and *BaX*, rather than only one, are unfavorable (favorable). That is, if *A*'s attitude toward *B* is unfavorable and *B*'s attitude toward *X* is unfavorable, *A*'s attitude toward *X* may very likely be favorable. One may like something because his enemy does not.

Now let us define "strain toward symmetry" as *A*'s intention to minimize the difference between his attitude toward *X* and *B*'s; that is, to minimize $(AaX - BaX)$. If this intention is greater than 0.5, *A* strains toward symmetry; if it is less than 0.5, *A* strains toward *asymmetry*. Let $P_A[\min(AaX - BaX)]$

represent the probability that A strains toward symmetry, and $P_A[\max (AaX - BaX)]$ represent the probability that A strains toward asymmetry.

We can now formulate the following hypotheses.

1. As

$$[P(AaX)^+ \mid (AaB)^+ \text{ and } (BaX)^+] - \left[P(AaX)^+ \; \middle| \; \text{or} \begin{array}{l} (AaB)^+ \text{ and } (BaX)^- \\ (AaB)^- \text{ and } (BaX)^+ \end{array} \right]$$

increases,

$$P_A[\min(AaX - BaX)]$$

also increases.

2. As

$$[P(AaX)^+ \mid (AaB)^- \text{ and } (BaX)^-] - \left[P(AaX)^+ \; \middle| \; \text{or} \begin{array}{l} (AaB)^+ \text{ and } (BaX)^- \\ (AaB)^- \text{ and } (BaX)^+ \end{array} \right]$$

increases,

$$P_A[\max(AaX - BaX)]$$

also increases.

Complementary hypotheses can be obtained by changing all the plus superscripts to minuses, and the minus superscripts to pluses.

The advantage of a symbolic statement of this hypothesis over a statement of it in words becomes apparent when we try to express the first one in words.

As the difference between (1) the probability that A's attitude toward X is favorable (given that his attitude toward B and B's toward X are favorable), and (2) the probability that his attitude toward X is favorable (given that either his attitude toward B or B's toward X is unfavorable), increases, then A's intention to minimize the difference between his and B's attitude toward X also increases.

The second hypothesis covers a possibility not considered by Newcomb: if A's attitude toward B is unfavorable and his attitude toward X depends on his attitude toward B, and B's attitude toward X is unfavorable, A may strain for asymmetry with B with respect to X.

Now consider Newcomb's second conclusion: "the greater the likelihood of increased symmetry as a consequence of one or more communicative acts." Let us define a communicative act as the sending and receipt of a message containing a specified amount of syntactic information in the absence of pragmatic noise. Then we can formulate the following hypothesis.

3. As

$$[P(AaX)^+ \mid (AaB)^+ \text{ and } (BaX)^+] - \left[P(AaX)^+ \middle| \text{or} \begin{array}{l} (AaB)^+ \text{ and } (BaX)^- \\ (AaB)^- \text{ and } (BaX)^+ \end{array} \right]$$

increases, then the greater is the probability that a communicative act
between A and B will reduce

$$[(AaX)-(BaX)\,|\,(AaX) \neq (BaX)];$$

and as

$$[P(AaX)^+\,|\,(AaB)^- \text{ and } (BaX)^-] - \left[P(AaX)^+ \,\middle|\, or \begin{array}{l} (AaB)^+ \text{ and } (BaX)^- \\ (AaB)^- \text{ and } (BaX)^+ \end{array} \right]$$

increases, then the greater is the probability that a communicative act
between A and B will increase $[(AaX)-(BaX)]$, given that this difference is
not maximum.

Similar hypotheses can be formulated about beliefs, but this entails a
considerable increase in complexity. There is no single summary belief that
parallels attitude. The closest approximation is belief in probability of outcome, which reflects belief in probability of choice and efficiency. The believed
probability of outcome is almost certainly no simple function of the interaction of belief in probability of choice and belief in efficiency. We have
followed Newcomb in hypothesizing what would happen if attitudes to B
and X varied while beliefs remained constant. For a science of communcation
it would be necessary also to determine what would happen as the various
parameters of belief varied.

We have tried to show (1) how loosely formulated hypotheses can be
tightened up, and (2) how a conceptual system assists in doing so. In connection with the second it should be recalled that measures of belief and
attitude, so central to this discussion, were developed in earlier chapters.
Without these measures the hypotheses formulated here would be empty,
no matter how precise their formulation.

Rapoport's Hypotheses

Consider the following relatively simple hypothesis. If $(AaB)^+$, $(BaA)^+$,
and $(AaX) \neq (BaX)$, then two-way communication between A and B about
X will produce a decrease in $[(AaX)-(BaX)]$. That is, if A and B have
favorable attitudes toward each other but their attitudes toward X differ,
communication between them will decrease this difference. This hypothesis
suggests the question: If $(AaB)^-$, $(BaA)^-$, and $[(AaX)-(BaX)] \neq$ max, then
will communication between A and B reduce the difference $[(AaX)-(BaX)]$?

In his discussion of the effectiveness of debates in resolving conflicts,
Rapoport (1960) suggests several ways of increasing this effectiveness. These
suggestions can be translated into hypotheses formulated within the conceptual system developed here. For example, Rapoport suggests that if two
hostile persons must debate on a subject on which they disagree, they are
more likely to reach agreement if each is required to formulate the other's

point of view in a way that the other accepts. This can be translated as follows. If

1. $(AaB)^-$, $(BaA)^-$, and $[(AaX) \neq (BaX)$,
2. A sends a message to B connoting what A believes to be B's attitude toward and beliefs about X, and B accepts these connotations, and
3. B sends a corresponding message to A that A similarly accepts,

then the probability that subsequent communication between A and B will reduce the difference, $(AaX) - (BaX)$, increases, as compared with what would happen if either condition (1) or (2) were not satisfied.

Now let us consider how this hypothesis could be tested. First, we must be able to measure four attitudes: (AaB), (AaX), (BaA), and (BaX). We have already considered (in Chapter 6) how this can be done. Next we require a sample of pairs of people who satisfy condition (1) with respect to an X. (At the time of this writing, for example, if X were U.S. policy in Viet Nam, they would be easy to find.) The attitude of each person toward the other and X would also be determined. We would then randomly divide these hostile pairs into two groups of equal size. Pairs in one group would be told to try to reach agreement on X within a specified time. Pairs in the other group would be told to do the same thing only after they had satisfied conditions (2) and (3) above. At the end of the designated time, the attitudes of each member of each pair toward X would again be measured and the differences obtained. A comparison of the before and after differences would confirm or disconfirm the hypothesis.

Rapoport's second hypothesis involves the effect of each party's "delineating the region of validity of the opponent's stand." He explains as follows.

> It is not unusual in debate to point out grounds for considering the position of the opponent *invalid*. It is argued, for example, that some or all of the premises assumed by the opponent do not hold. In the approach where the removal of threat is a major consideration, this procedure must be reversed. The logical implications remain formally the same; by delineating the conditions under which the opponent's point of view *is* valid, we imply the residual conditions, under which it is *not* valid. But the emphasis is on the former, not on the latter. Showing examples which support the opponents' point of view is a continuation of our message to him that he has been heard and understood (p. 287).

This hypothesis involves a message or messages from each party of the conflict to the other, which states the conditions in which he believes (1) the other's beliefs about X to be valid and (2) his attitudes toward X to be justified. It asserts that if there is such an interchange, differences between attitudes toward X will be reduced by subsequent communication. These assertions can also be translated into the conceptual system being developed here.

Once A and B have each produced a statement of the other's beliefs and attitudes toward X, which the other has accepted, if A sends a message to

B that connotes the conditions in which *A*'s beliefs and attitudes toward *X* would be the same as *B*'s in current conditions, and *B* does the same, then the probability that subsequent communication between *A* and *B* will reduce the difference, $(AaX) - (BaX)$, increases.

Communication of almost any form between conflicting parties does seem to reduce the tendency to conflict. In several laboratory experiments on conflict and cooperation in which the interaction takes place in conditions that remain the same except for the presence or absence of communication, a significantly greater tendency to cooperative behavior has been found where communication is possible. (See, for example, Ackoff et al. 1966.)

REFERENCES

Newcomb, T. M. "An Approach to the Study of Communicative Acts." In *Communication and Culture,* edited by A. G. Smith, pp. 66–79. New York: Holt, Rinehart & Winston, 1966.

Rapoport, Anatol. *Fights, Games, and Debates.* Ann Arbor: The University of Michigan Press, 1960.

Author Index

281

Subject Index

284